The Administration Of An Institutional Church: A Detailed Account Of The Operation Of St. George's Parish In The City Of New York...

George Hodges, John Reichert

Nabu Public Domain Reprints:

You are holding a reproduction of an original work published before 1923 that is in the public domain in the United States of America, and possibly other countries. You may freely copy and distribute this work as no entity (individual or corporate) has a copyright on the body of the work. This book may contain prior copyright references, and library stamps (as most of these works were scanned from library copies). These have been scanned and retained as part of the historical artifact.

This book may have occasional imperfections such as missing or blurred pages, poor pictures, errant marks, etc. that were either part of the original artifact, or were introduced by the scanning process. We believe this work is culturally important, and despite the imperfections, have elected to bring it back into print as part of our continuing commitment to the preservation of printed works worldwide. We appreciate your understanding of the imperfections in the preservation process, and hope you enjoy this valuable book.

St. George's Parish
In the City of New York

GEORGE HODGES

JOHN P. PETERS

WITH INTRODUCTION BY
PRESIDENT ROOSEVELT

NEW YORK AND LONDON
1906

The Administration Of an Institutional Church

A DETAILED ACCOUNT OF THE OPERATION OF

St. George's Parish

In the City of New York

BY

GEORGE HODGES

DEAN AND PROFESSOR OF PASTORAL THEOLOGY
EPISCOPAL THEOLOGICAL SCHOOL, CAMBRIDGE, MASS.

AND

JOHN REICHERT

CLERK OF THE VESTRY OF ST. GEORGE'S CHURCH
NEW YORK CITY

WITH INTRODUCTIONS AND COMMENTS BY
PRESIDENT ROOSEVELT, BISHOP POTTER
AND DR. RAINSFORD

NEW YORK AND LONDON
HARPER & BROTHERS PUBLISHERS
1906

Copyright, 1906, by HARPER & BROTHERS.

All rights reserved.

Published November, 1906.

TO
HUGH BIRCKHEAD
THIS DESCRIPTION OF THE GOODLY HERITAGE
INTO WHICH HE IS ENTERING IS
AFFECTIONATELY DEDICATED

CONTENTS

CHAP.		PAGE
INTRODUCTION:		
	I.—By President Roosevelt	ix
	II.—By Bishop Potter	xi
	III.—By Dr. Rainsford	xiv
	IV.—By the Authors	xvii
I.	General Management	1
II.	The Plant	13
III.	The Records	49
IV.	Services and Sermons	73
V.	Religious Instruction of the Youth	101
VI.	Work with Boys	166
VII.	Work with Girls	195
VIII.	Men and Women	221
IX.	The Ministration of Relief	252
X.	The Finances of a Free Church	273
XI.	General Principles	307
	Index	317

ILLUSTRATIONS

W. S. RAINSFORD		*Frontispiece*
ST. GEORGE'S CHURCH	*Facing p.*	x
ST. GEORGE'S RECTORY	"	xii
ST. GEORGE'S MEMORIAL HOUSE	"	16
PLANS OF ST. GEORGE'S CHURCH AND ST. GEORGE'S MEMORIAL HOUSE	"	22
ST. GEORGE'S DEACONESS HOUSE	"	26
DEACONESS HOUSE—FIRST FLOOR PLAN	*Page*	29
DEACONESS HOUSE—SECOND FLOOR PLAN	"	30
DEACONESS HOUSE—THIRD FLOOR PLAN	"	31
DEACONESS HOUSE—FOURTH FLOOR PLAN	"	33
DEACONESS HOUSE—BASEMENT PLAN	"	34
TRADE-SCHOOL—FIRST STORY PLAN	"	35
TRADE-SCHOOL—SECOND STORY PLAN	"	37
TRADE-SCHOOL—THIRD STORY PLAN	"	39
TRADE-SCHOOL—BASEMENT PLAN	"	41
SEA-SIDE COTTAGE—FIRST FLOOR PLAN	"	43
SEA-SIDE COTTAGE—SECOND FLOOR PLAN	"	45
SEA-SIDE COTTAGE—UNDER THE PAVILION	"	47
ST. GEORGE'S EVENING TRADE-SCHOOL	*Facing p.*	166
THE RIFLE RANGE	*Page*	181
ST. GEORGE'S CHURCH COTTAGE	*Facing p.*	266

INTRODUCTION

I.—BY PRESIDENT ROOSEVELT

The Church must be a living, breathing, vital force or it is no real Church; and therefore not only all good citizens but especially all earnest Christians are under a real debt of obligation to the Rev. William S. Rainsford for what he has done with St. George's Church in New York. Every serious student of our social and industrial conditions has learned to look with discomfort and alarm upon the diminishing part which churches play in the life of our great cities—for I need hardly say that no increase in the number of fashionable churches and of wealthy congregations in any shape or way atones for the diminution in the number of the churches in the very localities where there is most need for them. If ever the Christian Church ceases to be the Church of the plain people, it will cease to be the Christian Church.

Dr. Rainsford has stood pre-eminent among the clergymen to whom it has been given to prevent this condition of things from obtaining. His remarkable physical and mental equipment, and the appeal that ethical considerations make to him, put him in the forefront of those both able and eager to do the task. He was keenly alive to everything that appeals to men as men, and his broad and deep sympathies made him acutely sensitive to the needs of others no less than to the way in which these needs could be effectively met.

INTRODUCTION

With such an equipment, he took an empty church and filled it. He filled it with the men and women of the neighborhood. He made these men and women feel that whether they were rich or poor mattered nothing, so long as they were Christians who tried to live their Christianity in a spirit of brotherly love and of sane, cheerful helpfulness towards themselves and towards one another. He brought the church close to the busy, working life of a great city. With his strong human hand he felt the throbbing pulse of the people among whom he worked, and he fired their hearts with the spirit that was in his own. As a preacher, as an executive, as a citizen among his fellow-citizens, Dr. Rainsford made St. George's Church the most notable institution of its kind in the world. He did lasting work for social and civic righteousness. Not only New York City but the nation as a whole owes him a debt of gratitude for his moulding of American citizenship in the form in which it should be cast. The kind of citizenship for the upbuilding of which he labored is that which rests its sense of duty to city and country on the deep and broad foundation of the eternal laws of spiritual well-being.

I keenly regret Dr. Rainsford's retirement from active duty, and I welcome this book as giving a record of a life-work full of inspiration for his fellow-men. To Dr. Rainsford can be applied the words of the German poet:

> "Wer nicht gelitten, hat nur halb gelebt;
> Wer nicht gefehlt, hat wohl auch nicht gestrebt;
> Wer nicht geweint, hat halt auch nur gelacht;
> Wer nie gezweifelt, hat wohl kaum gedacht!"

Theodore Roosevelt

THE WHITE HOUSE,
Washington, D. C., *April 7, 1906.*

ST. GEORGE'S CHURCH
Stuyvesant Square

INTRODUCTION

II.—BY BISHOP POTTER

When I came to the Rectorship of Grace Church, New York, in 1868, Dr. Tyng was still Rector of St. George's Church, which, with its chapels, had come to be by far the most influential parish on the east side of the city. The chapels, of which there were two, afforded a felicitous outlet for energies and enthusiasms gathered in St. George's during Dr. Tyng's ministry; and over all he presided with characteristic energy and emphasis. It would be a stupid blunder to ignore the theological warfares of the time, which divided the city and diocese of New York into two strongly marked schools or camps, each of which regarded the other with an equal distrust and suspicion. From the beginning of his ministry in New York, nobody was in any doubt on which side Dr. Tyng ranged himself; and he drew about him, undoubtedly, a large constituency of earnest and devout people who regarded St. George's Church and pre-eminently Dr. Tyng as its Rector, as standing for scriptural and evangelical truth, in its purity and integrity.

It was not unnatural, therefore, that when advancing years warned Dr. Tyng that he should seek for a colleague, he turned in that direction from which men likeminded with himself had most largely come. The Rev. Dr. Walter Williams, at that time Rector of a church in Georgetown, D. C., and a graduate of the Theological Seminary of Virginia (where I came to know and love him), was a man of singularly winning and engaging character, of ample learning, and of distinguished intellectual power. He frankly owned, however, after due experiment, that the situation was one for which he could find no solution.

The reputation of the present Rector had then reached

INTRODUCTION

New York, and his work in Toronto, Canada, and his occasional visits to New York, had enabled many who had heard him to recognize his exceptional gifts. I remember very well the morning on which he came to see me in Grace Church Rectory, the questions he asked, and the counsel that I ventured to give him. One thing was certain: the old traditions of St. George's as a "pewed parish church," with a large constituency of well-to-do and cultivated people, could not much longer expect to be maintained. Originally, New York had been a largely homogeneous community; and, though growing annually with rapid strides from foreign immigration, had retained those primitive characteristics with which, originally, its Dutch and English settlers had stamped it. But all this, long before Dr. Tyng's resignation, had begun to be changed; and when Dr. Rainsford accepted the Rectorship of St. George's, he was confronted by a situation familiar enough down-town in New York, but wholly unlike that with which the earlier history of New York was identified. Some recent statistics of a so-called "social" sort have indicated the steady progress, northward, of New York's social centre. When I came to New York, it was between Union and Madison squares; but by 1880 it had advanced above the latter, even as, now, it is reported to be above Fifty-ninth Street. It was inevitable that this never-ceasing movement should affect parishes, and, fortunately for St. George's Church, Dr. Rainsford had the wisdom to recognize the situation and to deal with it in a statesman-like way. He made the church free, and gathered into it the congregations of the various chapels. In all this he was seconded by a vestry of exceptional character and ability, and assisted, as in the case of the gift of the stately Memorial Parish House, by Mr. J. Pierpont Morgan, by

ST. GEORGE'S RECTORY
209 East 16th Street

INTRODUCTION

a steadfast sympathy, expressing itself by an unwearied munificence.

But the history of St. George's Church for the last quarter of a century has illustrated, most of all, the power of a single and noble manhood. Eloquence there may be; the genius of organization; personal magnetism; tenacity of purpose, and qualities like them; but they are all inferior to that loftiest quality which makes men sensible of *divine authority and of human sympathy*. In the union of these two powers, I think that the ministry of the present Rector of St. George's Church has been altogether exceptional. He has the characteristics of his race and temperament; and the superficial listener or observer may not always be enamoured of these; but he has made St. George's Church a witness for his Master, Jesus Christ, among a population as dense as any city in the world contains, and that throngs and crowds St. George's pews whenever its doors are opened. The poor and heavy-laden, the "forgotten of their fellow-men," who turn to its altar for strength, comfort, and refreshment, know that a great human heart is there to translate to them the divine heart of Love that broods above us all, with matchless Sympathy and Help!

A feature of the history of St. George's Church, without reference to which I cannot close this hasty sketch, is the singular genius of its Rector as illustrated in the selection and assimilation of his curates. I have used that last word, "assimilation," advisedly, though it is not precisely that which I want. But no one who knows anything of the relations of a Rector and his assistants can be unmindful of the fact that sympathy and a mutual understanding between them is somewhat rare. In this respect, St. George's Church and its clergy are altogether exceptional. They seem to devise, and

INTRODUCTION

think, and act, in all that concerns the well-being of the parish, as one mind; and the steadfast enthusiasm, large insight, and untiring activity of their Rector seems to be shared by all of them. Every department of the parish life and work (how I wish I could speak of them as they deserve!) throbs and thrills with the same mystic energy and purpose.

It is a sore grief to me, as to all his clergy and people, that, while I write these words, their Rector is far away from them in search of health and strength. May God speedily restore to him both; but whatever shall be the Divine Ordering, be it ours to bless Him for a ministry so rare and Christlike as that of which the story is here recorded!

Henry C. Potter

LUXOR, EGYPT, *January 8, 1906.*

III.—BY DR. RAINSFORD

I HOPE that the following pages may be found of interest and value to the increasing company of men and women who are engaged in the work of the Institutional Church.

My secretary and friend of more than twenty years standing, Mr. John Reichert, has in my absence put together the materials out of which this book is made. But his part in its production is not merely that of compiler. The forms here printed, the expedients here set forth for keeping the business of a great parish in order,

INTRODUCTION

are as much his work as mine. These are what remain after many experiments and many failures. We drew them up together, sending them out by thousands at a time, then changing or suppressing or repeating them. I can truthfully say that they represent a great deal of time and study.

Dean Hodges, of the Episcopal Theological School in Cambridge, has most kindly consented to undertake the arduous task of editing the whole work, rewriting and rearranging the material as his experience suggests. Under his hands, I am sure that it will help many a young minister to undertake new tasks both of addition and of subtraction. Most young men attempt far too many organizations, and do not put enough persistent work into those which exist already.

No book, so far as I know, supplies such information as is here offered. For years, many letters day by day have come to me from clergymen and laymen seeking answers to such questions as these:

"How do you run your Men's Club?"

"How do you keep in your Sunday-school boys over sixteen years of age?"

"How do you reach the wage-earners in your neighborhood?"

"How do you train your teachers?"

"How do you work your envelope system?"

"How do you manage to have a large choir at small cost?"

"I am about to build a parish house. What is the plan of yours?"

It is of course true that some of these questioners may be mere copyists. They may argue that what has proved to be effective in one place will therefore fit the needs of another, and perhaps very different, place. I

INTRODUCTION

am sure that much of the organization in hundreds of parishes is worse than useless; it is burdensome and misleading. But I am also sure that when, under circumstances of real difficulty, such as are presented in the lower part of east New York, things have been accomplished that were never accomplished before, the methods that were used to obtain these results are worth studying.

We began in 1883 at St. George's in a very small way. The church was almost empty. The rich people—except three or four families—had moved away, and the poor had never come. We had, therefore, to begin from the very bottom. The task before us was not so much to revive an old parish as to create a new one. And this we had to do under circumstances so discouraging that a large number of churches had already retreated from the neighborhood and sought other fields. The following pages tell the story of our difficulties—how we met them, and how, to some extent, we overcame them.

1. We gave our very best to the little children, and they grew in time to be men and women thoroughly attached to the church which had sought them out.

2. We gave to every one who was willing to do any sort of work for setting forward the kingdom of the Lord Jesus an opportunity to do it; and wherever possible we gave them the work which they *liked* to do.

3. We sought carefully for capable men as assistant ministers. We made them free of the parish; gave each of them all conditions of men and women to visit, rich as well as poor; gave them abundant opportunities to preach and to have their sermons sympathetically criticised. The dearest, truest, most loyal friends I have to-day are the men who have served with me in St. George's during the past twenty-three years. There are more than thirty of them. They are a power for good wherever

INTRODUCTION

they minister, and they all tell me that their years of assistantship were of great value to them. I, on my part, can assure them that what is good and lasting in our work is theirs as much as mine.

4. We have had the invaluable support of a devoted band of trained deaconesses, living in community, leaving the parish seldom, and serving for long terms, as contrasted with the necessarily shorter terms of office of the assistant ministers.

5. And, lastly, we have been ever and always supported and advised by such a vestry as few churches have known.

To these five causes, under God, our success in the Free Church of St. George's has been due.

W. S. Rainsford

SCOTLAND, *October, 1905.*

IV.—BY THE AUTHORS

THIS book is not only a response to innumerable requests for information, but is also a record of the methods and achievements of a great parish. We therefore begin our account of these industries with a sketch of the parochial history. For most of the facts contained in this chapter we are indebted to an unsigned paper which was printed in the *St. George's Chronicle* for January, 1894.

The first church in New York which bore the title of St. George stood in the fort, near the present site of Bowling Green. It was built by the English in 1664,

INTRODUCTION

when they came into possession, and there confronted a Dutch church which was dedicated to St. Nicholas. In this St. George's Chapel, also called King's Chapel, the worship of the Church of England was held until the erection of Trinity Church, in 1696.

Trinity Church, and the little town about it, prospered and increased until, in 1748, the parishioners felt the need of what the wardens and vestry in their resolution called a "chapel of ease." Such a chapel was therefore built in the "Beekman pasture," on land given by Colonel Henry Beekman and Gertrude Van Cortlandt, his wife. There it stood, quite in the country, on Beekman Street, in the midst of meadow-land and orchards, on what was then called "the Cliffs," overlooking the East River. This was Trinity's first colony, and it was named St. George's, in memory of the church in the English fort.

St. George's Chapel, as the building was entitled, was consecrated in 1752. The Rector of Trinity, Dr. Barclay, his assistant, Dr. Auchmuty, with the wardens and vestry, and the charity scholars, met the mayor and other officials at the city hall in Wall Street, and marched in procession to the chapel. There, in 1787, Bishop Provost held an ordination service, the first in the city and one of the first in the country. There Washington worshipped.

In 1811, St. George's became an independent parish, losing its church by fire in 1814, but building another the next year, during the leadership of Dr. Milnor, the first rector. The first meeting of the wardens and vestry was held November 23, 1811. The wardens were Gerrit H. Van Wagenen and Harry Peters. The vestrymen were Robert Wardell, Isaac Carow, John Greene, Francis Dominick, John Onderdonk, Edward W. Laight, Isaac Lawrence, Cornelius Schermerhorn.

INTRODUCTION

The new church had galleries on either side, and another for the choir and organ at the west end. Three glass chandeliers hung from the panelled ceiling. The semicircular chancel contained a desk, pulpit, and clerk's desk. These, together with the rail and the frame of the organ, were made of mahogany, contributed, it was said, by a sea-captain who lost his masts in a storm, and replaced them from a mahogany forest. All the rest of the wood-work was painted white. The marble font, showing the carved heads of saints, had been captured from a French ship during the French war. The bell in the steeple was given by the neighbors, the inhabitants of "Montgomery Ward." Ten pounds of the building fund came from the Archbishop of Canterbury.

In this church Dr. Milnor served for thirty years. When he died, in 1846, Dr. Tyng succeeded him. In that year it was resolved to move up-town, accepting a generous provision of land for that purpose by the liberality of Mr. Stuyvesant. The second rector, like the first, championed the cause of what was then called Evangelical Churchmanship. It was a time when party differences were unhappily magnified. St. George's was known as a stronghold against the Oxford Movement, which was then arousing the hopes and fears of church people.

Then, even in its new location, the church saw uptown change to down-town. Every year substantial families changed their residence and transformed their interest to new parishes, and the population which took their places was of a very different order. The St. George's plan of that period was the universal plan of all the churches of all names. It was based upon the unit of the family. It proceeded upon the theory that on Sunday morning the father and mother would lead a procession of their children to the parish church, to occupy the family pew. But a great many of the new people had no such tradition. Some of them were unattached persons, making their individual way in the world. An increasing number were affected by the disintegrating influences of tenement-house life, one effect of which is to remove the restraints of neighborhood opinion. These conditions made the old, orderly, domestic life difficult, if not impossible. Here and there an individual out of a family group came to church; the children often came to Sunday-school; but the family pew was not rented.

Dr. Tyng saw the beginnings of this change, but upon his successor, Dr. Williams, it came in full force. He tried in vain to meet it. It was impossible to minister to the new conditions in the old way. And that, at the moment, was the only way. The new way had not been discovered. Dr. Williams frankly acknowledged his defeat. He finally resigned, on the ground that it was impossible to hold the church together. At that time only about twenty families of the old congregation remained in the parish. The church was empty; nothing increased but the annual deficit. Even the Roman Catholics, it was said, would not take St. George's as a mission. The only thing to do, in Dr. Williams's opinion, was to move away.

Under these circumstances, Dr. Rainsford was called to be the Rector. Dr. Rainsford has himself written the history of his ministry in *A Preacher's Story of his Work*. We will not go again into the difficulties and successes which he has so graphically and forcibly described. There they are set down in the pages of a good book, full of interest, instruction, and inspiration. The man who made St. George's what it is to-day is in that book. The heart of the St. George's plan is his splendid personality. But our business here is with the expression of that per-

INTRODUCTION

sonality in organization. William Stephen Rainsford was born in 1850, in Dublin. His father was a clergyman; so was his mother's father. He was graduated with the bachelor's degree in arts at St. John's College, Cambridge, in 1872. He went naturally into the ministry, and began his work as curate at St. Giles's, in Norwich. Presently he spent two years in the United States and Canada, devoting himself to evangelical work, conducting "missions" in large cities of the East and South. He returned to England, but was soon called to be Assistant Rector of the Cathedral of Toronto. There he was found, when Dr. Williams resigned, by the vestry of St. George's.

In these ten years of ministry, Mr. Rainsford showed the personal characteristics which have since become familiar not only to the people of his parish, but to the religious world at large. He plunged into the midst of things with an apparent superabundance of physical energy, which, however, needed such occasional recuperation as could be had only in the wilderness. He had times of deep depression of spirit, from which he escaped by the stress and peril of the hunting of big game in the deep woods or in the high mountains. He was at the same time keenly sensitive to the criticism of adverse public opinion, and no less than reckless in the absolute independence of his thought and speech. Sometimes he preached well, and the church was crowded; sometimes, for weeks he says, he preached ill, and the congregation fell away. He needed, for his own strength and inspiration, to be positively certain; and there were times when the old evangelical doctrines which he had learned from his father and the new truths which were appealing to him in the great books of his time, and in the experience of daily life, seemed sadly out of accord. That contention he was compelled to work out for himself with pain, and in the process he gave pain to others. When he felt a thing to be true, he said it in plain words without counting the consequences. And conservative people did not like it. Moreover, he had a temperamental objection to all hindering conventionalities; tested all forms and ceremonies by their effective value; had no interest in worn-out machinery; and cared only for the thing that would work. He was in quest of results. There was a big freedom about him which frightened cautious persons. This was the man who became Rector of St. George's in 1883.

The most important contribution which Dr. Rainsford made to this parish—excepting, of course, the great gift of himself, which passes all estimation—was the contribution of a new method. He found a church trying to minister in the old way to new conditions, and he changed the way so as to fit the conditions. He compared the old St. George's to "a fisherman accustomed to earn his bread at catching herrings; presently the run of herrings goes away from that section of the sea; in their place comes a tremendous run of smelts. If the fisherman could change his net he would be a richer man than before, because smelts are better fish; but he starves because he cannot change the size of the meshes." Dr. Rainsford proceeded immediately to change the size of the meshes. The old methods had been adapted to the family, the new methods were adapted to the individual. The essential principle of the Institutional Church is in that change.

Dr. Rainsford agreed to undertake the rectorship on three conditions: first, the church must be made free; secondly, all committees, except the vestry, must be abolished; thirdly, there must be an appropriation of

INTRODUCTION

ten thousand dollars a year for three years, to be used by the Rector at his own discretion. These conditions were cordially accepted, and the work began which it is our privilege to describe.

In these descriptions we have been courteously aided by the clergy and the deaconesses of the parish, and by the officers of the various organizations. We are indebted to them for manifold suggestions. The book, like the parish, is a co-operative work.

George Hodges

John Reichert

THE ADMINISTRATION OF AN INSTITUTIONAL CHURCH

THE ADMINISTRATION OF AN INSTITUTIONAL CHURCH

I

GENERAL MANAGEMENT

I. The Corporation.—II. The Staff.

An institutional church is like a business house in its use of two essential elements of executive success. The first of these is the centralization, and the second is the distribution of authority. Power must first be concentrated in the possession of a small company of responsible persons; it must then be so disseminated that every humblest worker shall have some of it, and in consequence shall work with a sense of freedom, of initiative, and of personal loyalty. The rector who does everything is almost as incapable as the rector who does nothing. "Never do anything yourself which you can get anybody else to do," is the maxim of every good administration; it being taken for granted that all this delegated work is diligently kept in mind and looked after and directed by the chief executive.

In an institutional parish, as in every other kind of parish in the Episcopal Church, the small company of responsible persons by whom the work is governed is divided into two groups—one charged with the temporalities, the other with the spiritualities. The group which directs the temporalities is the Corporation; the group which directs the spiritualities is the Staff.

I.—THE CORPORATION

The Corporation in the parish which we are describing is legally entitled "The Rector, Church Wardens, and Vestrymen of St. George's Church, in the City of New York." The two wardens and the nine vestrymen who, with the Rector, compose the Corporation, are chosen at an annual meeting, which is held on the Tuesday immediately after the First Sunday in Advent. Electors at such a meeting must be men of full age who have been regular attendants at the worship of St. George's for one year prior to the election, and have contributed to the support thereof. No person is eligible for the office of vestryman unless he is a qualified voter and has been baptized. No person is eligible for the office of church warden unless he is a qualified voter and a communicant in the Episcopal Church. The term of one of the wardens and of three of the vestrymen expires annually. Thus provision is made on the one side for continuity and on the other side for change. The Corporation has a clerk and a treasurer, a committee on envelopes, in charge of collections, an auditing committee, a finance committee, and a committee on the property.

The following are the wardens and vestrymen of St. George's as Dr. Rainsford's rectorship ends and Mr. Birckhead's rectorship begins. The date against each name denotes the year when such officer's term of service began.

GENERAL MANAGEMENT

WARDENS

John Pierpont Morgan, 1868   John Noble Stearns, 1871

VESTRYMEN

R. Fulton Cutting, 1883   William Jay Schieffelin, 1896
William Foulke, 1892   H. H. Pike, 1896
Seth Low, 1893   John Seely Ward, Jr., 1896
Henry W. Munroe, 1895   James W. Markoe, M.D., 1899
           Charles S. Brown, 1905

II.—THE STAFF

The Staff, of seven men and six women, all of whom receive salaries, is composed of the Rector, four assistant ministers, the Rector's secretary, the organist, three deaconesses, three parish workers, one of whom is a trained nurse, and the branch secretary of the Girls' Friendly Society. All of these persons give their entire time to the work of the parish.

From the beginning of Dr. Rainsford's rectorship, St. George's has been a training-school for young clergymen. These young men have come, for the most part, straight from the seminary. They have commonly been chosen, of late years, by young men who are already members of the Staff. The seminary graduate of two or three years' standing is still in sympathetic touch with the men who were under-classmen when he was a senior. He knows them by personal acquaintance. He chooses now one and now another whom the Rector may invite to spend the summer vacation at St. George's. These men, who have still a year of their seminary life before them, take part in this summer work, while others of the Staff are on their holidays. Thus the men get an idea of what the work is, and the Rector and his associates get their measure of the men. Then, when the time comes, the right men are called.

When a man has been asked by the Rector to become an assistant, he enters into a definite contract, in which certain duties are assigned to him, his salary is specified, and a study and bedroom are given him, in company with his brethren, on the top floor of the Parish House.

His first duty is to visit in a certain district. For purposes of visitation, the city is divided into four such districts. The people in the locality committed to him are of all classes, rich and poor, educated and uneducated. "At first," says Dr. Rainsford, "there was a remonstrance all over the parish against my sending the young clergy to visit. Some said, 'We do not want these young pastorettes coming around visiting us,' so I had to tell them, 'Then you had better go to some other church. It is quite impossible for me to visit you all. When you are sick or when you need me, I will come. But meanwhile I look to you people to aid me in training and keeping my junior clergy. Receive my clergy and give them opportunities to know you.'" Accordingly, the young parson calls on all the people of his district as their pastor, and visits them socially. He is to be on the watch for volunteer workers. He is to see that the young people, so far as they need it, join the classes and societies. He waits for no specific assignments, but moves about freely, commonly spending his afternoons in this occupation. It is found that in order to maintain the life of a parish of the size and character of St. George's, each of the four assistants must make from thirty-five to forty visits each week. Thus, in addition to calls in cases of special need, each man visits everybody in his district twice a year.

Among the people whose social engagements are many,

he avoids wasting his time in fruitless calling by use of this card, which he sends ahead of him a few days in advance:

> **ST. GEORGE'S RECTORY,
> 209 EAST 16TH ST.**
>
> One of my clergy will be calling in your neighborhood
> ....
> about............P. M. ....
> I hope you can make time to see him.
>
> [Signed by the Rector.]

A second duty of an assistant minister is to represent the Rector in some organization. For example, he is assigned to the trade-school. There he meets a board of directors, a number of supervisors, a corps of salaried teachers, and three hundred boys and young men. He is to come into acquaintance with all these persons, to advise with them if they desire, to help to maintain the spirit of enthusiasm and loyalty, but to hold no office. He is to bring new volunteer workers to take the places of those who fall out, and to get in new boys from the Sunday-school.

A third duty is in the Sunday-school. There he has a class or a department. Now one class and now another, and this year this department and next year that, so that he may be thoroughly trained in all the details of the business.

An important office which is held by every assistant in turn is that of "clergyman on duty" for the week. During his week he acts as senior assistant. "At first," says Dr. Rainsford, "we had a system that included senior and junior clergy, but I found that necessarily seniority was accounted by length of time, and not by competency, and I found that the senior, being only human, arrogated to himself certain rights which were not helpful to himself or to his junior brothers. Then I got the inspiration that each of my clergy should be the senior assistant for one week in a month; during that week he is officer of the week, so to speak, as a cadet at West Point is selected to be officer of the day; he must see the people, take the funerals, preach, and make emergency calls. This plan has worked delightfully; it gives each man as many rights as the others, and in addition gives more leisure to the others to read." They, also, all have the same chance to take responsibility and to master the executive details. The senior curate takes the morning service. He answers all the letters which the Rector turns over to the clergy. He sees all the people who come to the parish house for help, for advice, or for information. He takes the baptisms, marriages, and burials of the week, unless another member of the staff is asked for.

The clergy, except the one on duty for the week, are expected to keep their mornings sacred to study and to the preparation of sermons. The Rector advises them as to their reading, sending them books, calling their attention often to notable matters in the daily papers and in the magazines. And these matters he discusses with them freely.

For deaconesses, women of refinement, who have executive ability, know how to care for the sick, and are likely to be influential among boys and girls and mothers, are chosen. Young college women are invited to the deaconess house in the summer, while some of the regular workers are taking their vacation, and are thus enabled to put their sense of vocation to a practical test.

GENERAL MANAGEMENT

ST. GEORGE'S STAFF—DISTRIBUTION OF WORK, 19—, 19—

STAFF	REPRESENTING THE RECTOR IN THE ORGANIZATIONS	VISITING DISTRICTS	COMP. CLASSES	SP. SERV., CHURCH	SUNDAY-SCHOOL						
Rev. H. B.	Sund.-sch., Sr. Dept.; Choir; Up-town Sund.-sch.; Miss.-Socs.	14th–72d St., including Avenues	✓			Hosp. Cl.					
Rev. H. S.	Men's Club, Ath. Branch	2nd–3d St.; 73d–115th St., and Aves.	✓	3 P.M., Sun.	Lesson Com. Class Org. Men's B. Cl.						
Rev. A. T.	Primary Dept.; Trade-sch.	116th–121st St., and Aves.	✓	Wed. 8 P.M.							
Rev. C. H.	Battalion; Dramatic Soc.	15th St. and down, and Aves.; Brooklyn, etc.	✓	Sun. 3 P.M. Wed. 8 P.M.	Jun. 1 and 2 Class Org.	Catechism Class					
Deaconess S.	K. D's.; Chancel Com.	Half of 16th St.; 12th, 11th, and 10th Sts.; 6th St. and down, and Aves.	✓		Jun. 3, B. Cl., P.M.	Miss. Soc.	Holy T'ble	Bapt.	Mothers' Meeting		
Deaconess Y.	Miss. Soc.; Dramatic Soc.	Special Visiting	✓		Lesson Com. Teach. Meet. Bible Cl.						
Deaconess W.	Library; Wom. Ind. Soc.; Relief Dept.	18th–27th St.	✓		Class, Sen. Dept.	G. F. S.					
Miss Tp.	Care of Deaconess House; Sewing-school	13th–15th Sts., and Aves.	✓		Class, Sen. Dept.	G. F. S.	K. D's.	Cat. Cl.	Afternoon Service		
Miss. Tl.	Care of Sick; Married Women's Soc.	7th, 8th, and 9th Sts.			Class, Sen. Dept.	G. F. S.	Catechism Class	Afternoon Service			
Miss. M.	G. F. S.	Special Visiting				G. F. S.					
Miss. R.		Half of 16th, and 19th Sts and Aves.			Bible Class						

To be revised May, 19—

The deaconesses receive assignments of duty such as we have described regarding the clergy.

The plan on page 7 shows the distribution of the work among four clergymen, three deaconesses, and four other workers. It is made out for a year.

Once every week, with unfailing regularity, the members of the staff meet the Rector in his study. The hour is immediately after the nine-o'clock service on Monday morning. Only the most imperative excuse is accepted for absence from this conference. The impressions of Sunday are fresh in mind, and successes and failures are frankly considered. In one of the departments of the Sunday-school the attendance was unsatisfactory; what was the matter? Yesterday, at the evening service, the Rector heard one of the assistants preach. The Rector tells what he thought of the sermon—praise or blame, as is deserved or needed. There is a great bundle of letters in three piles; one clip holds those which the Rector answers by his stenographer; another, those which he assigns to his secretary to answer; the third lot he submits to the staff for discussion. The members of the staff, in turn, bring up the condition and problems of the various organizations, confessing failures and asking for direction. Cases of individuals are considered.

A page from the secretary's note-book will show with what care and particularity the interests of individual parishioners are studied.

Miss C. H., 40 East — St.	EXPLANATIONS
1. Old member returned, Oct. 5. 2. Has been abroad for years. 3. name given to Deaconesses. 4. To be called upon for work Oct. 8, 05. 5. To be called upon to join Envelope System, Oct. 8, 05. 6. Reports received. Will work in	Lines 1 and 2 explain themselves; 3 and 4 mean that the name was given at the staff meeting to one of the Deaconesses to get the person interested in the work for which she is most suited; 6 and 7 mean that the lady has taken up work in two organizations and

GENERAL MANAGEMENT

~~7. The G. F. S. and Sunday-school teacher.~~
~~8. Mailed letter to join Envelope System ✓ Oct. 8, 1905.~~

that she has given the name to the secretary of the G. F. S. and Sunday-school superintendent; 8 means that letter was mailed, and the ✓ next to it means that reply was received. The X through the whole indicates that all is finished and entered in the various records.

M. B., 1 Lexington Ave.

~~1. Rev. Mr. ———, of New Brunswick, in letter of Oct. 1, 1905~~
~~2. asks Rector to have this man~~
~~3. looked after. Has just come into the State.~~
~~4. Name given to clergy, Oct. 8, 05.~~
~~5. Has joined ...... church on Madison Avenue.~~

Lines 1, 2, and 3 explain themselves; 4, name given to clergyman to get the young man interested; 5, the young man told the clergyman that he had joined another church; X means that we can do nothing more.

Mrs. J. W. and Son, 405 — Ave

~~1. Met her in church, says want~~
~~2. to join church   Oct. 1, 05.~~
~~3. Mailed family record and literature.~~
~~4. About Envelope System, Oct. 3, 05 ✓~~
~~5. Name given to clergy, Oct. 8, 05.~~
~~6. Family came on visitors' night to go over building, Oct. 15, 05.~~

Lines 1 and 2 explain themselves; 3 and 4 mean that the secretary mailed family record and literature concerning Envelope System, ✓ check means both received; 5 and 6 mean that the clergyman called and invited them to view the work; X means done.

C. H. and sister, 111 E. — St.

1. Asked for Year-book, Nov., 1905.
2. Saying we have attended
3. for several years, but not
4. yet presented letter from......
   Church.
5. Called upon by Deaconess.
6. Asked to meet Rector Monday even'ng.
7. Asked to join Envelope System.

The meeting ends with a prayer, after which each person, including the Rector, submits a written report of the week's work. These figures are entered in a book under the respective names.

ADMINISTRATION OF AN INSTITUTIONAL CHURCH

St. George's Church, New York
Weekly Report — Clergy

	SERMONS AND ADDRESSES	VISITS	CLASSES AND MEETINGS	P. COM.	VISITS REC.
Sun.					
Mon.					
Tues.					
Wed.					
Thur.					
Fri.					
Sat.					
Total					

Week ending _____

Name _____

St. George's Church, New York
Weekly Report — Lay Workers

	VISITS	CLASSES MEETINGS	VISITS REC.	
Sun.				
Mon.				
Tues.				
Wed.				
Thur.				
Fri.				
Sat.				
Total				

Week ending _____

Name _____

GENERAL MANAGEMENT

Besides this formal meeting, the members of the staff are always welcome at the Rector's study, and see much of him in the Parish House. It is expected, however, that they will so far as possible work out matters of detail individually, or by consultation among themselves.

Once in awhile, say every three years, is held a general conference of workers. The Rector presides, and the head of each department reads a paper; except where the head is one of the staff, in which case it is read by another member.

These reports are made in the following form:

REPORT

Conference of Workers in St. George's Parish

Wednesday, February 24th, 8 P.M., Memorial Building.

Name of organization _____

Purpose of   "   _____

Number of workers _____
     (Officers, teachers, associates, etc.)

Number of members _____

Times and place of meeting _____

Running Expenses _____

    1. Appropriation
    2. Collected
    3. Total

Work done during past year _____

Present weakness of organization _____

Remarks:

This report must not take more than three minutes to read.

ADMINISTRATION OF AN INSTITUTIONAL CHURCH

After each report there is a discussion, in which new ideas are contributed, and every member is given some acquaintance with the general aspects of the parish industries.

The following letter bids the workers to the meeting:

ST. GEORGE'S RECTORY
209 EAST 16TH ST.

My dear Friend:

Will you oblige me by laying all other engagements aside and attending a meeting of St. George's Workers, Wednesday, February 24th, 8.30, in the chapel. I beg you to do as I ask if you possibly can. Come too, please, prepared to remain till 10.30.

Your friend and Rector,
W. S. Rainsford.

February —, 19—.

II

THE PLANT

I. The Church and Rectory—II. The Memorial House—III. The Deaconess House—IV. The Trade-School—V. The Sea-side Cottage.

I.—THE CHURCH AND RECTORY

The gates of the church stand open, like the gates of the New Jerusalem. By the door, in the yard, is a sign bearing the invitation, *Church open. Come in, rest and pray.* The church is thus at the service of the people, all the year round, from 8 A.M. until 5 P.M. This privilege was much used in the days when the church was in the midst of private residences. At present, that condition having changed, and the location being off the line of the daily movement of the people, on a quiet street, not so many come as formerly. But the tenement-house offers such scanty opportunities for privacy that the open church becomes a refuge and a silent benediction. In some open churches a shelf of good books is provided for these transient visitors. Two assistant sextons are always present, except during the hour for luncheon, then some pensioner of the parish is on duty.

In the vestibule is a framed list of the services. Just inside the church door is the Rector's box, designated for communications or contributions. On a small table at the head of each aisle are family-record blanks, forms for envelope subscriptions, forms of application for the year-book, and other such printed matter. Under one of the tables is a little closet, in charge of the head usher, containing smelling-salts and other simple remedies to be used in cases of fainting or other sudden illness. A space in one of the vestibules is curtained off and contains a couch for such emergencies. In another corner of the vestibule is the ushers' closet for hats and coats.

St. George's Church holds 1575 persons. The following figures are given to show the accuracy with which all the facts pertaining to the parish are ascertained and recorded: The nave seats 1020; north and south galleries, 408; east gallery, 50; choir, 82; chancel stalls, 15. Each pew is supplied with prayer-books and hymn-books, and these are regularly inspected to see that the right proportion is kept and that all ragged books are removed. By resolution of the vestry, as a precaution in case of fire or other alarm, no chairs are ever placed in the aisles or chancel. For the same reason the church doors open outward.

In one corner of the vestry-room is a closet for the vestments, with the names of the clergy over the hooks. There is a lavatory in another corner. A third corner contains a desk in which are kept the service-book—that is, the book of record of services—and forms for returns of baptism, marriage, and burial. A closet under this desk contains extra surplices, with stoles and hoods, and markers for the books. The communion linen, in charge of a deaconess, is kept in a set of drawers. The chancel committee meets here on Saturdays to repair the vestments of the clergy and choir. The laundry work is given to a reliable woman who is paid for it. The following prayer is printed and framed on the wall of the vestry-room, and is intoned by the clergyman in charge of the service, with responses by the choir, before the beginning of the processional hymn:

THE PLANT

> *V. Lord, hear our prayer*
> *R. And let our cry come unto Thee.*
> *V. O Lord, open Thou our lips*
> *R. And our mouth shall show forth Thy praise.*
> *O Lord, help us worthily to magnify Thy glorious name; prepare our hearts for Thy worship. Help us now with soul and body to offer to Thee an acceptable service, and save us through Jesus Christ, our Lord. AMEN.*

A plan of the church, such as is here given, is also framed in the vestry-room. A card sets forth certain facts about fees for marriages. The fee for the clergyman is optional. "Clergy are always glad to marry without any fee those who cannot afford to pay anything." No fee is to be paid to the sexton unless for extra work done, or unless the marriage takes place at an hour when the church is not commonly open. The organist has ten dollars for the small organ and twenty-five if he uses both organs. The choir is to be paid according to the number employed. When the church is used at other hours than from nine to five, there is a charge of ten dollars, and five more if the electric light is used.

There are two rooms for the choir—one for the men and boys, the other for the women. Each is lined with closets for vestments, and for prayer-books, hymn-books, and music. All the music for the choir is substantially bound and kept in covered boxes. These boxes are arranged alphabetically for convenience in finding anthems. The duty of the librarian is to arrange the needed music for rehearsals and services in stiff folio covers. Each singer has his own hymn-book, which is kept in a compartment numbered to correspond with the number on his surplice.

The rectory adjoins the church.

II.—THE MEMORIAL HOUSE

Dr. Rainsford saw very soon after his coming to St. George's that "in order to do the work of Christ at all effectually in a city like New York, it is absolutely necessary to reach a large number of our people not only once in seven days, but during the working-days of the week. Thousands of young men and women, not always of the poorest class, go to the devil for need of some place where they can enjoy innocent recreation without the presence of active temptation." This statement appealed to a wise and wealthy parishioner, and the Parish House was built in answer to it. "Those of us who have comfortable homes," the Rector said, "little dream what temptations beset the young men and women of our city, who, many of them far from home, have no place of resort but the tenement-house or the boarding-house. On Sundays and week-nights, the public room in the boarding-house, if they belong to the more well-to-do class, is the only place open to them." Thus the Parish House was meant to be not only a place for the Sunday-school and other classes, but a "palace of delight," where young people could play games or read or dance or listen to music. Some people who read the parable of the prodigal son with great seriousness miss the fact that a part of the wisdom of the good father consisted in providing his son with music and dancing on the evening of his return. It is possible that had there been

ST. GEORGE'S MEMORIAL HOUSE
203, 205, 207 East 16th Street

THE PLANT

ORDER OF WORK—ST. GEORGE'S PARISH

SUNDAY	Holy Communion: Every Sunday, 8 A.M. 1st " 11 A.M. 3d " 0 P.M	Sunday-sch'l, 9.30 A.M. Sen. and Jun.	Men's Bible Class, 9.50 A.M.	Morning P. and S., 11 A.M.	Men's Club open from 1 to 10 P.M.
	Children's Services, 3.15 P.M.	Sunday-school, Primary Dept., 3 P.M.	Library, 4 to 5 P.M.	Holy Baptism: 1st Sun. in month, 4 P.M.; 3d Sun. in month, 7 P.M.	Evening Prayer Service, 8 P.M.
	Bible Class for Women, 3 P.M.				
MONDAY	Morning Prayer, 9 A.M.	Meeting of Staff with Rector in Rectory, 10 A.M.	Trade-school, 7.30 to 9.30 P.M.	King's Daughters, 8 P.M.	G. P. S., 8 P.M.
	Wom. Ind. Soc., Work-rooms, 8 A.M. to 4 P.M.	Men's Club and Gym., 8 A.M. to 11 P.M.	Men's Club and Gym., open for visitors, 8.30 P.M. to 10.30 P.M.	Men's Club Elect. Com., 9.30 P.M.	Battalion Club, 7.30 to 10 P.M. Battalion Elect. Com., 8 P.M.
	Dramatic Club, 8 P.M.				
TUESDAY	Morning Prayer, 9 A.M.	Wom. Ind. Soc., 10 A.M.	Wom. Ind. Soc., Work-room open from 8 A.M. to 4 P.M.	Men's Club and Gym., 8 A.M. to 11 P.M.	Happy-hour Club, 2.30 P.M.

And so on.

more of such pleasures earlier in the story the prodigal son might have remained contentedly at home. Anyhow, these Scriptural joys, and some others, were set forth in the parish house, and have been abundantly justified by experience.

In the main entrance hall of the memorial house, facing the door, is a board showing the days and hours of all the parochial industries.

In the office of the secretary the floor-plans of the house are framed. On these plans are indicated the organizations to which special rooms are assigned for the year, according to the days of the week. Commonly, a society keeps the same room year after year. It is found best, however, to make the assignments year by year in order to provide for changes. When a society is disbanded, or needs less space, or more, some unpleasantness is avoided if it is understood that the arrangements are for twelve months only.

The six plans here follow, each with its accompanying explanation:

EXPLANATION OF THE USE OF THE FIRST FLOOR

A—Main Entrance Hall.

 On left of entrance, memorial tablet. Hung on elevator casing "Order of Work" (see page 17), and sign, "No smoking or loitering in the halls of the building."

 Back of the elevator, railed in enclosure used as follows: Telephone with switches. Local 'phones to sexton, engineer, and church. Closets for locking up consignments received for the various organizations, and book showing when elevator man (there are two) received these consignments.

 Key-board containing keys to all rooms and closets in the building.

 In the elevator, "In and Out" board for the clergy,

THE PLANT

and mail-rack. Notice for entertainments are often also placed in the elevator.

B—Girls' Entrance Hall.

Room C—Reception-room.
All people who call to see the clergy are first received there. It is also the office of the Sunday-school secretary, and here is the reference library of the Sunday-school.

Room D, called "the large room, ground floor," used as follows:

Sunday.	Junior I. and II. of Sunday-school, at	9.30 A.M.
	Kindergarten of Sunday-school, at	3.00 P.M.
Monday.	Girls' Friendly Society (Missionary work)	8.00 P.M.
Tuesday.	Women's Industrial Society (Cutting-out Committee)	10.30 A.M. – 1.00 P.M.
	(Also sale of the garments)	
	Girls' Friendly Society:	
	(Kitchen garden)	4.00 P.M.
	(Calisthenic)	8.00 P.M.
Wednesday.	Missionary Society (2d Wednesday in month)	10.30 A.M.
	Women's Industrial Society (sale of clothing, 1st and 3d Wednesdays)	9.00 A.M.
	(2d and 4th Wednesdays)	2.00 P.M.
Thursday.	Married Women's Society (Tea-room), from	2.00 – 5.00 P.M.
	Girls' Friendly Society (Calisthenic)	8.00 P.M.
Friday.	Girls' Friendly Society (Calisthenic)	8.00 P.M.
Saturday.	Sewing-school	9.30 A.M.

Rooms E and F, called "the library-room" because the parish library is there:

Sunday.	Junior IV. and V. Sunday-school	9.30 A.M.
	Library	4.00 P.M.

ADMINISTRATION OF AN INSTITUTIONAL CHURCH

Monday.	Kindergarten	9.00 A.M. – 12.00 M.
	Library	7.30 P.M.
Tuesday.	Kindergarten	9.00 A.M. – 12.00 M.
	Girls' Friendly Society:	
	(Embroidery. Candidates)	3.00 P.M.
	(Embroidery)	8.00 P.M.
Wednesday.	Kindergarten	9.00 A.M. – 12.00 M.
	Library	7.30 P.M.
	Selling of groceries	2.00 P.M.
Thursday.	Kindergarten	9.00 A.M. – 12.00 M.
	Married Women's Society	2.00 P.M.
	Girls' Friendly Society (Embroidery)	8.00 P.M.
Friday.	Kindergarten	9.00 A.M. – 12.00 M.
	Library	7.30 P.M.
Saturday.	Sewing-school	9.30 A.M.

Room G—Grocery store for the Relief Department, open Wednesday from 2 P.M. on; otherwise used as cloak-room.

Rooms H, I, and J.

Sunday.	Junior IV.*b*, Sunday-school	9.30 A.M.
Monday.	Work-rooms of the Women's Industrial Society	8.00 A.M. – 4.00 P.M.
	Girls' Friendly Society (Missionary)	8.00 P.M.
Tuesday.	Work-rooms of the Women's Industrial Society	8.00 A.M. – 4.00 P.M.
	Girls' Friendly Society:	
	(Cooking. Candidates)	4.00 P.M.
	(Cooking)	8.00 P.M.
Wednesday.	Work-rooms of the Women's Industrial Society	8.00 A.M. – 4.00 P.M.
	Girls' Friendly Society	8.00 P.M.
Thursday.	Married Women's Society	2.00 P.M.
	Girls' Friendly Society (Cooking)	8.00 P.M.
Friday.	Women's Industrial Society	8.00 A.M. – 4.00 P.M.
	Girls' Friendly Society (Cooking)	8.00 P.M.
Saturday,	Sewing-school	9.30 A.M.

THE PLANT

EXPLANATION OF THE ROOMS ON THE SECOND FLOOR

Room A is the Vestry-room.

On the second Monday of each month the vestry holds its regular meeting here. On Sundays this is used for a Bible Class of the Sunday-school. At all other times the room is used by the secretary.

On one side of the room is a large safe, built in the wall. On one side of it are kept the records of the parish, the old ones and the new ones. On the other side of the safe are kept matters concerning the corporation — such as the minutes of the vestry and papers which have to be filed. In another corner is the safe of the corporation treasurer. In another corner of the room can be found a set of closets with pigeon-holes.

The first set holds all the entries for the parish books, such as:

Change of addresses.
New names.
Transfers.
Marriage records for entry.
Baptism   "   "   "
Burial   "   "   "
Confirmation "   "   "

The second set of pigeon-holes holds the blank forms in use in the parish.

The third set of pigeon-holes contains, in a classified way, all the matters concerning the parish, such as copies of letters which have been sent out, plans of festivals, lists of special services, memorials, dedications, and so on.

In another corner is the secretary's desk.

Room B is called "the chapel."

Sunday.	Senior department of the Sunday-school	9.30 A.M.
	Primary department of the Sunday-school	3.00 P.M.
Monday.	King's Daughters	8.00 P.M.
Tuesday.	Girls' Friendly Society (Calisthenic. Candidates)	4.00 P.M.
	Girls' Friendly Society	8.00 P.M.

ADMINISTRATION OF AN INSTITUTIONAL CHURCH

Wednesday.	(Kept open for special events.)	
Thursday.	Married Women's Society	3.00 P.M.
	Mothers' meeting	8.00 P.M.
Friday.	Girls' Friendly Society (Calisthenic)	8.00 P.M.
Saturday.	Sewing-school	9.30 A.M.

Room C.

Girls' Friendly Society club-room. Girls who live too far away to go home from their work and get back to the Girls' Friendly Society in time for meetings can come here to prepare their own suppers. Also used as office of the branch secretary. On Sundays as a young women's Bible class.

Rooms D and E.

Monday.	King's Daughters	8.00 P.M.
Tuesday.	Girl's Friendly Society (Drawn-work and basketry)	8.00 P.M.
	Women's Industrial Society (Cooking class)	2.30 P.M.
Friday.	Girls' Friendly Society (Basketry)	8.00 P.M.

MEZZANINE STORY—(THE GALLERY FLOOR)

Rooms A, B, C, D, E, and F.

Sunday.	Sunday-school—Senior V., two men's Bible classes, and two Bible classes for young women held in the respective rooms	9.30 A.M.
Monday.	King's Daughters use all the above rooms except room *F*.	8.00 P.M.
Tuesday.	Girls Friendly Society (Dress-making and millinery) use all the above rooms with the exception of *A* and *F*.	8.00 P.M.
Thursday.	Girls' Friendly Society (Embroidery, drawn-work, and literary) use all the rooms with the exception of rooms *A* and *F*.	8.00 P.M.
	Married Women's Society	3.00 P.M.

ST. GEORGE'S CHURCH,
STUYVESANT SQUARE, NEW YORK

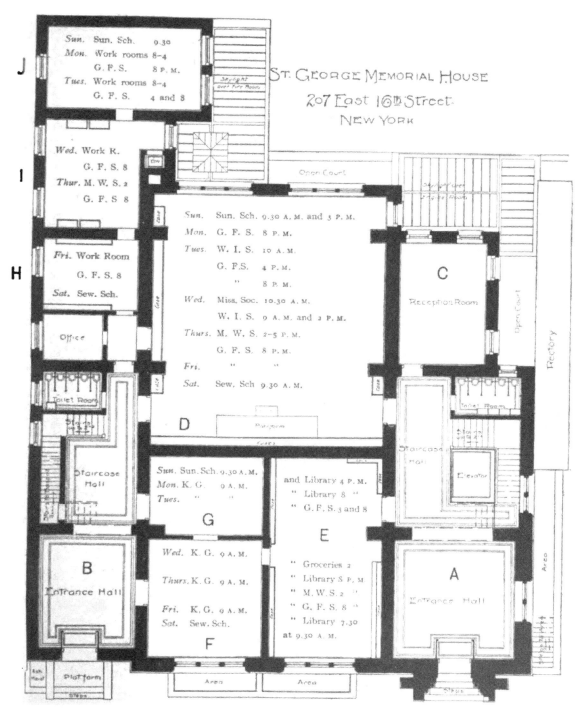

FIRST STORY PLAN
Scale 4 ft to an inch

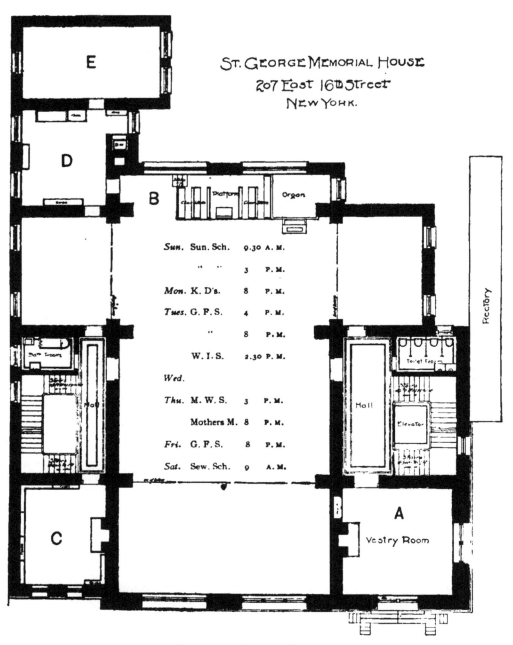

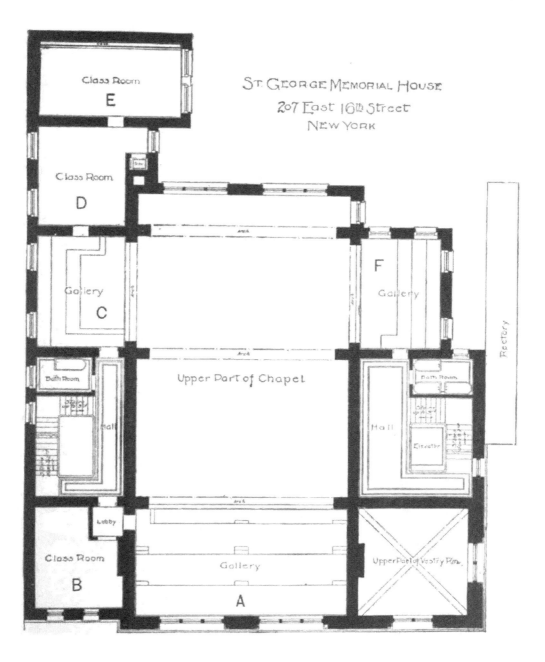

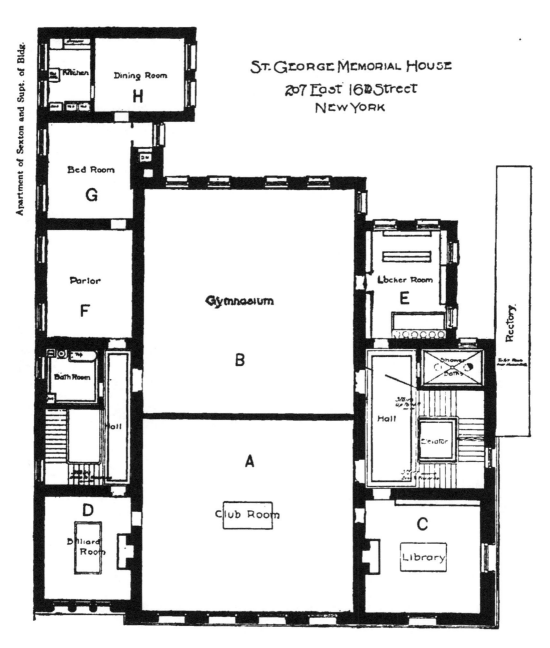

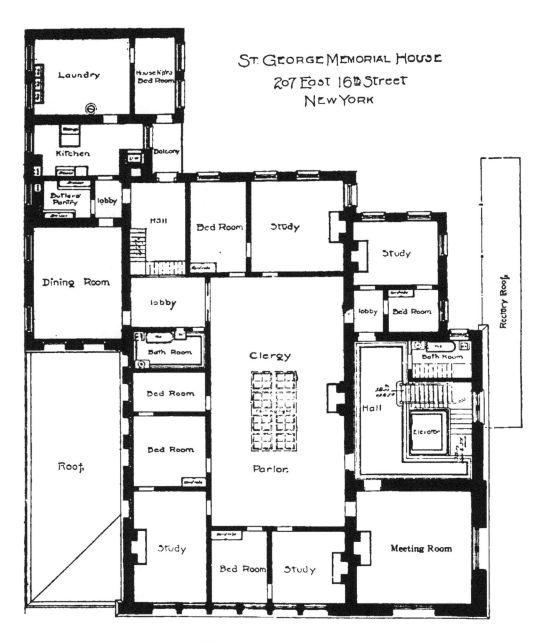

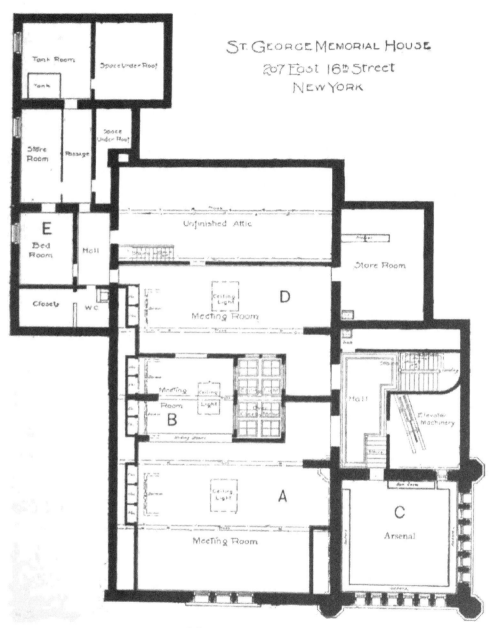

FIFTH STORY PLAN
Scale 4 ft to an inch

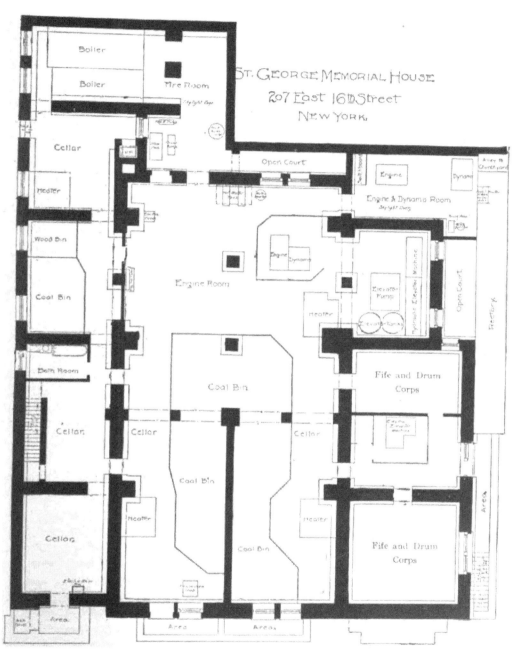

BASEMENT STORY PLAN
Scale 4 ft to on Inch

THE PLANT

Friday. Girls' Friendly Society (Dress-making and millinery) use all the rooms with the exception of rooms A and F . . . . 8.00 P.M.
Saturday. Sewing-school . . . . 9.30 A.M.

THIRD FLOOR—(CALLED MEN'S CLUB FLOOR)

The front rooms, A, D, and C, are the club-rooms of the Men's Club. Room A the general room, D the billiard-room, C the library; open daily to its members from 8 A.M. to 11 P.M., and on Sundays from 1 P.M. to 11 P.M., in the mornings the club-room and library being used for two young men's Bible classes. In the rear is the gymnasium, with locker-room and shower-baths.

The gymnasium (open daily from 8 A.M. to 11 P.M.) is as-assigned to the organizations as follows:

Tuesdays for the Girls' Friendly Society, from 8 to 9 P.M.

Thursdays for the Battalion, from 8 to 10 P.M.

Saturdays for the younger boys (divided into classes), beginning at 12 M., ending at 3 P.M.

At all other times for the use of the members of the Men's Club. And Sunday mornings it is used for classes by the Sunday-school for one of the junior departments.

Rooms F, G, and H form the apartments of the superintendent, who is also the sexton of the church.

FOURTH FLOOR—(OR CLERGY HOUSE)

Around the clergy parlor are the clergy rooms, for each clergyman a study (which is for the clergyman alone, but during the preparation for Confirmation they hold their classes there, and aside from that hold business meetings there for committees of the organizations in which they represent the Rector) and bedroom, a guest-room, and a meeting-room, two baths, dining-room, kitchen, laundry, and a room for the housekeeper. The clergy keep house and pay expenses out of their salaries, the vestry giving them a small appropriation to pay for refurnishing household goods and towards extra expenses. Heat and light the church also gives.

The reception-room is used to hold various gatherings. On Monday evenings the "At Home" of the Rector and clergy; at other times it is used for conferences of the teachers, receptions, the Rector's Confirmation Class for men and women on Sunday afternoons.

In the meeting-room is held on Sunday mornings a Sunday-school class, and in the afternoons a Bible class for mothers.

On week-days the room is used for various meetings.

FIFTH FLOOR

Up to a few years ago this story was an open garret, but the work grew rapidly, and therefore it was changed into rooms. The rooms A, B, C belong to the Battalion Club, open daily from 8 P.M. to 10.30 P.M., room C being the arsenal.

Room D belongs to the Dramatic and Literary Society.

Room E is the servants' room of the clergy house.

On Sunday mornings, first Sunday in month, breakfast is served in rooms A, B, and D, after the eight-o'clock communion, to the young communicants of the Sunday-school and the teachers.

BASEMENT STORY

The basement contains the furnaces for heating the building, electric light switches, elevator pump, etc. Two rooms designated to the Battalion for its Fife and Drum Corps, and a shooting-range for the Battalion have been improvised here also.

The largest room in the Parish House is used on Sunday for the school. On some other days it is much in demand by various organizations for dances, plays, and lectures. In order to avoid coincidence of events, and undue preference for any one society or kind of entertainment, such a plan as on page 25, revised annually, is framed for public reference:

THE PLANT

1905–1906

	OCT.	NOV.	DEC.	JAN.	FEB.	MARCH	APRIL	MAY	JUNE
	WED.	WED.	WED.	WED.	WED.	WED.	WED.	WED.	WED.
	4 Trade-school	1 *Communicants' Class*	6 Men's Club dance	3 *Communicants' Class*	7 Trade-school	7 Lecture in Church	4 Exhibition (also Tues.)	2 Trade-school commencement. *Communicants' Class*	6 G. F. S. dance
	11 General dance	8 G. F. S. dance	13 Married Women's Society	10 G. F. S. Quarterly	14 Married Women's Society	14	11 *Holy Week*	9 G. F. S. Quarterly	13
	18 Dramatic Society	15 Battalion dance	20 Christmas Festival Kindergarten	17 Ath. Com. Wrestlers dance	21 Men's Club dance	21	18 Men's Club	16 General dance	20
	25 G. F. S. Convention (also Thurs.)	22 G. F. S. Quarterly	27 Christmas Festival	24 Dramatic Society	28 *Ash Wednesday* *Communicants' Class*	28 *Communicants' Class*	25 Battalion dance	23 Sun-school graduation	27 *Communicants' Class*
		29 *Communicants' Class*		31 *Communicants' Class*				30 Married Women's Society. *Communicants' Class*	

CHAPEL, St. George's Memorial House. Schedule for year 1905–1906. To be revised May, 1906.
N. B.—This is passed upon by the staff and the heads of the various organisations. Please note the Communicants' Classes. They are put down here for the reason that no entertainment is allowed to conflict with the serious and religious side of the work.

ADMINISTRATION OF AN INSTITUTIONAL CHURCH

Many things come up which have to be arranged for as the need arises. For these a calendar like the following is prepared:

| January | THURSDAY, 4 | 1906 |

To the Supt.: Speak to me about arrangement of Confirmation Classes.

———, Secretary.

FRIDAY, 5

S. S. "Class 1909"	Large room ground floor (Dance)	8 P.M.	J. R.[1]
S. S. "Class 1905"	Meeting-room, top floor.	8 P.M.	H. B.
Trade-school.	Dramatic-room (Rehearsal)	8 P.M.	A. T.

[1] Initials on side represents the name of person who made the entry in the book.

DEACONESS HOUSE
208 and 210 East 16th Street

THE PLANT

Thus the superintendent of the building need ask no questions as to how the rooms are to be used for the day. He goes daily to the office and looks at the plans and calendar, and so knows how each room is to be arranged.

III.—THE DEACONESS HOUSE

To supplement the work in the Parish House, it was necessary to have a staff of trained women workers living in community. Dr. Rainsford wrote: "It is hopeless to expect to raise the fallen or support the weak, under the conditions presented in our great city, by merely volunteer aid. We want the best women, the most cultivated in our land, to undertake this work; but for it they must be trained. Personally, I myself am sure that the day will come—I hope it may come soon—when the ministrations, nay, the fascinations of the deaconess life will touch the imagination of multitudes of our women, and lead them to give not a mere driblet of their time, but years of life to that work among the young and the sick, and the very poor and oppressed, to which by instinct and sympathy they are so certainly called of God."

It has been found that five people, living in community, can do more parish work satisfactorily than ten people living in their own homes.

With the exception of the office, the Deaconess House is meant to be used quite differently from the parish building; it is not intended to house the organizations. Aside from being a residence for the deaconesses, it is meant to be a place where the volunteer workers may hold their meetings. Every Thursday afternoon the deaconesses are "at home" to the ladies of the parish, and tea is served; in this way many new-comers are attracted to the work and become interested in it. Women of means, in need of a retreat or rest, are invited to come for short periods, paying the expenses incurred by their stay.

Plans of the various floors of the Deaconess House follow, with accompanying explanations.

FIRST FLOOR

In the hall can be found the "In and Out" board of the deaconesses. The deaconesses eat on one side of the large dining-room; the other side is used for small committee meetings—such as meetings of the Associates of the G. F. S., the Missionary Committee, the Associates of the Married Women's Society, the leaders of the King's Daughters, teachers' meetings, and confirmation classes. The whole room is at times used for suppers on special parish occasions. Visitors are received in the reception-room. In the office is kept a complete list of the families of the parish, living in tenement-houses, arranged alphabetically and according to streets. Lists of people out of work are kept here. The deaconess on duty can be seen here during office-hours every day, and the poor come here for relief and advice.

SECOND FLOOR

The parlor is used for "At Homes," receptions, special meetings, and confirmation classes.

On this floor is a small apartment for the house mother. The idea is that the deaconesses should not be hampered in their work in the parish by the duties of housekeeping.

THE PLANT

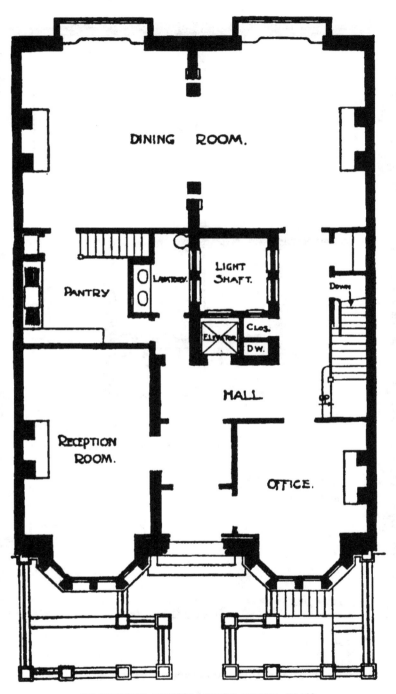

DEACONESS HOUSE—FIRST FLOOR PLAN

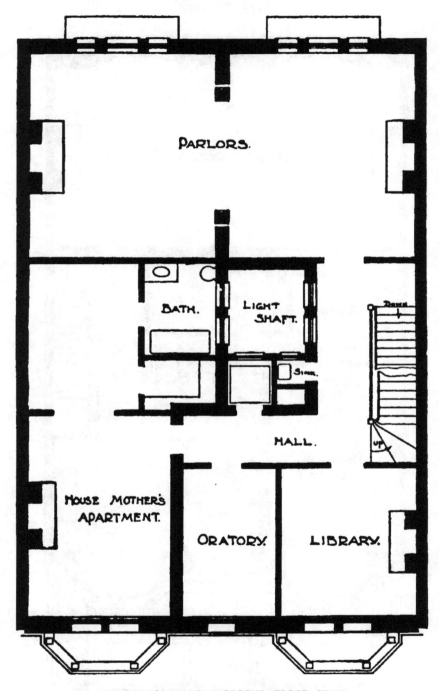

DEACONESS HOUSE—SECOND FLOOR PLAN

THE PLANT

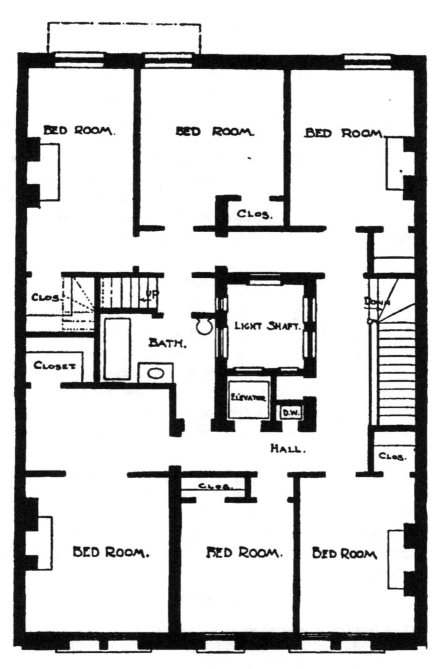

DEACONESS HOUSE—THIRD FLOOR PLAN

THIRD FLOOR

On this floor are the bedrooms of the deaconesses. Each deaconess has a large, airy, heated room. The four corner rooms are provided with open fire-places. The deaconesses, like the clergy, keep house, only with this difference: the clergy pay for the support of housekeeping out of their salaries, while the deaconesses receive a monthly appropriation from the church, out of which the household expenses are paid. All other expenses, such as repairs, coal, and wood, electric current, taxes, and insurance, are paid by the corporation treasurer.

FOURTH FLOOR

The three front rooms on the fourth floor make the infirmary, which is used for convalescent patients not yet strong enough to go back to tenement rooms. Many women and girls who have been sick in hospitals are necessarily discharged before they are fully able to resume their duties. Here they come and are provided with pleasant surroundings and nourishing food. Some who have not actually been sick, but are in immediate danger of breaking down, come here and are saved from serious illness. The floors are made of terrazzo, so that they can be flooded. A diet kitchen and drug-room adjoin the infirmary. A roof-garden with glass roof and southern exposure opens from this floor. In the rear are the servants rooms.

BASEMENT

The basement contains, the hot-water heating apparatus, the electric and gas meters, the wood and coal bins, a store-room, the kitchen, and the laundry.

THE PLANT

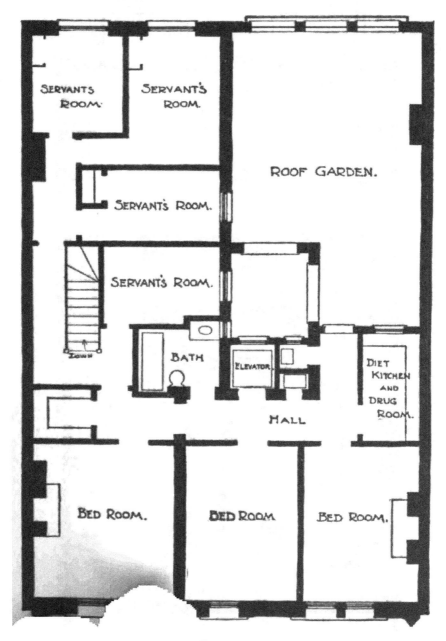

E—FOURTH FLOOR PLAN

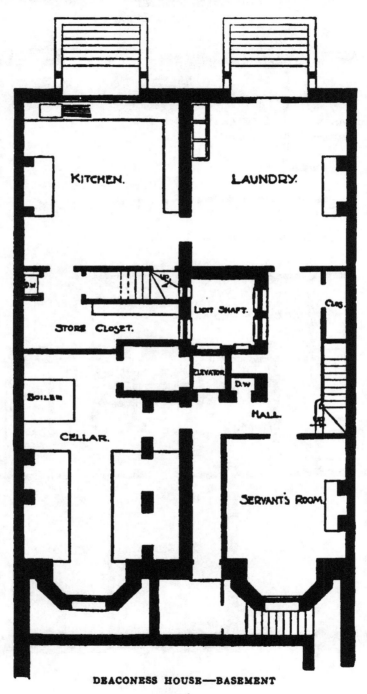

DEACONESS HOUSE—BASEMENT

THE PLANT

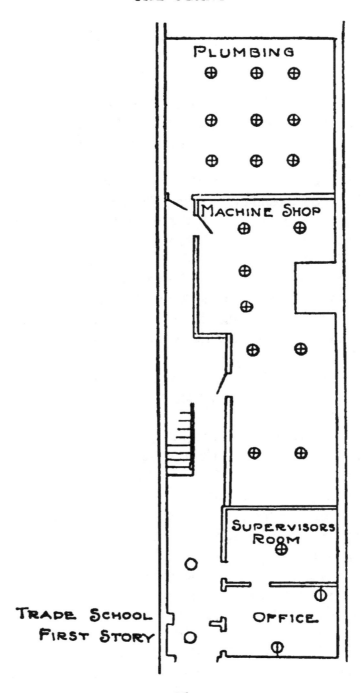

ADMINISTRATION OF AN INSTITUTIONAL CHURCH

IV.—THE TRADE-SCHOOL

FIRST FLOOR

The entrance is by a double front door, opening outward, which admits to a vestibule. Out of the vestibule the main outlet is by double doors, opening outward into the main hall of the building. There is also an entrance from the right of the vestibule into the office of the superintendent. After the time has arrived for the opening of the school, the inner double doors of the vestibule are locked, and late pupils must pass through the office, and thus to their class-rooms. In this way an account is taken of all who are late.

The office contains a desk for the superintendent and another for the secretary. In this room are two card-index systems, for enrolment, and for marking changes and keeping the records of the members of the school. Adjoining the office is the room of the supervisors—volunteer workers—for whose convenience tables, chairs, and desks are provided.

The first room on the right, going down the hall, will eventually be a machine-shop, but is used at present as an assembly hall and library. Here are magazines and papers of a technical nature, together with games and reading matter for the interest of boys. The library is in charge of a committee of ten members, two of whom are on duty every night, attending to the giving out of the books and games, and keeping order.

On the same floor, in the rear, is a plumbing room, having two work-benches (12 × 3), with Bunsen burners to heat the pots for the solder, and stands to hold the pipes while being soldered. The tables contain many drawers for the plumbing tools. Against the wall ad-

THE PLANT

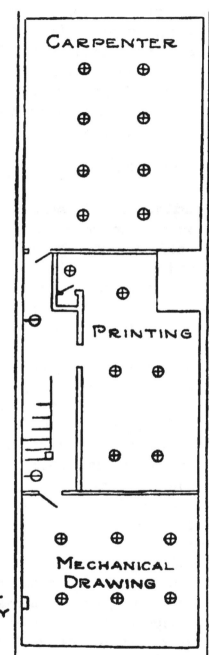

joining the machine-shop is a table for threading pipes and for other heavy work. Under this table are kept the pipe supplies. In the corner, on the right hand as one enters, is a rack containing thirty-two compartments (12 × 12) for keeping the boys' work, each boy having his own compartment. Beside this rack is a closet for the plumbing supplies. Along the wall are hooks for hats and coats.

SECOND FLOOR

The first room on the second floor is a carpenter-shop. Here are ten carpenters' benches containing two vises each, a place of forty-eight compartments for the boys' work, and a closet similar to the plumbing closet for the storage of materials and for the tools used by the instructors. Along the wall, on the left hand as one enters, are sixteen compartments (24 × 12 × 18) each containing a complete set of carpenters' necessary tools —mallet, back-saws, one cross and one rip, hammer, screw-driver, six chisels, try-square, bevel-gauge, nail-set, single-iron and double-iron jack-planes, and marking-gauge. The equipment of the instructors consists of such tools as are not in constant use by the boys, such as large saws, rabbets, planes, plough, brace and bit. On a stand near the carpenters' closet is a glue-pot heated by gas. Along the walls are frames containing free-hand drawings suggestive of good plans for young carpenters.

The printing-room contains two presses: one a foot-power and the other a hand press. It is intended to add another to be driven by an electric motor. The presses are by the wall of the carpenter-shop. Near them, in a closet, is kept the stock of paper. Along the sides of the room are sixteen frames holding the usual type-cases. In the middle of the room is the desk of the instructor,

THE PLANT

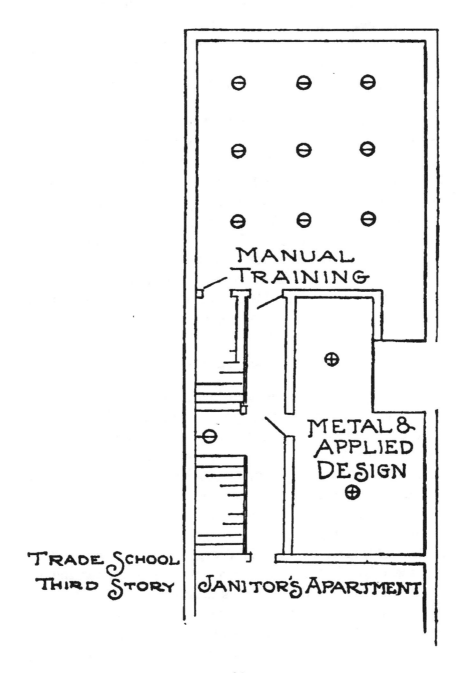

and a marble slab for locking-up the forms, together with the galley-stand.

Next to the printing-room is the mechanical-drawing department. Against the printing-room wall a closet (12 × 2 × 6) holds racks for seventy-five drawing-boards, and compartments for cases of instruments. Along the other three sides of the room drawing-shelves are built about thirty-six inches high, with a slight slant for the drawing-boards, and a three-inch level piece against the wall for pencils and ink. The boys stand at their work or sit on tall stools. In the middle of the room is a broad table, supported by two wooden horses, at which thirty boys work at one time, each having ample space. On Wednesdays the first and second carpentry classes, of fifteen boys each, take mechanical drawing here. On the other evenings the room is used by the two mechanical-drawing classes.

THIRD FLOOR

On the next floor, in the rear, at the head of the stairs, is the manual-training room, arranged for twenty-four boys. Each boy is separated from his neighbors, and all face the same way. In front of each boy is a table for his drawing-board. At his side is fastened a pencil-box, containing a pencil, pencil-compass, four thumb-tacks, a knife, and eraser. Under the table hang a T-square, a triangle, a scroll-saw, and an adjustable saw-table. Opposite the door is a large closet for the storage of materials. In this room are seventy-two compartments (14 × 8 × 12) to hold each boy's unfinished work. As soon as any piece is finished, it is stored away and a record is made. The teacher has his own bench, with vise and tools.

Adjoining this room is the department of metal-work

THE PLANT

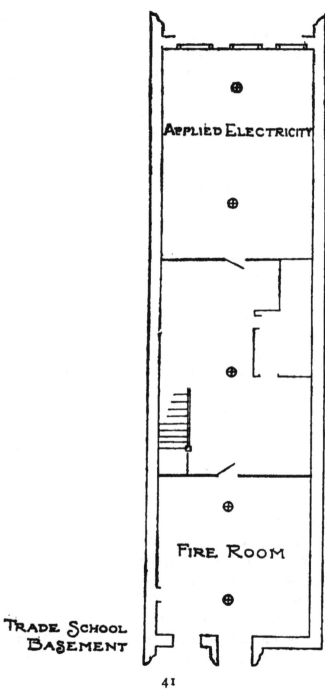

TRADE SCHOOL BASEMENT

and applied design. Here are shelves along the wall, as in the drawing-room, and heavy tables for the hammering of brass. There is a large closet for the storage of materials.

The walls of all these rooms are of white, glazed tile-brick, which makes the building easy to light. The floors are of cement, an inconvenient substance, hard to walk upon, dusty, and dulling every tool which touches it. There are green shades over all the electric lights. Every class-room has a wash-stand with running water. Transoms give ventilation.

BASEMENT

The basement contains in front the fire-rooms for the hot-water heating apparatus, the gas and electric meters, and the wood and coal bins. The rear room will eventually be used for classes in applied electricity, wiring, bells, and motors. At present it is a paint-shop for the carpentry and manual-training classes. Here are paint-tables, shelves arranged for paints, aprons for the painters, and ample space for unfinished work. At the end of the school year all of the work is on exhibition, and after that each boy takes his own work home.

V.—THE SEA-SIDE COTTAGE

This refuge from the heat of summer is at Rockaway Park, on Long Island, sixteen and a half miles from the city. It is an unpretentious house, most of the money having been spent on making the interior comfortable and homelike. Adjoining the house is a large pavilion, having an unbroken floor-space of fifty by seventy-five feet. It is two hundred feet from high-water mark. The front of the pavilion faces the surf, and both sides are open. One side is on the street, the other looks out

THE PLANT

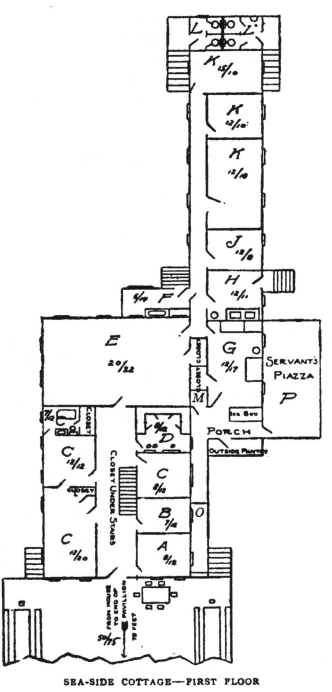

SEA-SIDE COTTAGE—FIRST FLOOR

over the cottage grounds, a hundred and twenty-five feet back. Facing south, the pavilion offers a wide ocean view and gets all the breezes.

Down the sides of the pavilion are long tables covered with white oil-cloth, chairs, and benches, where the excursionists take lunch. At the end which joins the house is a table, also covered with white oil-cloth, where the clergyman and deaconess who accompany the excursionists for the day, and any visitor they may bring, with the superintendent and his wife, take their lunch after the hurry of serving the tea, coffee, and milk on the pavilion and feeding the people in the house is over.

FIRST FLOOR

The main entrance to the house opens on this pavilion. Entering the broad hall, the first door to the right opens into room A, which is used by the clergyman of the day as a study. The next room, B, is a similar room for the deaconess. The third room, C, is the superintendent's dining-room. The fourth and last room on that side, D, is the linen-room. Around three sides of this room are spacious linen-closets; in the corner near the window is the sewing-machine, and here the mending of linen and bathing-suits is done. On the shelf along the wall, d, are boxes containing twine, buttons for bathing-suits, cotton, needles. The space, dd, is a key-board containing all the keys used at times by different people doing the work—in fact, all the keys not on the housekeeper's key-ring.

On the left are three connecting rooms, C, the sitting-room, bedroom, and bath-room of the superintendent. Facing the hall door is the door which opens into the large, pleasant dining-room, E, where the people who

THE PLANT

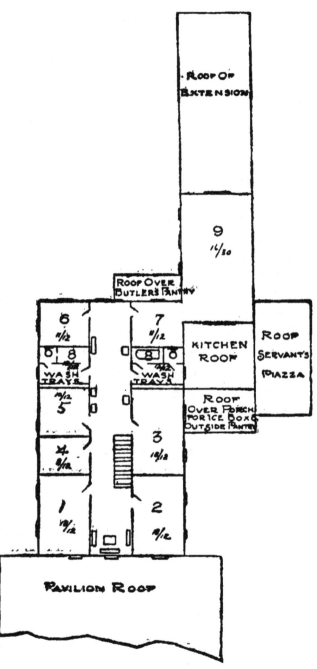

SEA-SIDE COTTAGE—SECOND FLOOR

stay for the week take their meals. Adjoining that is the pantry, *F*, where all the dishes are washed, bread cut, butter-balls made. These two rooms open also on another long hall, with windows down one side.

On the other side of this hall are, first, room *G*, a comfortable kitchen from which you get a view of the ocean; room *H*, a laundry, room *J*, a store-room where grocery supplies are kept. This is supplied with keepable groceries for the whole season, bought at the beginning at wholesale. The three rooms marked *K* are servants' rooms, in which seven people can be accommodated, with single beds and separate wash-stands. The rooms marked *L* are outside toilet-rooms with modern plumbing. They are not connected with the house by doors.

In front of the kitchen is a porch connecting with a long, narrow piazza which runs along the side of the house to the pavilion. This is used by the workers only. At the end, the space marked *M* is the closet where the dishes for the pavilion lunches are kept. Line *O* is a table which is hinged to the house and is let down to cross the passage at noon, and on it are placed the kettles containing hot tea and coffee, and the pitchers of milk which the clergyman, deaconess, and visitors pour out for the thirsty excursionists. The superintendent stands behind the table and sees that the kettles are replenished. On the porch to the left of the kitchen door is built the large ice-box and a small room called the "outside pantry," containing cleaning-cloths and pails. The space marked *P* is a large, covered piazza with rocking-chairs for the servants.

SECOND FLOOR

Up-stairs, the hall runs from back to front, with windows at both ends, and is furnished with seats and a

THE PLANT

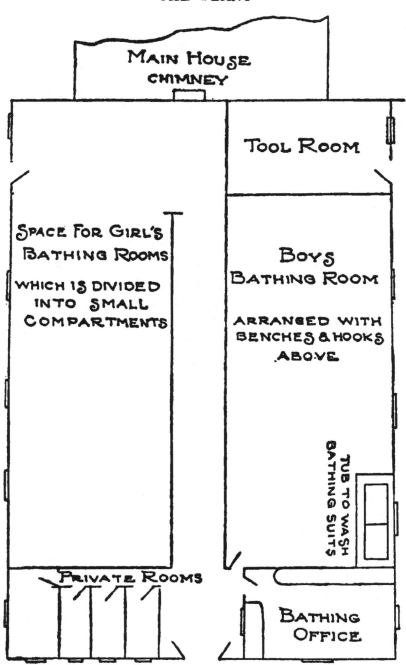

SEA-SIDE COTTAGE—UNDER THE PAVILION

table. It is used as a sitting-room on the few days when the pavilion is not habitable; or by mothers who have put their young babies to bed in the adjoining rooms, and are waiting for them to fall asleep. The rooms marked 1, 2, 3 are family rooms. That is, if a mother comes with five or six children, most of them small, she is put alone with her family in one of these rooms. They are large, with many windows, and furnished with big double beds, cradles, cribs, bureaus, and chairs. Room 4 is a small one with two single beds, and here we put two friends or relations who wish to be quiet. Rooms 6 and 7 are given to friends or relatives, and room 9 is a dormitory with eleven single beds, where we put young boys or girls. This has two windows looking out on the ocean, two overlooking the bay at the back, and two on the street side, with a ventilating skylight in the ceiling. It has all the air and sunshine Rockaway is able to furnish. The two rooms marked 8 are lavatories, with toilet-rooms, for night and rainy-day use. The room marked 5 is for an assistant to the superintendent's wife.

BASEMENT

Under the pavilion are the bathing-houses: on the right of the entrance, the office where the suits and towels are given out; on the left, in front, the rooms for the staff and visitors. Back of these is the long room divided into small rooms for the girls, and on the other side a large room for the boys. The carpenter-shop and tool-room are also here. Under the main building is the cellar.

III

THE RECORDS

I. The Parish Register—II. The Record of Statistics—III. The Mailing-Book—IV. The Record of Services—V. Where is What?—VI. The Parish Calendar—VII. The Year-Book.

I.—THE PARISH REGISTER

At the door of the church, before the eyes and beside the hands of every new-comer, are blanks for family records, and for the enlistment of all persons in the system of envelope offerings. (See pages 50, 51.)

The names and facts thus obtained are entered in the Parish Register. Such registers, in conventional form, and adapted to the uses of most parishes, may be had of church publishers or booksellers. The Bishop Paret register is excellent, so is the one arranged a good many years ago by the Rev. Mr. Hayes. The Young Churchman Company, in Milwaukee, publishes a convenient one. In all of these registers, however, a difficulty is found in the registration of families; partly because none of them is so arranged as to secure the notation of all the needed facts, and partly because, in many places, the family list is subject to such changes that a permanent record becomes unwieldy. This difficulty is met at St. George's by the use of a loose-leaf ledger. Such ledgers are to be had from the Perpetual Account Book Company, 33 Sullivan Street, New York City. They are somewhat expensive. A card-catalogue of families is the next best arrangement. A specimen leaf is inserted. (See pages 52, 53.)

ADMINISTRATION OF AN INSTITUTIONAL CHURCH

RECORD OF FAMILY

FOR

ENTRY IN THE PARISH REGISTER

OF

St. George's Church

The parishioners are *earnestly* requested by the Rector to fill this blank with the names of *only the members of the family attending St. George's Church*, and send it to the Rector, 209 East 16th Street, *at their earliest convenience*.

FAMILY NAME	RESIDENCE	CHRISTIAN NAMES	YEAR OF BIRTH	B.	C.	C.

THE CANON LAW CONCERNING REMOVALS

A communicant removing from one parish to another *shall* procure from the Rector (if any) of the parish of his last residence, or, if there be no Rector, from one of the wardens, a certificate stating that he or she is a communicant in good standing; and the Rector of the parish or congregation to which he or she removes shall not be required to receive him or her as a communicant until such letter be produced.— *Title II., Canon* 12, § 1.

SPECIMEN

FAMILY NAME	RESIDENCE	CHRISTIAN NAMES	YEAR OF BIRTH	B.	C.	C.
Brown	171 E. 40	John, } Parents		B.	C.	C.
		Mary,		B.	C.	C.
		Thomas	1890	B.	C.	C.
		Ellen	1895	B.		
		Edward	1900	B.		

(OVER)

N. B.—B. C. C. means Baptized, Confirmed, Communicant.

THE ENVELOPE SYSTEM

Those who find a church home in St. George's are invited to pledge themselves to make a free-will offering weekly, monthly, or yearly for its maintenance. When the subscription slip below is returned, a package of envelopes will be mailed, containing one for every Sunday or every month, as the case may be. The offering should be put in the envelope and placed upon the plate each Sunday, or if absent one or more Sundays, the offerings and envelopes to correspond should be enclosed.

For further information an appointment should be made with the Rector's secretary, who will call and explain this system.

REMARKS:

St. George's Church
Stuyvesant Square, N. Y.

OFFERINGS FOR SUPPORT OF CHURCH AND CLERGY

Name (Mr., Mrs., or Miss)..................................

Address...

Weekly offering...

Monthly " ....

Yearly " ....

Date from which offerings begin............................

When filled in, mail to
                    THE RECTOR,
                      209 *East 16th Street.*

ADMINISTRATION OF AN INSTITUTIONAL CHURCH

THE PARISH REGISTER. ST. GEORGE'S CHURCH, NEW YORK.

ENTRY	B	C	C	NAME	RESIDENCE	R	BIRTH	S	M	B	G	REMARKS
1883	✓	94	✓	Meyer, James F.	200 East — St.	✓	1878		✓			Transferred to St. James's Church, Massachusetts, October, 1905
1885	✓		✓	Mengelson, Mrs. Frederick	— St. Ann's Ave.	✓						Rec. through transfer from —— Church, N. Y. C., January, 1885.
1885	✓	97	✓	" Charles	"		1880		✓			
1886	✓	92	✓	Merz, George	— Second Ave.	✓	1872		✓			
1887	✓	90	✓		"		1884		✓			See over leaf, married.
1890	✓	04	✓		"			✓				Married to James Merle, October, 1905.
1901	✓			Mead, Mrs. F. W.	105 East — St.							Née Pauline Stone.
1904	✓		✓		— Irving Place	✓						Rec. through transf. from —— Church, San Francisco, 1904. Transferred to St. —— Church, Phila., January, 1906.
Dec., '05		✓	✓	Merchant, John W.	106 West — St.	✓						
"		✓	✓		"							Died January 15, 1906.

52

THE RECORDS

"	✓	✓				"	Rebecca	✓	1885	
"	✓	08				"	Rudolph		1887	
"	✓					"	Jane		1890	
Jan., '06	✓				✓	511 East — St.	Mears, William	✓		
"	✓			✓	✓	"	" Mrs. Katherine			
"	✓	✓	✓	✓		"	" Florence			✓
"	✓	✓	✓	✓	✓	"	" James	✓	1889	✓ ✓
"	✓				✓	"	" August		1887	✓ ✓ ✓
"	✓					— Madison Ave.	Meade, John M.	✓		With letter of introduction, St. —— Ch., Pres., January, 1906.

The letters *B, C, C* stand for baptized, confirmed, communicant. The date under the first *C* indicates the year of confirmation. *E* represents the envelope system. It shows who is contributing and who is not contributing to the support of the parish. *S* signifies Sunday-school; *M*, Men's Club; *B*, Battalion; *G*, Girls' Friendly Society. Thus appears the relation of each person to the activities of the parish.

The family record is arranged alphabetically, and is accompanied by a card-list of families according to their residence, the streets being also alphabetically arranged.

Each member of the staff has on his desk a change-of-address pad, on which he enters all such removals as come to his knowledge, and turns the records in to the secretary.

```
┌─────────────────────────────────────────────┐
│          St. George's Church, New York      │
│                                             │
│  Full name.................................│
│                                             │
│  Old address..............................│
│                                             │
│  New address..............................│
│                                             │
│  If person has left the church, state here..│
│                                             │
│  ...........................................│
└─────────────────────────────────────────────┘
```

The cards of the members whose addresses have been lost through removal and their failure to notify us, are laid aside and from time to time the office boy is set to work to procure the new addresses in various ways—viz.: Looking through the city and social directories and telephone-book; inquiring of their old neighbors; at the tradespeople where they might be supposed to have dealt; also at the livery-stables. This covers the ground for rich and poor.

THE RECORDS

For accuracy in the entries of baptisms in the Parish Register, the following form is filled out in each case by the officiating clergyman, and transferred at once to the permanent record:

St. George's Church, New York
BAPTISM

₊ It is important that this form should be filled in very legibly.

1. Christian name IN FULL

   ....

2. Parents

   ....

3. Residence of parents

   ....

4. Sponsors

   ....

   ....

   ....

5. Date of birth

   ....

6. Date of baptism

   ....

7. Officiating clergyman

   ....

Holy Baptism is administered on the first Sunday of every month, at 4 P.M.

All printed forms in use in the parish are on pads for convenience. Where two forms are exactly of the same size, the paper is made of a different color.

ADMINISTRATION OF AN INSTITUTIONAL CHURCH

The officiating clergyman also, at the time of the baptism, fills out and gives to the parents the following certificate:

In the Name of the Father and of the Son and of the Holy Ghost, Amen.

DIOCESE OF NEW YORK

St. George's Church
Stuyvesant Square, New York

This Certifies that

....

was received into the congregation of Christ's flock, by

HOLY BAPTISM

on the..........*day of*............*A.D., 190*..

Place of birth........ *Date of birth*.........

....
.... } *Sponsors*
....
....

The record of a confirmation is entered in the register from such cards as this:

St. George's Church

Confirmation, 1902

PALM SUNDAY, MARCH 23d, AT 8 P.M.

Name.......................... *Age*......

Address..

W. S. RAINSFORD

Candidates to be in church at 7.45 P.M.
This card to be presented at the door.

THE RECORDS

The record of a burial is entered in the register from blanks filled out either by the officiating clergyman or by the sexton and undertaker.

St. George's Church, New York

BURIAL

Date of burial

....

Full name

....

Age

....

Place of residence

....

Date of death

....

Cause of death

....

Place of service

....

Place of interment

....

Officiating clergyman

....

Baptisms, confirmations, marriages, burials, are vital facts, of permanent value, and should not therefore be kept on cards which are liable to be lost. The same is true of the list of communicants. These are all entered, chronologically, not alphabetically, in one or more substantially bound books, and with ink chosen with reference to its durable quality.

II.—THE RECORD OF STATISTICS

In order to show month by month the exact condition of the parish membership, a book of Record of Statistics is kept, with the gains entered on one side and the losses on the other. In the leaf from this book here shown, *Ind.* means individuals; *Cf.*, confirmed; *Tr.*, gained or lost by transfer; *Oth.*, gained or lost in other ways; *Fam.* means families. From this summary the report is made up as required by the Diocesan Convention.

RECORD OF STATISTICS, FROM EASTER, 19__, TO EASTER, 19__

19__	GAINED							LOST						
		IND.	COMMUNICANTS				FAM.	IND.	COMMUNICANTS				FAM.
			CF.	TR.	OTH.	TOTAL			TR.	DEATH	OTH.	TOTAL	
April	5												
On record		7521				4600	1877						
May	1	15		1	5	6	2	8	1	1	3	5	1
June	9	15		2	4	6	2	8	1	..	4	5	1
July	9	30		4	8	12	3	20	..	..	10	10	1
Aug	15	30		5	10	15	3	20	1	3	6	10	2
Sept	8	20		3	9	12	3	20	1	1	8	10	2
Oct	7	20		..	..	..	2	..	..	..	..	..	..
Nov	15	40		7	14	21	5	20	..	..	15	15	4
Dec	30	50		5	10	15	8	30	1	2	5	8	4
19__													
Jan	30	70		8	8	16	7	35	1	2	5	8	5
Feb	20	10		1	6	7	2	5	2	1	1	4	1
March	25	215	180	5	20	205	5	45	10	2	8	20	3
		515	180	41	94	315	42	211	18	12	65	95	24
		7521				4600	1877	—plus number last reported.					
		8036				4915	1919						
		211				95	24	—minus persons lost.					
April	..	7825				4820	1895	—number on record Easter, 19__.					

III.—THE MAILING-BOOK

Another volume of the parish records is the Mailing-Book. At various seasons and for various purposes,

THE RECORDS

letters, notices, and appeals are sent to members of the parish. But some of these persons are rich and some are poor, some are interested in this and some in that. It is therefore necessary to make such distinctions as will enable the secretary to know to whom a particular communication should be sent.

In this list, *P.M.* means parish missions. Collections are taken for this purpose in March and November. Those whose names are checked receive letters of reminder. *Th. G.* stands for Thanksgiving dinners; letters asking for contributions are sent to names indicated. *Xmas* is for Christmas festival; *East. F.* for Easter festival. These persons pay for these festivities, for the garnishing of the church, for the Sunday-school treat. *Dec.* means decorations; letters are sent to those who are to be asked to aid the committee at Easter and Christmas in this work. Thus the adornment with flowers and greens is done not by hired florists, but by the people themselves with their own hands. It is a social occasion, a time of parish joy, magnifying the significance and sacredness of these seasons. *Big A* denotes special sums from special persons for special purposes. 7 stands for any list not already designated, for money, for workers, for a special meeting. (See page 60.)

IV.—THE RECORD OF SERVICES

Besides the Record of Statistics and the Mailing-Book, a third additional volume of memoranda is the Record of Services. This is kept in the vestry-room, and entries are made in it by the clergymen on duty immediately after each service. (See page 61.)

MAILING-BOOK—ST. GEORGE'S CHURCH, NEW YORK

P.M.				TH. C.	XMAS.	EAST. P.	DEC.	BIG A.	7
✓	Stone	Miss S.	— Wash. Sq.		✓				
✓	Storer	J. W.	— East 28th St.	✓	✓	✓	Mr. and Mrs.		
✓	"	Mrs. J. W.	"						
✓	Stout	John F.	— Mad. Av.		✓				
✓	Scott	Mrs. James	— Irving Place.				✓		
✓	Stover	Mr. and Mrs. C. L.	40 West — St.		✓		✓		

THE RECORDS

RECORD OF SERVICES, ST. GEORGE'S CHURCH, N. Y.

DATE		DAY	HOUR	SERVICE	OFFICIATING CLERGY	NO. COM'NTS	NO. BAPT'D	REMARKS
Dec., 1903	22	Tues.	9	M. P.	Rev. ——			
	23	Wed.	9	M. P.	"			
	24	Thurs.	9	M. P.	"			
	"	12	H. C.	Rev. —— and Rev. ——	15			
	25	Friday	7	H. C.	Rector and Staff	750		Xmas Day, Rector Address
	"	10.30	M. P., H. C., Sermon	"	360		Sermon, Rector
	26	Sat.	9	H. C.	Rev. —— and Rev. ——	4		St. Stephen's Day
	27	Sun.	8	H. C.	Rev. —— and Rev. ——	8		St. John the Evangelist
	"	11	M. P	Rector and Staff			
	"	3.15	Children's Service	Rev. —— and Rev. ——			
	"	8	Musical Service	Rev. —— and Rev. ——			
	28	Mon.	9	H. C.	Rev. —— and Rev. ——	4		Holy Innocents
	29	Tues.	9	M. P.	Rev. ——			
	"	3.30	Jun. S.S., Festival	Rev. —— and Rev. ——			
	"	8	Sen. S.S., Festival	Rector and Rev. ——			
	30	Wed.	9	M. P.	Rev. ——			
	31	Thurs.	9	M. P.	Rev. ——			
	"	12	H. C.	Rev. —— and Rev. ——	8		
	"	11 P.M.	Watch-night Serv.	Rector and Staff			
Jan., 1904	1	Fri.	12.05	H. C.	Rector and Staff	350		

61

ADMINISTRATION OF AN INSTITUTIONAL CHURCH

V.—WHERE IS WHAT?

Finally, in the secretary's desk is a small card-catalogue called *Where is What?* This was started to make it easy to find the things which, in a large place equipped with small office facilities only, are scattered all over the parish building and rectory. This catalogue tells where to find things in the secretary's desk, in the pigeon-holes, in the pigeon-holes of the safe, in the bookcase in the office, in the cabinet on top of the desk, in the set of closets in the hall. This key is attached to the catalogue:

Things in the desk are marked on the card	D.
Things in the pigeon-holes are marked on the card	P.
Things in the pigeon-holes of the safe are marked on the card	S.
Things in the bookcase in office are marked on the card	B.
Things in the bookcase in another room are marked on the card	B.B.
Things in the closet on top of desk are marked on the card	T.D.
Things in the closet in the hall are marked on the card	H.C.

For instance, to find matters relating to parish missions, the following card, under "P" in the catalogue, is consulted:

Parish Missions   P.—Box 7
   (1) Rector's letter to the congregation

Parish Mission Record   T.D.—No. 4
   Showing payments
   and pledges

THE RECORDS

This means that the circular letter, a sample for each year, can be found in the pigeon-hole No. 7, and that the records showing payments can be found in the closet No. 4, on top of the desk.

VI.—THE PARISH CALENDAR

The calendar tells at a glance what notices should be given out in the church and what arrangements should be made for seasons and services. It contains in detail a description of the manner in which days are kept from year to year, when such and such offerings are taken, when the time comes to pray for Congress, together with such suggestions for doing these things better as occur to the clergy as these days come and go. It is like the monastic consuetudinary. It assists the Rector to keep such a resolution as General Braddock made as he fell at Fort Duquesne, "I will do better another time!" That is a frequent resolution with which the cares and distractions of the parish deal as the Indians dealt with General Braddock. It can be kept alive and made effective only by being put into a book.

Sample pages of such a book are shown on pages 64 and 65. With such memoranda the clergy are enabled to form and maintain parish customs, which make a pleasant and helpful continuity of parish life, and give the people a sense of the thoughtfulness and reasonableness of the ecclesiastical arrangements.

Another form of parish calendar is kept on good-sized cards, which are dated according to the church year, having the secular dates written, if at all, in pencil. Thus seven cards hold the memoranda of the first week in Advent: changes of colors, special notices—as of collection for Christmas expenses, suggestions of themes for

ADMINISTRATION OF AN INSTITUTIONAL CHURCH

PARISH CALENDAR FOR

DATE	NAME OF DAY	HOUR OF SERVICE	COLLECTION	SERVICE
1905 Sun., Nov. 5		11 A.M.	Com. alms	Holy Com.
" Nov. 5		4 P.M.		Bapt.
" Nov. 12		11 A.M.	Parish missions	
" Nov. 19		7 P.M.		Bapt.
" Nov. 26	23d Sun. after Trinity	11 A.M.		
Thurs., Nov. 30	St. Andrew's	9 A.M.		Holy Com.
" Nov. 30	Thanksgiving Day	10.30 A.M.	Widows and orphans of clergy	
Sun., Dec. 3	1st Sun. in Advent	11 A.M.	Com. alms	Holy Com.
" Dec. 3		4 P.M.		Bapt.
Tues., Dec. 5		9 A.M.		
Sun., Dec. 17		7 P.M.		Bapt.
Thurs., Dec. 21	St. Thomas's	9 A.M.		Holy Com.
Fri., Dec. 22		8 P.M.		
Mon., Dec. 25	Xmas.	7 A.M.	Endowment	Holy Com.
Mon., Dec. 25	Xmas.	11 A.M.	Endowment	Holy Com.

THE RECORDS

THE YEAR 1905-1906

ORDER OF SERVICE AND REMARKS	CHANGES FOR THE NEW YEAR
When does Congress meet? (Prayer for Congress.)	
First notice of election: one warden, three vestrymen.	
(1) Special lesson, Deut. viii.; 1 Thes., v., 12-24. (2) Psalm for Venite. (3) Benedicte — Jubilate. (4) Clergy enter rail after Prayer for church militant. Choir recess back of altar.	
Second notice of election: one warden, three vestrymen.	
Vestry election. Notify newspapers. Call vestry meeting.	
Decorating church for Xmas. (Clergy and deaconesses get young people to help.) Supper at Deaconess House afterwards.	Supper in Parish House again.
Have Xmas carols in seats.	
Hymn 51—Carol—Shortened M. P.—(Nicene Creed) Hymn 58—ante com.—Hymn 59—Sermon and Offertory—Prayer for church militant—Dresden Amen—Holy Com.—(Gounod's Sanctus) Hymn 225, before reception—Blessing—Hymn 60—Have Psalms found in P. B.	

ADMINISTRATION OF AN INSTITUTIONAL CHURCH

Advent services, promotion in the Sunday-school. Then seven cards for the second week, and so on. Each week, when ended, with such betterings as experience has suggested, has its record taken from the front of the box of cards and put at the back, ready to appear again in its turn when the year comes round. Guide-cards show the different seasons and the great days. The following card would be preceded by a guide-card marked *Confirmation*. It is given to show with what particularity the details of such services are set down in a great parish.

Order of Service		Changes for New Year
8 P.M. Conf.	Processional Hymn 90—Conf. service—Hymn 289—(Antiphonally just before Confirmation) to be announced; sung kneeling—conclusion of Confirmation—Hymn 602—Bishop's address—Hymn 216—Offertory and Closing Collects—Recessional 507—white stoles. Remember: 1. All clergy stand aside for Bishop to pass within the rail—then to stalls. Rector to reading-desk, takes opening and gospel. 2. Distribution of clergy after 289: (*a*) one behind the Bishop to hold Book; (*b*) one behind Rector; (*c*) two ahead of steps. 3. Galleries reserved for families until 7.30 P.M. 4. Boys to take alms basins. 5. Candidates middle aisle; boys south aisle; girls north aisle.	

VII.—THE YEAR-BOOK

Once a year a full report is made to the parish of the work of the past twelve months. At the end of each year the following letter is sent to all the heads of departments:

New York, April 22, 1906

———————————

———————————

The Year-Book of St. George's Church will soon be made ready for press. It is of first importance that all reports, reviews, and records of work be sent in before May 22d.

Will you personally see to it that the reports as below for the year beginning Easter, 1905, ending Easter, 1906, are forwarded to me prior to that date?

In order to secure manuscript of uniform size, we ask that you will please make your report upon the paper which is sent under separate cover, writing on one side only. Besides the descriptive matter, a full and corrected list of officers and members is needed.

Very truly yours,

———————————

SECRETARY,
207 East 16th Street

Report of..................................
    "   ....
    "   ....
    "   ....
    "   ....
    "   ....
    "   ....

ADMINISTRATION OF AN INSTITUTIONAL CHURCH

The Year-Book is arranged as follows:

1. Corporation

> **LEGAL TITLE**
> _____
>
> **RECTOR**
> _____
>
> **WARDENS**
> _____   _____
>
> **VESTRYMEN**
> _____   _____   _____
> _____   _____   _____
> _____   _____   _____
>
> **CLERK OF THE VESTRY**
> _____
>
> **TREASURER**
> _____
>
> **COMMITTEE IN CHARGE OF ENVELOPES**
> _____   _____
>
> **PROPERTY COMMITTEE**
> _____   _____
> _____   _____
>
> **DELEGATES TO THE DIOCESAN CONVENTION**
> _____   _____   _____

2. Treasurer's report.
3. List of special church collections during the year.
4. Canon law concerning removals.
5. Rector's or Vestry's Introduction.
6. Members of the staff—names.
7. List of ushers.
8. Hours of services.
9. Statistics for year ending 19—
    (*a*) Work of the staff.
    (*b*) Number of services.
    (*c*) Membership: last reported.
       Individuals and communicants, how gained, how lost. Present number.

THE RECORDS

10. Persons baptized—names.
11. Persons confirmed—names.
12. Persons married—names.
13. Persons buried—names.

> N.B.—This practically ends the vestry's report of the work (and from the foregoing can be made the annual report to the Diocesan Convention). Then follow the reports of the clergy, deaconesses, and officers of the various organizations.

1. Choir.
2. Chancel Committee.
3. Christmas Festival contributors—names.
4. Easter Festival contributors—names.
5. Parish building: short history of the same, followed with a list of classes and meetings according to days.
6. Deaconess House: Same as parish building.
7. Missionary Society—Foreign and Domestic.
8. Sunday-school.
9. Library.
10. Parish relief:
    (a) Relief Department.
    (b) Care of the sick.
    (c) Hospital work.
    (d) Woman's Industrial Society.
    (e) Fresh-air work.
11. Reports of the institutional organizations:
    (a) Men's Club.
    (b) Girls' Friendly Society.
    (c) Married Women's Soc.
    (d) King's Daughters.
    (e) Battalion.
    (f) Trade-school.
    (g) Sewing-school.
    (h) Dramatic Society.
12. Forms of Bequest.
13. Index.
14. Clerical staff for the new year.
15. Inside cover: names and places of parish buildings.

When the Year-Book is ready for distribution the following letter is placed in the pews, the same in substance year by year, but changing with the changed conditions:

ADMINISTRATION OF AN INSTITUTIONAL CHURCH

**ST. GEORGE'S RECTORY
209 EAST 16TH ST.**

New York, November 1, 19—.

MY DEAR FRIENDS:

I want you to read the "Year-Book" for 19— carefully. I wish you to see in it not merely a partial description of what we have set ourselves to do, but a call to you to join hands with us and help us in the doing of it. If you are going to get good from Christ's Church and help for your own soul and life, it will be because you are willing to give the service of your life to that Church. So many stand aloof and look on. So many leave others to do their share, that those who are working are often distracted and necessarily wearied for lack of aid and help that is often held back through sheer thoughtlessness. Many of you who read this book can do something to make St. George's work easier to those engaged in it, more helpful to those who are sought by it. What can you do?

1. If you attend the church, let me have your name. A common habit of to-day of floating round from church to church can do no good, weakens the churches, and does not help the wanderer. If you come to St. George's regularly, it is due to me and to my assistant clergy and deaconesses that we should know where you live.

2. If possible lend us a hand. As you read this "Year-Book," you may think to yourself that we have workers in abundance, all we need, and more; but this is not so. We are sometimes at our wit's end to find round pegs to put in round holes. We need teachers in the Sunday-school; associates in the Girls' Friendly Society and King's Daughters. If you can only give up two hours a week to trying to know your fellow-citizens, and bring to them from the richness of your life what their lives lack, you can help us much. We want young men and young women in our classes, in our societies, in our clubs. We want the parents to send their children. We want college men to come and give us help with our boys' clubs and in the trade-school. Can you not lend us aid in some of these works? If you want more information, come and visit the Memorial House on Monday evenings. From eight to eleven you will find the Rector and the clergy there.

3. As you are able to give, I want your financial aid. St. George's is almost entirely supported by its envelope system. This system means voluntary giving. Through this system you may give once a year, once a month, or once on Sunday, whichever way pleases you best. Some will say, "I can only give a very small sum; it would not be worth my while to take an envelope." It is worth your while to help forward order and system. It is worth your while to help us to carry out a plan which is vital to the church's support. If you have confidence in those who manage the church, it surely is worth your while to prove your confidence by your works. We have now nearly one thousand envelope subscribers, and these one thousand gave last year $19,727.62. If you wish to join the envelope system, fill out the slip on the second page, tear it off, and return it to me. If you do not understand the system, say so under the heading of Remarks, and my secretary will call and explain it to you.

It is not an easy task to carry on successfully the work we have attempted in St. George's. Perhaps you are doing all you can. Perhaps you are standing in the market-place idle. I cannot judge for you. Judge for yourself. And oh, remember the night cometh, and cometh soon, when none of us can any longer work.

I am, your faithful friend,

W. S. RAINSFORD,
Rector.

ADMINISTRATION OF AN INSTITUTIONAL CHURCH

ENVELOPE SYSTEM FOR SUPPORT OF ST. GEORGE'S CHURCH

Name..

Address...

How much will you give per week?.................

If you care to give once a month, state how much.................

If once a year, how much ....

When will you commence?.........................

REMARKS

....
....
....
....
....

(OVER)

On the back of the leaf to be detached is printed, *Take this letter home and read it, and mail this slip to me or put it in my box next Sunday. Also, Please send me a Year-Book.*

Name....................

Address..................

The letter has proved its usefulness. It has brought in many names of new people, has enlisted new workers, diminished appeals from the pulpit, and greatly increased subscriptions. It has helped to put the material side of the parish life on a sound business basis.

IV

SERVICES AND SERMONS

I. The Congregation—II. The Services—III. The Choir—IV. The Sermons.

I.—THE CONGREGATION

THE congregation is continually recruited by invitation and by correspondence. From time to time, all the members of the staff, together with volunteer workers, make a systematic house-to-house visitation. Also in January of each year a great number of addresses are taken from the city street directory of the neighborhood, and others are obtained from the janitors of apartment-houses and the keepers of lodging-houses. To these persons a letter is sent, sometimes in print, sometimes in facsimile, calling their attention to the church, and offering them its hospitality.

**ST. GEORGE'S RECTORY
209 EAST 16TH ST.**

January, 19—.

I find that there is a large number of people moving into the neighborhood of St. George's Church who have no connection with any religious organization. I therefore think it well to send around the enclosed card, on which the services of the church are stated — and beg to assure all who may read it of a most hearty welcome always, at

St. George's Church, Stuyvesant Square;
St. George's Memorial House, 207 East 16th St.;
St. George's Rectory, 209 East 16th St.;
St. George's Deaconess House, 208 East 16th St.

W. S. RAINSFORD,
Rector.

ST. GEORGE'S RECTORY
209 EAST 16TH ST.

January, 19—.

St. George's Church is absolutely free and always open—at all services. Won't you come and worship with us?

In these days of hurry we all need to take a little time in which to be quiet. We cannot be religious alone—we are so made as to need the help of others. The Christian Church is the association of people who are trying to be good themselves, and to make the world better.

Come and join our company—you will be made welcome.
Sunday mornings at 11.
Sunday evenings at 8.
Children come at 9.30 Sunday morning.

Your friend and neighbor,
W. S. RAINSFORD.

ST. GEORGE'S CHURCH
STUYVESANT SQUARE, NEW YORK

January 10, 19—.

Let me offer you (or you and your family, as the case may be) a neighborly welcome to St. George's Church. We all know that it takes trouble to keep our souls alive. The strain and hurry of our great city we all feel. Once a week at least we need a rest, a quiet hour, a time to THINK, *to* PRAY, *to* WORSHIP. *If you belong to any other church, this letter is not meant for you. But if you do not go regularly to*

SERVICES AND SERMONS

any other church, will you not accept this note as an invitation to St. George's? Our church is democratic, and all the seats at all the services are free. We believe the Christian Church was meant by Jesus Christ to be a place where men meet as men, and not as poor men or rich men. Come, then, and meet with us, and let us try to be good ourselves and to make our city good.

W. S. RAINSFORD,
Rector of St. George's Church.

The stranger who responds to such an invitation finds a personal welcome awaiting him. The seating of the congregation is in charge of a member of the vestry. The ushers are chosen by him in conference with the Rector, though suggestions as to suitable persons may be made by any member of the staff. The ushers stand at the entrance to the aisles and tell all strangers that the church is absolutely free, and that they may sit wherever they can find a place. After the church is so full that single seats here and there are all that remain empty, then the ushers conduct persons to these seats, filling the pews from the chancel to the door. The Rector and other clergy are at the end of the church fifteen minutes before the service, to welcome the people. After the evening service, they come down the aisles to shake hands.

The customary duties of ushers are set forth in the following card, which is given to every man who is appointed to that office:

ST. GEORGE'S CHURCH

INSTRUCTIONS TO USHERS

I. The ushers on duty at the morning service are expected to be at the church every Sunday, not later than 10.30 A.M. Those on duty in the evening, not later than 7.30 P.M.

II. No pews are to be reserved under any circumstances. Persons coming early are privileged to take the same pew every Sunday, if they so desire.

III. The ushers shall not put more than five persons in the long pews or more than four in the short ones until all the pews are filled. Should there still remain some persons unseated, one additional person may be put in each pew. The ushers, however, are not to interfere with persons who voluntarily attempt to go into a pew that already has four or five persons in it.

IV. No one shall be allowed to pass up the aisles during prayers, during the reading of the lessons, or during the sermon. In the latter case, however, persons may be allowed to take seats near the door. There shall be no conversation, even about church work, after the service has begun.

V. When an usher cannot be in his place, it is expected that he will notify the chairman, that another may be appointed to take his place during his absence.

At the time of the Holy Communion, the head usher and his assistants stand in the aisles and regulate the number of those who may conveniently come forward at one time by moving slowly down the aisles.

II.—THE SERVICES

Every Sunday the Holy Communion is celebrated at 8 A.M., with a second celebration on the first Sunday of each month at eleven, and on the third Sunday in the evening at nine o'clock. The evening communion is the solution of various attempts to find a time for this sacrament for persons who, by the conditions of their lives, cannot well come at the conventional hours. An early service on Wednesdays was tried, but did not meet the need. All the services of the parish are determined by the principle that the church is made for the people, not the people for the church.

Morning Prayer is said on Sundays at eleven o'clock, and Evening Prayer at eight, in each case with a sermon. There is a children's service at 3.15.

SERVICES AND SERMONS

During the week there is daily Morning Prayer at nine o'clock, for which the Holy Communion is substituted on saints' days. There is an evening service on Wednesdays at eight o'clock, a continuation of the evangelistic meetings which were held in the old Avenue A mission. The service begins with fifteen minutes of hymn singing, the hymns being chosen by the congregation; then there is a brief evening prayer, followed by an address, very direct and intimate; and the service closes with the blessing pronounced in the pulpit. Every Thursday the Holy Communion is celebrated at noon.

Baptism is administered on the first Sunday of each month at four o'clock, and on the third Sunday evening at seven.

The following notes are taken for the most part from the parish calendar, and indicate special observances.

IN ADVENT

The Benedicte is used instead of the Te Deum.

As Christmas approaches, the following letter is used to procure assistance from the congregation in the decorating of the church:

December, 1902.

My dear M——:

It will give the Rector and the committee on church decorations pleasure if you will help in dressing St. George's Church for Christmas. This is to be done on Monday, December 22d. We should appreciate it if you will kindly let us know whether we may expect you on the afternoon or evening of that day.

Sincerely yours, M. J. S.,
Chairman.

ADMINISTRATION OF AN INSTITUTIONAL CHURCH

This letter is signed by the chairman of the decorating committee, which is responsible for the garnishings at Christmas and Easter, and also for the adornment of the Lord's Table with flowers on Sundays and feast days. The Rector also makes an appeal from the pulpit for aid in the Christmas decoration. The occasion is made a pleasant one socially; all the clergy and deaconesses are present, and there are refreshments in the Parish House.

Before Christmas, the Rector sends to every communicant a copy of such a letter as follows:

St. George's Rectory
209 East 16th St.

> Let us meet together again at the Table of our Lord. Christmas morning —
> Let us come. asking Him to bless and pardon us all. —
> Services are at 7. and 11. a. m.
>
> Your Friend and Rector.
> W. S. Rainsford
>
> Advent 1902

ON CHRISTMAS DAY

Carols are sung at the Holy Communion at seven o'clock, and there is a carol after the processional at the

SERVICES AND SERMONS

eleven o'clock service. Gounod's Sanctus is sung in the Communion.

The children's festival takes place two or three days after Christmas, in the evening at eight o'clock. The service is as follows: Sentence, Lord's Prayer and versicles, a carol in place of the psalm, then collects and the grace; then an address, followed by the distribution of gifts. The recessional is without singing.

THE WATCH-NIGHT SERVICE

The service begins at eleven o'clock, the clergy and choir entering without singing. A hymn is then sung, the litany is said, followed by a hymn and by the ninety-first psalm. This takes half an hour. At half-past eleven prayers are said, and there is an address which closes at five minutes before twelve. These five minutes are kept for silent prayer, during which the clock strikes. There is then a celebration of the Holy Communion.

IN LENT

Cards such as that which is here shown are distributed at the beginning of Lent.

LENTEN SERVICES, 19—

St. George's Church
Stuyvesant Square, New York

Rev. W. S. RAINSFORD, D.D., Rector

ASH-WEDNESDAY
    Morning Prayer and Ante-Communion . . 9 A.M.
    Litany, with Penitential Office and Address 11 A.M.
    Evening Prayer . . . . 5 P.M.
    Mid-Week Service . . . . 8 P.M.

ADMINISTRATION OF AN INSTITUTIONAL CHURCH

MONDAYS
- Morning Prayer . . . . 9 A.M.
- Evening Prayer . . . . 5 P.M.

TUESDAYS
- Morning Prayer . . . . 9 A.M.
- Children's Service . . . . 5 P.M.

WEDNESDAYS
- Morning Prayer . . . . 9 A.M.
- Service and Address by Rector . . . 4.30 P.M.
- Mid-Week Service . . . . 8 P.M.

THURSDAYS
- Morning Prayer . . . . 9 A.M.
- Holy Communion . . . . 12 M.
  - With five-minute Address by the Rector
- Evening Prayer . . . . 5 P.M.

FRIDAYS
- Litany . . . . 9 A.M.
- Evening Prayer . . . . 5 P.M.

SATURDAYS
- Morning Prayer . . . . 9 A.M.

SUNDAY SERVICES
- Holy Communion . . . . 8 A.M.
- Morning Services, with Sermon . . . 11 A.M.
- Holy Communion (1st Sunday in month) . 11 A.M.
- Children's Services . . . . 3.15 P.M.
- Holy Baptism (1st Sunday in month) . . 4 P.M.
- Holy Baptism (3d Sunday in month) . . 7 P.M.
- Evening Prayer, with Sermon . . . . . 8 P.M.
- Holy Communion (3d Sunday in month) . 9 P.M.

HOLY WEEK

MONDAY
- Ante-Communion . . . . 9 A.M.
- Evening Prayer, with ten-minute Address . 5 P.M.

TUESDAY
- Ante-Communion . . . . 9 A.M.
- Children's Service . . . . 5 P.M.

WEDNESDAY
- Ante-Communion . . . . 9 A.M.
- Service and Address by Rector . . . 4.30 P.M.
- Service of Preparation for Easter Communion. Address by Rector . . . . 8 P.M.

SERVICES AND SERMONS

Maundy-Thursday
- Morning Prayer . . . . 9 A.M.
- Holy Communion . . . . 12 M.
- Evening Prayer, with ten-minute Address . 5 P.M.
- Holy Communion, in commemoration of the institution of the Lord's Supper . . 8 P.M.

Good-Friday
- Morning Prayer and Ante-Communion . . 9 A.M.
- Passion Service by Rector . . . 12 M. to 3 P.M.
- Litany . . . . 5 P.M.
- Short Service and Address . . . . . 8 P.M.

Easter Even.
- Ante-Communion . . . . 9 A.M.

Easter-Day
- Holy Communion and Address. . . . . 7 A.M.
- Morning Prayer, Sermon, and Holy Communion. Admittance till 10.15, by ticket only . . . . 10.30 A.M.
- Sunday-school Festival — Junior Department. . . . . 3.30 P.M.
- Sunday-school Festival — Senior Department . . . . 8 P.M.

CONFIRMATION CLASSES

For Men and Women, Sunday, 3 P.M.
  (Memorial Building) . . . . *Rector*
For Boys, Tuesday, 8 P.M.
  (Memorial Building) . . . . *Assistant Clergy*
For Girls and Women, Tuesday, 8 P.M.
  (Memorial Building) . . . . . . *Deaconesses*

The Bishop will visit the Parish, to administer the Rite of Confirmation, Palm-Sunday, March 27, 8 P.M.

SUBJECTS FOR WEDNESDAY TALKS
By Rector
Interpretations of Familiar Doctrines

(1) Some Meanings of Baptism.
(2) Significance of Confirmation.
(3) Ground of Christian Certainty—Character of Jesus.
(4) Fatherhood of God.
(5) Kingdom of God Among Us.
(6) Mediatorship of Jesus.

ADMINISTRATION OF AN INSTITUTIONAL CHURCH

COLLECTIONS

First Sunday in Month	Parish Poor
Ash-Wednesday	Parish Poor
Second Sunday in March	Parish Missions
Thursdays	St. Luke's Home for Aged Women
Good-Friday	Colored People of the South
Easter-Day	Sea-side Fund

Prayers are said daily, morning and evening, at 9 A.M. and 5 P.M. There is but one series of special instructions, given at the mid-week service. At the Thursday noon celebration there is a five-minute address. The emphasis of Lent is put upon this service.

On Palm-Sunday, at the morning service, there is a distribution of palms at the door of the church by the clergy after the recessional.

On Ash-Wednesday, Morning Prayer and Ante-Communion are said at 9 o'clock, and the Litany and Penitential office, with a sermon, at 11 o'clock. At this second service the clergy and choir come in and go out silently; a hymn is sung, kneeling, before the Litany; and a hymn is sung, kneeling, after the blessing.

In Holy Week there is a preparation for the Easter Communion at 8.30 P.M. The Holy Communion is celebrated on Maundy-Thursday at 8 P.M. On Good-Friday, the Passion service is conducted by the Rector from 12 A.M. to 3 P.M.; and there is a short service, with an address, in the evening.

ON EASTER-DAY

As a reminder of the Easter Communion and Collection, a letter such as the following is sent to every communicant, enclosing two Pay Envelopes, marked with lines for the contributor's name, address, and amount, one yellow, marked Sea-side Fund, the other white, marked Rector's Fund.

SERVICES AND SERMONS

ST. GEORGE'S RECTORY
209 EAST 16TH ST.

DEAR FRIEND:

I must write to you what I would far sooner say by word of mouth. Come to the Lord's Table Easter-Day.

Come seeking pardon for the past. Come seeking guidance and help for the future.

Try to forgive your enemies. Try to be true to your friends. Try to be patient to all men. Try to see some good in all.

Bring an offering which costs you something.

I want to use your alms for two purposes:

    (1) To send the tired and sickly to the sea-side.

    (2) For my private poor fund.

Dear Friend, "While we HAVE TIME let us do good unto all men, specially to those who are of the household of faith."

                       Your friend and Rector,

Lent, 19—.   *W. S. RAINSFORD.*

Holy Communion, Easter-Day, 7 A.M., 10.30 A.M.

The second service on Easter-Day begins at 10.30 A.M., but admission is by card until 10.15 A.M. This was done because the people of the parish were crowded out by strangers.

COUNTERSIGNED W. S. R.

St. George's Church
Stuyvesant Square

EASTER-DAY, APRIL 3, 1904
ADMIT BEARER TO SERVICE, 10.30 A.M.
ENTRANCE BY REAR DOORS OF CHURCH
UNTIL 10.15 O'CLOCK

KINDLY RETURN THIS TICKET TO THE
RECTOR IF YOU CANNOT USE
IT YOURSELF

This card is mailed to all envelope subscribers and their families, and cards can be had on application by those who are members but non-subscribers. This brings in every year the names of a good many people who come regularly to the church, but who have not previously made themselves known to the clergy. In mailing the cards to such persons, the following form, signed by the Rector, is enclosed, together with a blank for making out a family record and joining the envelope system.

> *I understand that you are a member of St. George's parish. If so, will you kindly fill out the enclosed Family Record and return same to me at an early day.*
>
> *Very truly yours,*
>
> _____

These names are submitted to a staff meeting, and distributed for visitation. The clergy and deaconesses follow the letter immediately. Reports are made at the next conference of the staff, and names are added in consequence to the lists of communicants, of subscribers, and of workers.

At the Easter children's festival there is a short evensong with carols, and plants in pots are given out to the children.

III.—THE CHOIR

"My one aim and desire," says Dr. Rainsford, "has been to have services in which all can heartily join. A hearty service, hymns universally sung, prayers in which all join audibly, are the best preparation for a helpful sermon. Let all, then, join in hymns, chants, and responses. If you see strangers without books, immediately supply them. Nothing of this sort is trivial."

Accordingly, the choir is a body of singers who are trained primarily for the purpose of leading the worship of the congregation. To this end, familiar music is sung to hymns and canticles. The same chants are used with the Venite, for example, or the Benedictus or Jubilate, for months in succession. The people sing with the choir. These hymn-tunes and chants are sung by the choir without "shading"; that is, without changes of time from fast to slow, or changes of tone from strong to soft. Such changes discourage and perplex a congregation, and make congregational singing impossible.

At the same time, while all hymn music and most of the chanting is thus simple, straightforward, and familiar, the choir-master has a wide range in the selection for the Te Deum and the anthems. These, too, when settings are found which please the people, are frequently repeated.

Nearly all of the members of the choir of St. George's are communicants. They kneel together in their surplices at the altar-rail. Their singing is an act of their own worship. Their service is a contribution which they make to the cause of the Christian religion. Most of the choir members are volunteers, who are paid only their car-fare. There are paid leaders, however, in each part, and a quartet of soloists.

In the maintenance of such a choir much attention is paid to the social side of their corporate life. At New Year's, the Rector gives the choir a supper. In the spring and fall, they go out together for a day in the country or by the sea. The choir is encouraged to provide entertainments of wholesome amusement. The singers go to concerts, sometimes to plays, on invitation of members of the parish. They are asked of an evening to the houses of parishioners. Thus their own interest in the church is emphasized by the interest which the people take in them. Theirs is a place of dignity, like that of the clergy and the deaconesses, recognized and appreciated.

The music of the Sunday-school is so chosen as to be a preparation for the music of the church. All the hymns and canticles are there sung in the same manner as in church. There are two vested choirs of boys, one in the junior room, the other in the senior room. These boys graduate from the junior to the senior choir, and thence to the church choir. There is also a volunteer choir of forty girls, who sing at the mid-week service. Out of this also graduations are made into the choir of the church.

A careful record has been kept of all the hymns and tunes sung at St. George's since the beginning of Dr. Rainsford's rectorship. The list has been changed from time to time according to the success of the selections for congregational use. We present here a complete list for all the Sundays and some of the Holy Days of the year. The tunes are in Hutchin's Hymnal. A numeral above the line indicates the first or second tune in the book.

PROPOSED CHANGES

First Sunday in Advent

8 A.M.	48^1	Come, Thou
	388	Come, Thou Almighty
	412^1	The King of Love
11 A.M.	43^1	Rejoice, Rejoice
	3^1	Come, My Soul
	39^1	Lo! He Comes
	406^1	Brief Life
8 P.M.	179^1	Hark! the Sound
	12^1	Abide with Me
	414^1	Guide Me
	407^1	For Thee, O Dear

SERVICES AND SERMONS

PROPOSED CHANGES

Second Sunday in Advent

11 A.M.	48^1	Come, Thou
	610	O Holy Saviour
	357^1	O Jesu, Thou
	490^1	Glorious Things
8 P.M.	506^1	Oft in Danger
	661^2	As Pants The
	284^1	O Word of God
	22^2	Sweet Saviour, Bless

Third Sunday in Advent

11 A.M.	311^1	Ancient of Days
	414^1	Guide Me
	317^1	Thou Art
	408^1	Jerusalem, the Golden
8 P.M.	39^1	Lo! He Comes
	10^1	The Sun Is Sinking
	32^2	Saviour, Again
	510^3	Go Forward

Fourth Sunday in Advent

11 A.M.	312^1	Christ, Whose
	415	Call Jehovah
	602	I Need Thee
	656^1	Breast the Wave
8 P.M.	331^1	Watchman, Tell
	329	Thy Kingdom Come
	325	Light of Those
	15^1	The Shadows

Christmas Day

7 A.M.	49	Oh, Come,
	58	O Little Town
	51^1	Hark! the Herald
11 A.M.	51^1	Hark! the Herald
	58	O Little Town
	59^1	It Came Upon
	60	Angels, From

The First Sunday after Christmas

11 A.M.	49	Oh, Come,
	53	Shout the Glad
	60	Angels, From
	51^1	Hark! the Herald
8 P.M.	59^1	It Came
	60	Angels, From

Watch-night Service

11 P.M.	203^1	A Few More
	621	Days and Moments
	503	Awake, My Soul
	423^1	Lead, Kindly Light

ADMINISTRATION OF AN INSTITUTIONAL CHURCH

PROPOSED CHANGES

Second Sunday after Christmas

- 8 A.M. 510² Go Forward
- 58 O Little Town
- 408¹ Jerusalem, the Golden
- 11 A.M. 523¹ Forward! Be Our
- 312¹ Christ, Whose Glory
- 228² And Now
- 404¹ I Heard a Sound
- 8 P.M. 65 As With Gladness
- 53 Shout the Glad
- 487 Rise, Crowned With

First Sunday after Epiphany

- 11 A.M. 66¹ Brightest and Best
- 254 From Greenland's
- 253² Fling Out the Banner
- 249¹ O Sion Haste
- 8 P.M. 510² Go Forward
- 432² Love Divine
- 606¹ Just As I Am
- 460² The God of Abraham

Second Sunday after Epiphany

249¹ O Sion Haste, instead of 261, to avoid repetition.

- 11 A.M. 62¹ From the Eastern Mts.
- 28¹ This Is the Day
- 261¹ Jesus Shall Reign
- 66¹ Brightest
- 8 P.M. 408¹ Jerusalem, the Golden
- 63 Earth Has Many
- 434¹ Jesu, the Very
- 15¹ The Shadows

Third Sunday after Epiphany

- 11 A.M. 507² The Son of God
- 459 Oh, Worship the King
- 421¹ Lead Us
- 444² O Saviour
- 8 P.M. 450¹ All Hail
- 624² My God, I Thank Thee
- 661² As Pants The
- 584¹ Go Labor On

404¹ I Heard a Sound, instead of 584, to avoid repetition.

Fourth Sunday after Epiphany

- 11 A.M. 368² Alleluia! Sing
- 344¹ Nearer, My God
- 412¹ The King of Love
- 510² Go Forward
- 8 P.M. 345¹ My Faith Looks
- 535¹ Now the Day
- 544 There Is a Green Hill
- 335² Jesu, Lover

SERVICES AND SERMONS

PROPOSED CHANGES			
			Septuagesima Sunday
	11 A.M.	408¹	Jerusalem
		415	Call Jehovah
		584²	Go, Labor On
		396	Ten Thousand
	8 P.M.	491	The Church's One
		336¹	Rock of Ages
319¹ Thou Didst Leave, instead of 624, to avoid repetition.		624²	My God, I Thank
		642	Tarry With Me
			Sexagesima Sunday
	8 A.M.	387¹	Round the Lord
		505¹	Fight the Good
28¹ This Is the Day, instead of 505, to avoid repetition.		345¹	My Faith
	11 A.M.	398¹	Hark! Hark
		329	Thy Kingdom
		228²	And Now
		490¹	Glorious Things
	8 P.M.	395²	Those Eternal
		616¹	He Leadeth Me
		363²	O Lamb of God
		438¹	Sing, My Soul
			Quinquagesima Sunday
249¹ O Zion Haste, instead of 491, to avoid repetition.	11 A.M.	491	The Church's One
		434¹	Jesu, the Very
		383	Holy, Holy, Holy!
Rector's selections for missions, 11 A.M.:		387¹	Round the Lord
194 God of Our Fathers	8 P.M.	489¹	Pleasant
346² Lord as to Thy		403¹	O Mother Dear
379² Come Gracious		23²	Our Day of Praise
403² O Mother Dear		261¹	Jesus Shall Reign
			First Sunday in Lent
	8 A.M.	438¹	Sing, My Soul
		342¹	Art Thou Weary
		432²	Love Divine
510² Go Forward, instead of 505, to avoid repetition.	11 A.M.	505¹	Fight the Good
		177	O King of Saints
		444²	O Saviour, Precious
	8 P.M.	81¹	Christian! Dost Thou
		335²	Jesu, Lover
319¹ Thou Didst Leave, instead of 407, to avoid repetition.		407¹	For Thee, O Dear
		12¹	Abide With Me
			Second Sunday in Lent
	11 A.M.	460²	The God of Abraham
		82	Weary of Earth
		610	O Holy Saviour
		406¹	Brief Life

ADMINISTRATION OF AN INSTITUTIONAL CHURCH

PROPOSED CHANGES			
			Second Sunday in Lent (Con'd)
	8 P.M.	544	There is a Green
		624²	My God, I Thank
		506¹	Oft in Danger
		398¹	Hark! Hark
			Third Sunday in Lent
	11 A.M.	516¹	Onward, Christian
		616¹	He Leadeth Me
		261¹	Jesus Shall Reign
		489¹	Pleasant Are
	8 P.M.	363²	O Lamb of God
		311¹	Ancient of Days
			Fourth Sunday in Lent
	11 A.M.	444²	O Saviour, Precious
		637	Come, Ye Disconsolate
		586¹	Lord, Speak to Me
		312¹	Christ, Whose Glory
	8 P.M.	179²	Hark! the Sound
		12¹	Abide with Me
404¹ I Heard a Sound, instead of 507, to avoid repetition		10¹	The Sun Is Sinking
		507²	The Son of God
			Fifth Sunday in Lent
	11 A.M.	261¹	Jesus Shall Reign
Come, My Soul, Thou Must Be, instead of 311, to avoid repetition.		311¹	Ancient of Days
		398¹	Hark! Hark
	8 P.M.	101	When I Survey Crucifixion
		88¹	Lord, in This
			Palm-Sunday
	11 A.M.	90	All Glory
		102²	O Sacred Head
346² Lord, as to Thy, instead of 507, to avoid repetition.		507²	The Son of God
		91	Ride On
	8 P.M.		*Confirmation Service*
		90	All Glory, Land
		289³	Come, Holy Ghost
		602	I Need Thee
		216 (13)	Thine Forever
		507²	The Son of God
			Easter-Day
	7 A.M.	121	The Strife Is O'er
		243	On the Resurrection
		225	Bread of the World
		122	Jesus Lives

SERVICES AND SERMONS

PROPOSED CHANGES

Easter-Day (Con'd)

11 A.M.	121	The Strife Is O'er
	112¹	Jesus Christ Is Risen
	243	On the Resurrection
	225	Bread of the World—or 227
	122	Jesus Lives
8 P.M.	121	The Strife Is O'er
	545²	Golden Harps
	368²	Alleluia! Sing to

First Sunday after Easter

11 A.M.	121	The Strife Is O'er
	112¹	Jesus Christ Is Risen
	109	Welcome Happy
	122	Jesus Lives
8 P.M.	112¹	Jesus Christ Is Risen
	109	Welcome Happy
	122	Jesus Lives
	121	The Strife Is O'er

Second Sunday after Easter

11 A.M.	110¹	Come, Ye Faithful
	459	Oh, Worship the King
	408	Jerusalem
	444²	O Saviour, Precious
8 P.M.	368²	Alleluia! Sing to
	12¹	Abide With Me
	125²	Hark! Ten Thousand
	403¹	O Mother Dear

Third Sunday after Easter

11 A.M.	491	The Church's One
	336²	Rock of Ages
	487	Rise, Crowned
	516¹	Onward, Christian
8 P.M.	408¹	Jerusalem
	344¹	Nearer, My God
	434¹	Jesu, the Very
	32²	Saviour Again

Fourth Sunday after Easter

8 A.M.	374¹	Crown Him
	228²	And Now, O
	519²	Saviour Blessed
11 A.M.	311¹	Ancient of Days
	344¹	Nearer, My God
	374¹	Crown Him
8 P.M.	602	I Need Thee
	606¹	Just As I Am
	335²	Jesu, Lover
	22²	Sweet Saviour

ADMINISTRATION OF AN INSTITUTIONAL CHURCH

PROPOSED CHANGES

Fifth Sunday after Easter

11 A.M.	396	Ten Thousand
	3[1]	Come, My Soul
	335[2]	Jesu, Lover
	394[1]	O Paradise
8 P.M.	261[1]	Jesus Shall Reign
	616[1]	He Leadeth Me
	363[2]	O Lamb of God
	438[1]	Sing, My Soul

Sunday after Ascension

11 A.M.	374[1]	Crown Him
	368[2]	Alleluia! Sing
	132	Our Lord Is Risen
	126[1]	See the Conqueror
8 P.M.	130	Look, Ye Saints
	179[2]	Hark! the Sound
	132	Our Lord Is Risen
	407[1]	For Thee, O Dear

Whitsunday

11 A.M.	386	Holy Father, Great Creator
	377[1]	Come, Holy Spirit
	375	Our Blest Redeemer
	312[1]	Christ, Whose Glory
8 P.M.	386	Holy Father
	375	Our Blest Redeemer
	374[1]	Crown Him

Trinity Sunday

8 A.M.	387[1]	Round the Lord
	228[2]	And Now, O Father
	383	Holy, Holy, Holy
11 A.M.	383	Holy, Holy, Holy
	311[1]	Ancient of Days
	385	Holy, Holy, Holy, Lord
8 P.M.	383	Holy, Holy, Holy
	487	Rise, Crowned
	385	Holy, Holy, Holy, Lord
	386	Holy Father

First Sunday after Trinity

11 A.M.	387[1]	Round the Lord
	450	All Hail the Power
	610	O Holy Saviour
	383	Holy, Holy, Holy
8 P.M.	460[2]	The God of Abraham
	434[1]	Jesu, the Very Thought
	505[1]	Fight the Good Fight
	194	God of Our Fathers

SERVICES AND SERMONS

PROPOSED CHANGES

Second Sunday after Trinity

11 A.M.	516[1]	Onward, Christian Soldiers
	3[1]	Come, My Soul
	660[1]	Oh, for a Closer Walk
	284[1]	O Word of God
8 P.M.	444[2]	O Saviour, Precious
	344[1]	Nearer, My God
	586	Lord, Speak to Me
	507[2]	The Son of God Goes

Third Sunday after Trinity

11 A.M.	418	O God, Our Help
	1	New Every Morning
	504[2]	My Soul Be On Thy
	398[1]	Hark! Hark! My Soul
8 P.M.	345[1]	My Faith Looks Up
	335[2]	Jesu, Lover
	414[1]	Guide Me
	408[1]	Jerusalem, the Golden

Fourth Sunday after Trinity

11 A.M.	194	God of Our Fathers
	624[2]	My God, I Thank Thee
	432[2]	Love Divine
	444[2]	O Saviour, Precious
8 P.M.	404[1]	I Heard a Sound
	342[1]	Art Thou Weary
	336[1]	Rock of Ages
	22[2]	Sweet Saviour

Fifth Sunday after Trinity

8 A.M.	3[1]	Come, My Soul
	228[2]	And Now, O Father
	363[2]	O Lamb of God
11 A.M.	519[2]	Saviour, Blessed
	394[1]	O Paradise
	344[1]	Nearer, My God
8 P.M.	387[1]	Round the Lord
	674	Peace, Perfect Peace
	422[2]	Lead Us, O Father
	22[2]	Sweet Saviour

Sixth Sunday after Trinity

11 A.M.	491	The Church's One
	335[1]	Jesu, Lover
	624[2]	My God, I Thank Thee
	284[1]	O Word of God
8 P.M.	253[2]	Fling Out
	673[1]	I Heard the Voice
	450[1]	All Hail
	16[2]	The Day Is Past

ADMINISTRATION OF AN INSTITUTIONAL CHURCH

PROPOSED CHANGES

Seventh Sunday after Trinity

11 A.M.	510²	Go Forward
	357¹	O Jesu, Thou Art
	377¹	Come, Holy Spirit
	490¹	Glorious Things
8 P.M.	414¹	Guide Me
	398¹	Hark! Hark
	487	Rise Crowned
	23³	Our Day of Praise

Eighth Sunday after Trinity

11 A.M.	489¹	Pleasant Are
	418	O God, Our Help
	433¹	How Sweet
	385	Holy, Holy, Holy, Lord
8 P.M.	520¹	Rejoice, Ye Pure
	505¹	Fight the Good Fight
	642	Tarry With Me
	407³	For Thee, O Dear

Ninth Sunday after Trinity

8 A.M.	444²	O Saviour, Precious
	216	Thine Forever
	507²	The Son of God
11 A.M.	507²	The Son of God
	363³	O Lamb of God
	130	Look, Ye Saints
8 P.M.	516¹	Onward, Christian
	423¹	Lead, Kindly Light
	679²	There Is a Blessed Home
	261¹	Jesus Shall Reign

Tenth Sunday after Trinity

11 A.M.	404¹	I Heard a Sound
	649	Lord, Forever
	584¹	Go Labor On
	490¹	Glorious Things
8 P.M.	506¹	Oft in Danger
	660	Oh, for a Closer
	583¹	Work, for the Night
	616¹	He Leadeth Me

Eleventh Sunday after Trinity

11 A.M.	311¹	Ancient of Days
	602	I Need Thee
	586¹	Lord, Speak to Me
	179³	Hark! the Sound
8 P.M.	374¹	Crown Him
	670¹	Father, Whate'er
	345¹	My Faith Looks Up
	496	Lord of Our Life

SERVICES AND SERMONS

PROPOSED CHANGES

Twelfth Sunday after Trinity

11 A.M.	521²	Thro' the Night
	623	I'm But a Stranger
	503	Awake, My Soul
	656¹	Breast the Wave
8 P.M.	582¹	Stand Up
	646¹	Thro' the Day
	606²	Just as I Am
	521²	Thro' the Night

Thirteenth Sunday after Trinity

8 A.M.	507²	The Son of God
	602	I Need Thee
	345¹	My Faith Looks Up
11 A.M.	496	Lord of Our Life
	3¹	Come, My Soul
	523¹	Forward Be Our
8 P.M.	253²	Fling Out
	629	We Would See Jesus
	357¹	O Jesu, Thou Art
	600	Jesu, My Lord

Fourteenth Sunday after Trinity

11 A.M.	444²	O Saviour, Precious
	487	Rise, Crowned
	610	O Holy Saviour
	450¹	All Hail the Power
8 P.M.	460²	The God of Abraham
	623	I'm But a Stranger
	597¹	Jesus, and Shall
	12¹	Abide With Me

Fifteenth Sunday after Trinity

11 A.M.	177	O King of Saints
	143	Jesus Calls Us
	422²	Lead Us, O Father
	516¹	Onward, Christian
8 P.M.	656¹	Breast the Wave
	363²	O Lamb of God
	624²	My God, I Thank
	408²	Jerusalem

Sixteenth Sunday after Trinity

11 A.M.	374¹	Crown Him
	306	Eternal Father
	375	Our Blest Redeemer
	490²	Glorious Things
8 P.M.	522²	On Our Way
	19¹	God, that Madest
	149¹	Jesus! Name
	432²	Love Divine

ADMINISTRATION OF AN INSTITUTIONAL CHURCH

PROPOSED CHANGES			*Seventeenth Sunday after Trinity*
	11 A.M.	176	For All the Saints
		434¹	Jesu, the Very
		377¹	Come, Holy Spirit
		179²	Hark! the Sound
	8 P.M.	496	Lord of Our Life
		14	At Even
		661²	As Pants The
		679²	There Is a Blessed

Eighteenth Sunday after Trinity

8 A.M.	249¹	O Zion Haste
	616¹	He Leadeth Me
	516¹	Onward, Christian
11 A.M.	249¹	O Zion Haste
	624²	My God, I Thank
	491	The Church's One
8 P.M.	396	Ten Thousand
	22²	Sweet Saviour
	615¹	O Jesus I Have
	462	Sing Alleluia

Nineteenth Sunday after Trinity

11 A.M.	311	Ancient of Days
	3¹	Come, My Soul
	336²	Rock of Ages
	386	Holy Father
8 P.M.	523¹	Forward! Be
	606²	Just As I Am
	143	Jesus Calls Us
	407¹	For Thee, O Dear

Twentieth Sunday after Trinity

11 A.M.	509²	Soldiers of Christ
	466	Now Thank We All
	586¹	Lord, Speak to Me
	487	Rise, Crowned
8 P.M.	489¹	Pleasant Are They
	674	Peace, Perfect Peace
	671²	While Thee I Seek
	583¹	Work, for the Night

Twenty-first Sunday after Trinity

	11 A.M.	177	O King of Saints
		414¹	Guide Me
		335¹	Jesu, Lover
		312¹	Christ, Whose Glory
311 Ancient of Days, instead of 505, sung on preceding Sunday.	8 P.M.	505¹	Fight the Good Fight
		667²	My God, My Father
		677¹	As, When the Weary
		22²	Sweet Saviour

SERVICES AND SERMONS

PROPOSED CHANGES	
610 Bad Processional.	
374 Good Processional, therefore transpose.	

Twenty-second Sunday after Trinity

11 A.M.
- 610 O Holy Saviour
- 344¹ Nearer, My God
- 374¹ Crown Him
- 408¹ Jerusalem

8 P.M.
- 444² O Saviour, Precious
- 676¹ One Sweetly Solemn
- 418 O God, Our Help
- 15¹ The Shadows

Twenty-third Sunday after Trinity

8 A.M.
- 357¹ O Jesu, Thou Art
- 588 (678)¹ Thro' Him
- 444² O Saviour, Precious

385¹ Holy, Holy, Holy, instead of 444, to avoid repetition.

11 A.M.
- 491 The Church's One
- 584¹ Go Labor On
- 249¹ O Zion Haste

8 P.M.
- 414¹ Guide Me
- 11¹ Son of My Soul
- 253² Fling Out
- 582¹ Stand Up

Twenty-fourth Sunday after Trinity

11 A.M.
- 510² Go Forward
- 143 Jesus Calls
- 432² Love Divine
- 679² There Is a Blessed

368² Alleluia! Sing to Jesus, instead of 679 (never have).

487 Rise, Crowned With Light, instead of 521 (never have).

8 P.M.
- 521² Thro' the Night
- 674 Peace, Perfect Peace
- 673¹ I Heard the Voice
- 403¹ O Mother Dear

Twenty-fifth Sunday after Trinity

11 A.M.
- 194 God of Our Fathers
- 261¹ Jesus Shall Reign
- 660¹ Oh, for a Closer
- 284¹ O Word of God

8 P.M.
- 317¹ Thou Art Coming
- 423¹ Lead, Kindly Light
- 363² O Lamb of God
- 408¹ Jerusalem

All Saints' Day

- 176 For All the Saints
- 398¹ Hark! Hark
- 177 O King of Saints
- 404¹ I Heard a Sound

Thanksgiving Day

- 194 God of Our Fathers
- 193 Come, Ye Thankful
- 196¹ Our Fathers' God
- 200 Lord God, We Worship

ADMINISTRATION OF AN INSTITUTIONAL CHURCH

IV.—THE SERMONS

The Rector preaches on Sunday morning, at which time his part in the morning prayer is to read the lessons. The assistant clergymen take the rest of the service. He takes also the Wednesday evening address in Lent. The other opportunities for preaching are open to the juniors. Thus every young man who joins the staff at St. George's is placed in a position of dignity as regards the service, and in a position of responsibility as regards the work of preaching. He commonly begins with a written sermon, brought from the seminary. Then, when he begins to gain confidence, he is encouraged to preach without manuscript, at first on Wednesdays, then on Sundays, in the evening. It is found with the congregation of St. George's that the sermon without manuscript carries better, and is more effective than one which is read.

Experience has shown that people are interested and helped by sermons preached in course, rather than by single sermons unrelated to that which has preceded and that which is to follow. It was Dr. Rainsford's habit to preach a series of sermons on one text, thus giving himself time to speak his mind fully on important subjects. His most effective utterances have been instructions rather than formal discourses. It has been found that strangers happening to hear one of such sermons came again to hear the others.

Lectures on vital current topics have sometimes been given in the church by competent speakers on Thursday evenings. The following advertisement of one such course was widely circulated among working-men. Posters were also placed on street corners, at the great thoroughfares, these brought in great congregations.

SERVICES AND SERMONS
LECTURES TO WORKING-MEN

UNDER THE AUSPICES OF

Right Rev. Henry C. Potter

Rev. Lyman Abbott	Richard Pattison
Isaac Cowan	Rev. W. S. Rainsford
Robert Fulton Cutting	James B. Reynolds
John Greenough	Dr. Albert Shaw
John S. Henry	Rudolph E. Schirmer
Abram S. Hewitt	Carl Schurz
Thomas L. James	Rev. Josiah Strong
Patrick McCarthy	Prof. Charles Sprague Smith

William J. O'Brien

St. George's Church
Stuyvesant Square, New York City

Men are cordially invited to attend. Admission free.

This course of lectures originated in my desire to give to the working-men of this city the views and suggestion of men whose broad sympathies towards working-men are well known and whose lives inspire confidence in the value of their thoughts upon the present condition of labor and capital. With this purpose in mind, I sought the assistance of those whose names appear on the front page of this circular, and a plan was developed for a course of lectures to be given at St. George's, at eight o'clock on the evenings shown on the foregoing programme.

Although they are to be given in a church, they are not to be theological or sectarian in character, nor are they to be political.

Men of all creeds are invited, and it is expected that the subjects will be treated on the broadest grounds of truth from which all will derive benefit.

The first lecturer is supplied by the People's Institute, through the kindness of Prof. Charles Sprague Smith.

Being convinced of the necessity of this movement, and having entire confidence in the speakers and their subjects, I ask all working-men to take this opportunity to join with me in making this course a success by attending the lectures. The speakers, although busy men, are giving their services, and you—men who represent the bone and sinew of industry—will, I am sure, show your interest in the great questions to be discussed by giving your presence.

WILLIAM S. RAINSFORD.

These lectures were given by Dr. Lyman Abbott, Dr. Washington Gladden, Hon. William Dudley Foulke, Dr. Canfield, of Columbia University, and others.

The lantern is sometimes used at Christmas and Easter and for missionary services, and is found effective. In some parishes the children are assembled on the evening of Good-Friday, and lantern pictures are shown, beginning with the entry into Jerusalem on Palm-Sunday, and ending with the Easter appearances, or with the Ascension. A similar service is held on the evening of Epiphany, showing the Christmas pictures, and others from the life of our Lord.

Little use is made of the newspapers in advertising or reporting the sermons or services, though they are used in case of special musical services, for Lenten notices, and for occasions to which people outside the parish are to be invited.

V

RELIGIOUS INSTRUCTION OF THE YOUTH

I. The Sunday-school—II. The Confirmation Classes—III. The Library.

I.—THE SUNDAY-SCHOOL

1. Importance.

The one ray of hope in St. George's parish when Dr. Rainsford began his work was the Sunday-school. There was, indeed, as he said afterwards, a great gulf between the school and the church. The two seemed to bear no relation one towards the other. But the school was getting hold. It was making an appeal to the actual neighborhood, to which there was a small but genuine and hearty response. There the great work began. Emphasis was immediately put upon the children. The utmost care was taken in their instruction in conduct, in creed, in the ways of the church. In them was seen the parish of the future. The beginning of a strong church, Dr. Rainsford insisted, is a good Sunday-school. The theory has been abundantly proved true by experience. A great deal of the enduring strength of St. George's Church is in the young men and women who have been trained in the school. They began as children. Now they are leaders and teachers in the various organizations of the church, filled with the spirit of the parish, and devoted to its interests.

At the same time it was felt, and is still felt, that Sunday-school instruction in general is inadequate; for the most part it continues the traditions of a past generation. But the public-school has left these traditions far behind. In discipline and in instruction the Sunday-school suffers by contrast with the methods and the lessons to which the children are accustomed during the week. The children come to it without much respect, and behave in a manner which would be impossible between Monday and Friday.

In order to meet the situation, care is taken at St. George's to bring the standards of the Sunday-school up to the high level of the public-school. The arrangements which we are now to describe have been perfected after many experiments. Their sole purpose is to use to more and more effect the opportunity presented by the youth of the parish. They have been found to work well under the conditions of a city parish. They cannot be adopted in detail to the advantage of the parish of St. John's-in-the-Wilderness, or even of St. Martin's-in-the-Fields, but the principle of order, the attention to little things, the insistence on punctuality, the giving of time and study and prayer to the lessons, and in general the appreciation of the importance of the school—these are the elements of a good school anywhere.

2. Officers.

The officers of the Sunday-school are the superintendent, the secretary, the treasurer, the treasurer of the missionary offerings, and the organist, who is also organist of the church. These five are appointed by the Rector, and are responsible to him for the condition of the school. The superintendent, who is a member of the vestry, is chairman of all committees.

Under the supervision of these five officers are the three heads of departments—primary, junior, and senior. Each of these has a secretary, who is responsible for the class-books, reports, and other records of his department.

The following card, which is posted in the Sunday-school office, sets forth the duties of a secretary:

RULES FOR SECRETARIES

1. Secretaries should be at their posts not later than 9.10 A.M.
2. Distribute class-books, etc., at the door as the teacher arrives.
3. Give the late teachers their class-books, etc., during the singing of the recessional hymn.
4. Count the attendance during the singing of the recessional hymn.
5. Under no circumstances are the secretaries to disturb the classes during the teaching of the lesson.
6. The offering is to be taken up during the singing of the hymn immediately after the lesson.
7. After the school closes the secretaries should gather up the class-books, etc., and return them to the office.

3. Records.

The Sunday-school is divided into four departments:
1. Primary (with kindergarten) meets at 3 P.M.
2. Junior (five grades) meets at 9.30 A.M.
3. Senior (five grades) meets at 9.30 A.M.
4. Bible classes (post-graduate) meet at 9.30 A.M.
   " " (for mothers) meet at 3 P.M.

In order to show the details of the method of receiving and placing scholars, of marking their proficiency and of keeping the records, we will take a lad of five and lead him along, step by step, from his entrance to his graduation. John Mark is brought one Sunday afternoon by his older sister. She asks that John may be received as a new scholar. She is given the following card, which she takes home to be filled out by her father or mother:

ADMINISTRATION OF AN INSTITUTIONAL CHURCH

CERTIFICATE OF PARENTS

TO BE SIGNED IN INK BY THE PARENTS AND RETURNED BY THE SCHOLAR

We, the parents of (here write child's name in full)..........
..
apply for the admission of our child, born....................
................, into St. George's Sunday-school, and agree to use our best efforts to encourage the child in regular attendance, in home study of the lesson, and full compliance with the rules of the school.

..Father.
..Mother.
Residence,...............................Street.
..........Floor, No.......... Date,....................
Parent's occupation,....................................
Is child baptized? (Yes or no.)........................
Is child confirmed? (Yes or no.)........................
..
Other members of the family in St. George's Sunday-school
..
Parents attend church at................................

RELIGIOUS INSTRUCTION OF THE YOUTH

QUESTIONS TO BE ANSWERED

Is this the first time you have been in this Sunday-school?

Have you ever gone to any other Sunday-school?

What school?

When did you leave it?

Why did you leave it?

Why did you come here?

What day school do you attend?

What class?

High,   Grammar,   Primary,

Visited by..

During that week the visitor of the primary department calls upon John Mark and his parents, and ascertains that his appearance at the school is recognized and desired by the family. The next Sunday Mary brings back her brother and the card. A secretary takes his name, address, and age, and duly enters these facts on the lists. She gives John a number which is against his name on the roll, and producing a little medal (Fig. 1) stamps the number upon it. This medal he will wear every Sunday. Another secretary gives him a blank-book in which she pastes a Bible picture. The Perry pictures are cheap and good for this purpose. John is instructed to place the book on his little chair, and to sit on it to keep it flat. He is told to take the book with him when he goes home, and to bring it again next Sunday for another picture. The secretary transcribes the facts contained in the certificate of parents upon such a card as follows (see page 107), and this is filed in the attendance record of that department.

FIG. 1

John's first year is preliminary to the work of the primary department, and is arranged according to the methods of the kindergarten. At the end of that year he is given a new medal (Fig. 2), and is promoted. Two more years he spends in the primary division.

FIG. 2

At the age of eight, after these three primary years, he enters the junior department. Here his name is enrolled in a class-book. This book is in paper covers, and bears on the outside the name of the school and blank spaces for the name and address of the teacher and the depart-

RELIGIOUS INSTRUCTION OF THE YOUTH

No..........	ATTENDANCE					
	MONTH	1	2	3	4	5
Name........................	Jan.					
	Feb.					
Address.....................	Mar.					
	April					
Parents' Names................	May					
	June					
....	July					
	Aug.					
Baptised.....................	Sept.					
	Oct.					
Entered......................	Nov.					
Left.........................	Dec.					

ment and the number of the class. On the first page appears the following rules:

RULES

1. LESSONS.—No lesson can be substituted for that assigned for the day without the express permission of the superintendent.

2. SCHOLARS.—No scholar can be admitted to any class, or transferred from one class to another, except by the superintendent or secretary of the school.

    NOTE.—The wishes of teachers are always consulted as to admissions or transfers, but the power to admit or transfer is reserved to the proper officers.

3. ORDER.—When the superintendent or officer in charge calls for order, all work and talking in the classes is to be stopped.

4. MARKS:

Attendance		Lessons		Conduct	
Early	10	Good	10	Good	10
Late	5	Fair	5	Fair	5
Very late	1	Poor	1	Poor	1
Absent	0	No work	0	Bad	0

NOTE.—Teachers are at liberty to use all the numbers from 1 to 10 in marking the scholars.

N. B.—Scholars who come to the class after the opening verse of the processional hymn are not to be counted early.

5. CLASS-BOOKS.—All class-books must be left in the school on the last Sunday in the month.

An outline of the course of study in the junior department occupies the next page. On the third are printed these counsels for teachers:

SUGGESTIONS TO TEACHERS

1. STUDY THE MEMORANDA, as to the order of the service, the organization for parish work, etc.

2. MARKING. — Marks are kept as a RECORD of what the scholars ACCOMPLISH. The teacher should therefore be careful to make this record of real value by careful marking. But in marking lessons and conduct, allowance should be make, according to the teacher's discretion, for the natural ability and disposition of each scholar.

3. ORDER.—The best way to preserve order is to interest the scholars. Disorder may be rebuked or punished in the teacher's discretion. In an extreme case a scholar may be sent away for the day, not strictly as punishment, but rather as a measure of self-defence and for the sake of the rest of the class. Sparingly used this is a useful resort. If frequently employed it loses its good effect and amounts to a confession of weakness.

4. WORSHIP, HYMNS, RESPONSES.—Show the scholars HOW TO FIND the service for the day, and try to get them to join in the responses. Subordinate your own worship to teaching them to worship. Set an example of hearty singing and urge your scholars to begin singing with the first word of each hymn.

RELIGIOUS INSTRUCTION OF THE YOUTH

5. VISITING.—The officers of the school will aid you in this as you may request, but it is better for teachers to visit personally, if possible. On application to the secretary, teachers desiring to meet their scholars during the week can obtain rooms in the Memorial House for the purpose.

6. TEMPORAL NEEDS.—Teachers should not attempt to supply the needs of families visited without consulting the deaconesses, and in case of sickness reporting to the trained nurse.

7. BIBLES AND PRAYER-BOOKS.—Every scholar should have a Bible of his own. They can be purchased of the secretaries. Testaments, 3 cents; Bibles, 5 cents; Reference Bibles, 10 cents; Prayer-books at various prices.

8. OFFERINGS.—Gradually bring the scholars to appreciate that giving is an act of worship. Encourage systematic giving. Although no teacher is urged to give, those who wish to do so will probably find it useful to adopt a system for themselves, whether by fixing a sum or making their offerings proportional to those of their classes.

9. CORRESPONDENCE.—Letters should be addressed either to Mr. H. P———, 114 ——— Street, or to Dr. E. B———, 156 ——— Ave.

10. PROMOTIONS.—Promotions take place the last Sunday in October. The class teacher is the best judge of who is fit for promotion. Every teacher, before she gives up the class in the spring, will therefore give to Dr. E. B——— a list of the scholars that seem fit for promotion, and a list of those that had better remain another year in the grade. A teacher leaving before the end of the term should hand in this list, as it may not be possible to provide the class with another regular teacher.

There is a page of information for scholars, giving the names, purposes, and hours and places of meeting of the various societies and week-day classes.

When he is entered on the records of the junior department of the Sunday-school, John Mark takes with him a circular of information for his parents. (See page 112.)

The blank pages for records follow: first for the permanent record; then for the statements week by week.

ADMINISTRATION OF AN INSTITUTIONAL CHURCH

PERMANENT RECORD OF JUNIOR V.

Joined Cl.	Card Cat.	Address	Name	Date of Birth	Bapt.	Conf.

MONTH OF

Class No.——		1st, 19—					8th, 19—				
		OFFERINGS $——					OFFERINGS $——				
TEACHER	Attendance	Lesson	Conduct	Total	Visited	Attendance	Lesson	Conduct	Total	Visited

RELIGIOUS INSTRUCTION OF THE YOUTH

CLASS No. 3. FOR 1908–9, ORGANIZED NOV., 1903

PARENTS' NAMES		Trade-School	Bat.	Sew'g School	King's D'rs	Girls' Pr.		Date of Leaving	%
Father	Mother								

OCTOBER, 19—

15th, 19—					22d, 19—					29th, 19—					
OFFERINGS $—					OFFERINGS $—					OFFERINGS $—					
Attendance	Lesson	Conduct	Total	Visited	Attendance	Lesson	Conduct	Total	Visited	Attendance	Lesson	Conduct	Total	Visited	

ADMINISTRATION OF AN INSTITUTIONAL CHURCH

Junior Department *Please keep this circular for reference*

St. George's Sunday-school

INFORMATION FOR PARENTS

SERVICES
1. Sunday-school, 9.30 a.m., every Sunday.
2. Catechism Service, 3.15 p.m., November to June.

Doors Open at 3 p.m.   Service Begins at 3.15 p.m.

NOTICE

The Junior department is graded. It takes five years to complete its work. At the end of each year the children who have done faithful home-work and passed a good examination will be promoted. The rest remain in the same grade another year.

Children who pass over ninety per cent. on their examination can skip a grade.

Parents are requested to notify us of cause of absence of their children; otherwise, if their absence is prolonged, their places will be filled.

RULES

1. No scholar may attend two Sunday-schools.
2. Children are expected to attend the catechism service, but any one will be excused from this service at the written request of their parents.
3. The catechism which is learned by those attending this service must be learned at home by those who are excused.
4. No children are confirmed in the Junior department.

Parents wishing an exception made to this rule must apply to Dr. E. B_____ before the last Sunday in November. Scholars for whom an exception is made will have to pass a special examination.

Children leaving the school are requested to take letters of transfer to the new Sunday-school.

ADDITIONAL INFORMATION

Sewing-school. Saturday, 10 a.m. November to June.

Trade-school. 505 East 16th Street. Every evening, 7.30. Apply to clergyman in charge, 7.30 p.m., Mondays, at Memorial House.

Battalion, Junior Company. Boys from fourteen to sixteen. Apply to Mr. C. C. H_____.

Junior Friendly Society. Girls over thirteen years, Thursday, 8 p.m. Girls under thirteen years, Friday, 3.30 p.m.

Parish Library. Free to all. Sunday, 4 p.m. Monday, Wednesday, and Friday at 8 p.m.

King's Daughters. Girls over twelve years. Mondays at 8 p.m. Apply to Miss C. S_____.

Mothers' Meetings. Thursday, 8 p.m.

Mothers' Bible Class. Sunday, 3 p.m. Miss C. S_____ in charge.

RELIGIOUS INSTRUCTION OF THE YOUTH

When John Mark has gone regularly through the five grades of the junior department, he is thirteen years of age. Then, upon examination, he is promoted to the senior department. He is given a promotion-card:

Grade....   *Class....*

St. George's Sunday-school
207 EAST 16TH STREET, NEW YORK CITY

[Sunday-school, 9.30 A.M., every Sunday in the year]

....

Present this card at.............entrance next Sunday morning, 9.15 a.m., and you will be shown to your class.

....
Superintendent.

Every member of the Junior Department is expected to attend the catechism service in the church at 3 p.m.

| Date of Birth. | Baptized? | Father's name. | Mother's name. |
| 19— | Yes. No. | | |

Now his name is entered in a new class-book, which differs from the one previously described in only a few details: chiefly in an arrangement of five blank spaces on the cover for the name and address of John's teacher as he changes from one to another through the five grades of the department, and he is only marked present or absent in the senior department, not according to attendance, lesson, and conduct.

These being passed, John, at eighteen, is given an engraved certificate of graduation. (See page 114.)

He may now leave the school, or enter a post-graduate Bible class, or serve as a teacher in the primary or junior departments. A large number of these teachers have served this apprenticeship.

> DIOCESE OF NEW YORK
> ### Sunday-school of St. George's Church
> IN THE CITY OF NEW YORK
> [SEAL OF CHURCH]
>
> *This certificate of Graduation is awarded to*
>
> ....
>
> *upon the completion of the regular course of Biblical instruction in this school.*
>
> *Dated, New York,.........A.D. 19..*
>
> ....
>   *Rector*
>
> ....
>   *Superintendent*

The general card-catalogues contain the records of the school. One is according to the letters of the alphabet. (See page 115.)

The other is according to department, grade, and class, as follows:

Date	Grade	Class
Name		
Address		
Remarks		

RELIGIOUS INSTRUCTION OF THE YOUTH

SUNDAY-SCHOOL RECORD

FAMILY NAME	FATHER	MOTHER
Mark	John	Margaret

RESIDENCE   400 East 14th Street

SCHOLAR'S NAME	YEAR OF BIRTH	ENTRY IN SCH'L	PROM. FROM P. D.	JUNIOR DEPARTMENT						SENIOR DEPARTMENT					BIBLE CLASS	GRAD-UATED
				5	4	3	2	1	A	5	4	3	2	1		
John	1900	1905	1908	Cl. 3 Nov. 1908	Cl. 3 Nov. 1909	Cl. 1 Nov. 1910	Cl. 5 Nov. 1911	Cl. 7 Nov. 1912		Cl. 7 Nov. 1913	Cl. 3 Nov. 1914	Cl. 3 Nov. 1915	Cl. 5 Nov. 1916	Cl. 1 Nov. 1917	Cl. 9 Nov. 1918	May 1918

ADMINISTRATION OF AN INSTITUTIONAL CHURCH

The general attendance, Sunday by Sunday, is noted on the following card, which is made out for each department. These cards are brought to the secretary of the senior department, who transcribes the figures in a book.

		Scholars			
Grade	Teachers	Male	Female	Total	Absent Teachers
Bible Classes					
Senior 1					
" 2					
" 3					
" 4					
" 5					

ATTENDANCE

A transfer slip is given with each promotion from grade to grade.

```
                (TRANSFER SLIP)
            St. George's Sunday-school
            ─────────────
Grade..................  Class..................
Name..............................................
Address...........................................
Year born..............  Month..................
Baptized..................
                PARENTS' NAMES
..................................................
                TRANSFERRED TO
Grade..................  Class..................
This slip to be returned to the secretary with the class-book.
..................................................
```

RELIGIOUS INSTRUCTION OF THE YOUTH

The card here shown, which he hands to the secretary on the evening of graduation, is used by graduates who desire to join post-graduate courses.

St. George's Sunday-school

Graduate's application for membership in classes taking post-graduate courses.

The undersigned desires to be entered as a member of the Bible Class taught by

....

for the school year 1903-4, and pledges ......self to as regular attendance as circumstances will permit.

Signature..............................

Address..............................

Last class..............................

This application requires to be renewed yearly.

The foregoing card is mailed to him, with the following letter from the Rector:

To the Graduate Members of the Sunday-school:

Dear Friends,—You have completed the course in our Sunday-school, and received your diplomas as a recognition of work regularly and faithfully done. You are now free to make a choice—you may leave the school honorably, with the best wishes of all your friends here, or you may enroll your name year by year in one of the Bible classes. We shall be glad to have you remain and thus give your loyal support to St. George's, but we shall fully understand your position should you decide to leave the Sunday-school at this time. Whichever way you choose, be sure that the love and interest which you have earned here will follow you out into the world, and nothing you may do or become

can separate you from the strong right hand of helpfulness which St. George's holds out to all who need. With a prayer that God may help you to do the best as you see it, I am
Faithfully your friend,
....

Twice a year a report is presented to the parents of each child, covering attendance, lessons, and conduct for the past months.

St. George's Sunday-school
JUNIOR DEPARTMENT

Grade..........   Class..........

Scholar's name.................................

Address.....................................

REPORT FOR

	Term ending February	Term ending June
Number of Sundays present early	......	......
Number of Sundays present late	......	......
Number of Sundays absent	......	......
Lessons	......	......
Conduct	......	......
Examination mark (100 the highest)	......	......

.... *Class Teacher.*

.... *Superintendent.*

This report must be signed by parent and brought back to class teacher the following Sunday.

FEBRUARY
....
Signature of Parent.

JUNE
....
Signature of Parent.

RELIGIOUS INSTRUCTION OF THE YOUTH

Forms such as these are sent to teachers in whose classes are reports of absent scholars.

St. George's Sunday-school
SENIOR DEPARTMENT

M...Teacher of

Grade.........Class.........

The following members of your class were absent two or more Sundays during the past month. Please secure some response from them by visiting or correspondence, and return this report to me. Use the other side of this form in reporting.

....
Superintendent.

NAMES	ADDRESSES

St. George's Sunday-school
SENIOR DEPARTMENT

M...Teacher of

Grade.........Class.........

Please give below the names and addresses of those scholars whom you consider as having left your class, and return this memorandum to me at the close of the school.

....
Superintendent.

NAMES	ADDRESSES

In case of failure to pass an examination, or to keep up to the standard of diligence demanded, a statement is mailed to the parents.

St. George's Sunday-school

207 EAST 16TH STREET, NEW YORK CITY

Sunday-school 9.30 A.M., every Sunday in the year

The Sunday-school work of.....................has not been such as to entitle h.... to promotion. Please see that ....he prepares h.... lesson every Sunday this year.

Your child is also expected to attend the catechism service in the church at 3.15 P.M.

Die Sonntagsschularbeiten $_{des}^{der}$ .... berechtigen $_{ihn}^{sie}$ nicht dazu versetzt zu werden. Bitte, achten Sie gefl. darauf das $_{er}^{sie}$ auf $_{seine}^{ihre}$ Lection jeden Sonntag vorbereitet ist.

Wir erwarten, das Ihr $_{Tochter}^{Sohn}$, dem Katechismus Unterricht um 3.15 Uhr Nachmittags in der Kirche beiwohnt.

SUPERINTENDENT.

---

4. Accounts.

The general expenses of the school are met by the church. The school receives an annual appropriation from the corporation. Of the disbursement of this appropriation the treasurer of the school keeps an account which he submits to the treasurer of the church.

The collections taken in the school are all for missionary purposes. The school is represented in the Missionary Society of St. George's, and through this society contributes to the missionary apportionment of the parish.

In the primary department, a small bag is used for the

RELIGIOUS INSTRUCTION OF THE YOUTH

class offering. In the junior department there is a small envelope, of stiff manila paper, imprinted as follows:

St. George's Sunday-school

JUNIOR DEPARTMENT

OFFERING

Teacher..............................

Grade.......... Class..................

Amount..............................

In the senior department, the envelope is $3\frac{3}{4}$ x 6 inches in size. It is specially made for this purpose by Raynor & Perkins, 115 William Street, New York City, and can be purchased from them. The printing, which is here shown, can be done by a local press.

St. George's Sunday-school

SENIOR DEPARTMENT

Grade.......... Class.......... Teacher..............................

190	Jan.	Feb.	Mch.	Apl.	May	June	July	Aug.	Sept.	Oct.	Nov.	Dec.
1st Sunday												
2d Sunday												
3d Sunday												
4th Sunday												
5th Sunday												
Total for Month												

ADMINISTRATION OF AN INSTITUTIONAL CHURCH

SENIOR I.

Month	April, 1905				May, 1905					June, 1905				
Number of Sun.	1	2	3	4	5	1	2	3	4	5	1	2	3	4	5
Class No. 1........	17	18	17	33											
" 2........	8		9	9											
" 3........	15	11	21	5											
" 4........	4	12	6	20											
" 5........	35	35	20	11											
" 6........	5		10	20											
" 7........															
" 8........	21	18	16	23											
	1.05	.94	.99	1.21											

RELIGIOUS INSTRUCTION OF THE YOUTH

SUMMARY

MONTH	APRIL, 1905					MAY, 1905					JUNE, 1905				
NUMBER OF SUN.	1	2	3	4	5	1	2	3	4	5	1	2	3	4	5
Bible Classes.........															
Senior I.............	1.05	.94	.99	1.21											
" II.............															
" III............															
" IV............															
Junior I............															
" II............															
" III...........															
" IV...........															
" V............															
Women's Bible Class.															
Up-town School....	22.16	19.18	21.36	21.10											

ADMINISTRATION OF AN INSTITUTIONAL CHURCH

The collections from the various rooms are given to the secretary of the senior department, who locks up the money in the church safe till Monday. On Monday evening the secretary and one of his assistants count it, dividing the coins by denomination and putting them into envelopes marked with the amount. On Tuesday the money is deposited with the treasurer of the church.

The secretary keeps a record of the collections in the form shown on pages 122 and 123.

At the beginning of Lent the children receive the usual mite-boxes from the Church Missions House, for the Easter offering. On Palm-Sunday these boxes are brought to the class, where they are opened, their contents counted by the teachers, and the whole offering of the class placed in a stout envelope. On Easter-Day, at the children's festival, when it is time for the offering, a representative of each class takes the class envelope, and all march in procession to the chancel, where the envelopes are placed in the alms basin.

```
┌─────────────────────────────────────────┐
│            EASTER OFFERING              │
│        St. George's Sunday-school       │
│                                         │
│   Grade...............  Class...........│
│                                         │
│   Teacher...............................│
│                                         │
│   Amount................................│
└─────────────────────────────────────────┘
```

5. Services.

The services are so arranged as to make the children familiar with the prayer-book. They are apportioned to the different rooms in such a manner that there is a continuous progress until the time of graduation. Every part of the Morning and Evening Prayer and of the Ante-Communion enters in order into these services. In the conduct of the services, the scholars are frequently called upon to repeat after the leader the collects and other portions which in church are said by the minister alone, in order to insure attention and understanding. Also, there are frequent explanations of the origin and the meaning of the service, and of the way in which the worshippers ought to take part in it. In Junior I. and II., one of the clergy takes the service; in the senior department the Rector takes the opening service, to emphasize its importance.

The service in use in the primary department is in print, and may be had of Thomas Whittaker, Bible House, New York City. The Creed and the Lord's Prayer in this service are set to music, and all the responses of the school are sung. The musical notes are given in the little paper-covered book which is entitled *Our Own Service*. The following is the order:

Hymn.
Leader. Let us praise God for another day.
School. Praise the Lord with gladness.
L. Praise God for life, health, and all the blessings He has given us.
S. *Praise the Lord with gladness.*
L. All Thy works praise Thee, O Lord.
S. *Praise the Lord with gladness.*
L. Every good gift comes down from the Father.
S. *Praise the Lord, praise the Lord, praise the Lord.*
Hymn.
L. We have one Father, who is over us all.
S. *Therefore let us love one another.*
L. All we on earth are brothers.

ADMINISTRATION OF AN INSTITUTIONAL CHURCH

S. Therefore let us love one another.
L. None of us liveth to himself, and none of us dieth to himself.
S. Therefore let us love one another.
All together. The Creed.
Hymn. *All kneeling.*
L. O Lord, keep us from sin and danger, for Jesus' sake.
S. Send Thy blessing, Lord, we pray.
L. O Lord, give us Thy Holy Spirit, for Jesus' sake.
S. Send Thy blessing, Lord, we pray, let us serve Thee day by day.

All together:
   Father, of Thee three things we pray:
     To know Thee more clearly,
     To love Thee more dearly,
     To follow more nearly,
       Every day.

The Lord's Prayer. *All sitting during the taking of the offering.*
L. All things come of Thee, O Lord, and of Thine own have we given Thee.

Offertory hymn. *All standing.*
   Small are the off'rings we can make,
   But thou hast taught us, Lord,
   If given for the Saviour's sake
   They lose not their reward.

Lesson.
Hymn. *All together bow heads.*
Our Heavenly Father, bless us and keep us, now and forever. *Amen.*
Recessional march.

In the first two stages of the junior department, the following is the opening service:

Processional Hymn.
V. Jesus said, "Suffer the little children to come unto me, and forbid them not.
R. "For of such is the kingdom of God."

RELIGIOUS INSTRUCTION OF THE YOUTH

V. Beloved, let us love one another.
R. For love is of God and God is love.
V. The Lord be with you.
R. And with thy spirit.

(Music, 528)

1. Jesus from Thy throne on high,
   Far above the bright blue sky;
   Look on us with loving eye:
      Hear us, Holy Jesus.

2. Be Thou with us every day,
   In our work and in our play,
   When we learn and when we pray:
      Hear us, Holy Jesus.

3. May we prize our Christian name,
   May we guard it free from blame,
   Fearing all that causes shame:
      Hear us, Holy Jesus.

4. May we grow from day to day,
   Glad to learn each holy way,
   Ever ready to obey:
      Hear us, Holy Jesus.

5. Jesus, whom we hope to see,
   Calling us in heaven to be
   Happy evermore with Thee:
      Hear us, Holy Jesus. *Amen.*

Let us pray.

Our Father, who art in heaven: Hallowed be Thy name. Thy kingdom come; Thy will be done on earth, As it is in Heaven. Give us this day our daily bread. And forgive us our trespasses, As we forgive those who trespass against us. And lead us not into temptation; But deliver us from evil; For thine is the kingdom, and the power, and the glory, for ever and ever. *Amen.*

After shall be said as followeth:

V. O Lord, open Thou our lips,
R. And our mouth shall show forth Thy praise.
V. Glory be to the Father, and to the Son, and to the Holy Ghost.

R. As it was in the beginning, is now, and ever shall be, world without end. *Amen.*
V. Praise ye the Lord.
R. The Lord's name be praised.
Psalm or Hymn.

The Apostles' Creed.
I believe in God the Father Almighty, Maker of heaven and earth:
And in Jesus Christ his only Son our Lord: Who was conceived by the Holy Ghost, Born of the Virgin Mary: Suffered under Pontius Pilate, Was crucified, dead, and buried: He descended into hell; The third day he rose again from the dead: He ascended into heaven, And sitteth on the right hand of God the Father Almighty: From thence he shall come to judge the quick and the dead.
I believe in the Holy Ghost: The Holy Catholic Church; The Communion of Saints: The Forgiveness of Sins: The Resurrection of the body: And the Life everlasting. *Amen.*
V. The Lord be with you.
R. And with thy spirit.
Let us pray.
V. O Lord, show Thy mercy upon us,
R. And grant us Thy salvation.
V. O God, make clean our hearts within us,
R. And take not Thy Holy Spirit from us.

(Use one or more of the following prayers.)

O Lord, we give thanks unto Thee, who hast kept us during the night past from all evils both of body and soul; and we humbly beseech Thee give us grace to cast off the works of darkness, and to walk as children of the light. Preserve us this day from all sin and from all perils and dangers, through Jesus Christ our Lord. *Amen.*

In the morning, at noonday, and evening we praise and bless Thee, O Lord of Love, and we pray Thee to direct our prayers as incense before Thee. Preserve us this day and evermore in our lives, and bring us at last to Thy heavenly kingdom above, through Jesus Christ our Lord. *Amen.*

O God, our Heavenly Father, make us truly sorry for all

the wrong things that we have done; and help us to grow better day by day. Keep us from all meanness and selfishness, and from hurting others by word or deed, through Jesus Christ our Lord. *Amen.*

Almighty and everlasting God, the Father of our Lord Jesus Christ, send down upon us the healthful spirit of Thy grace. May we never be ashamed to confess the faith of Christ crucified, but manfully to fight under His banner and continue His faithful soldiers and servants unto our life's end, through the same Jesus Christ our Lord. *Amen.*

Thine is the day, O Lord, and Thine the night. Grant that the Sun of righteousness may abide in our hearts to drive away the darkness of wicked thoughts, through Jesus Christ our Lord. *Amen.*

The grace of our Lord Jesus Christ, and the love of God, and the fellowship of the Holy Ghost, be with us all evermore. *Amen.*

Hymn.

After the lesson, the school closes with a hymn, and the prayer following:

Leader. Lord of all power and might, who art the Author and Giver of all good things, graft in our hearts the love of Thy name. Increase in us true religion, nourish us with all goodness, and of Thy great mercy keep us in the same, through Jesus Christ our Lord. *Amen.*

Leader. Look, O Lord, in mercy upon all near and dear to us; upon all little children, and especially those who are desolate and uncared for.

Scholars. Lord, hear this prayer, for Christ our Saviour's sake.

Leader. O Father of mercies, look down with pity upon all who are in trouble, sickness, or sin, and guide their feet into the way of peace.

Scholars. Lord, hear this prayer, for Christ our Saviour's sake. Amen.

Leader. May the very God of peace sanctify you wholly, and I pray God your whole spirit and soul and body be preserved blameless unto the coming of our Lord Jesus Christ. *Amen.*

I. Thess. v. 23.

Hymn.

ADMINISTRATION OF AN INSTITUTIONAL CHURCH

In the last three stages of the junior department, changes are brought in, each child having a prayer-book. The services undergo a change each year, so that at the time of promotion to the senior department the scholar has a fair knowledge and familiarity with the order of Morning Prayer. This shows a curriculum of service, same as a curriculum of lessons.

In the senior department, the opening service is shown in the following order. The closing service consists of the general thanksgiving, the collect of St. Chrysostom, and "The Lord bless us and keep us."

SUNDAY-SCHOOL OF ST. GEORGE'S CHURCH

OPENING SERVICE

The opening service shall not take more than fifteen minutes. To this end the psalms, prayers, and hymns may be shortened at the discretion of the leader.

FIRST SERVICE

Processional: Hymn.
Sentence.
Confession.
Lord's Prayer.
V. O Lord, open thou our lips.
R. *And our mouths shall show forth thy praise.*
V. Glory be to the Father, and to the Son, and to the Holy Ghost.
R. *As it was in the beginning, is now, and ever shall be, world without end. Amen.*
V. Praise ye the Lord.
R. *The Lord's name be praised.*

—| Venite
 | Psalm (Short)
　　　or
—| Lesson
 | Jubilate
　Creed

RELIGIOUS INSTRUCTION OF THE YOUTH

V. The Lord be with you.
R. And with thy spirit.
    Let us pray.
V. O Lord, show thy mercy upon us.
R. And grant us thy salvation.
V. O Lord, make clean our hearts within us.
R. And take not thy Holy Spirit from us.
Collects.
Recessional: Hymn.

SECOND SERVICE

Processional: Hymn.
Sentence.
V. The Lord be with you.
R. And with thy spirit.
    Let us pray.
Lord's Prayer.
V. O Lord, open thou our lips.
R. And our mouths shall show forth thy praise.
V. Glory be to the Father, and to the Son, and to the Holy Ghost.
R. As it was in the beginning, is now, and ever shall be, world without end. Amen.
V. Praise ye the Lord.
R. The Lord's name be praised.
Te Deum.
Creed (may be omitted).
V. The Lord be with you.
R. And with thy spirit.
    Let us pray.
V. O Lord, show thy mercy upon us.
R. And grant us thy salvation.
V. O Lord, make clean our hearts within us.
R. And take not thy Holy Spirit from us.
Collects.
Recessional: Hymn.

THIRD SERVICE

Processional: Hymn.
Sentence.
Confession.

ADMINISTRATION OF AN INSTITUTIONAL CHURCH

Lord's Prayer.
V. O Lord, open thou our lips.
R. And our mouths shall show forth thy praise.
V. Glory be to the Father, and to the Son, and to the Holy Ghost.
R. As it was in the beginning, is now, and ever shall be, world without end. Amen.
V. Praise ye the Lord.
R. The Lord's name be praised.
Psalm (short).
Magnificat or Nunc Dimittis or Gloria in Excelsis.
Creed.
V. The Lord be with you.
R. And with thy spirit.
   Let us pray.
V. O Lord, make clean our hearts within us.
R. And take not thy Holy Spirit from us.
Collects.
Recessional: Hymn.

FOURTH SERVICE

Processional: Hymn.
   Let us pray.
Collect: "Almighty God, unto whom all hearts are open, all desires known, and from whom no secrets are hid," etc.
The Commandments.
Kyrie.
Collect for the day.
Gloria in Excelsis.
Recessional: Hymn.

FIFTH SERVICE

Processional: Hymn.
   Let us pray.
Collect: "Almighty God, unto whom all hearts are open," etc.
Hear what our Lord Jesus Christ saith.
Thou shalt love the Lord, etc.
Lord have mercy upon us.
Christ have mercy upon us.
Lord have mercy upon us.
   Let us pray.

RELIGIOUS INSTRUCTION OF THE YOUTH

O Almighty Lord and Everlasting God, vouchsafe, we beseech Thee, to direct, sanctify, and govern, both our hearts and bodies, etc.

Collect for the day.
Epistle (may be shortened).
Announcement of Gospel.
Gloria Tibi.
Gospel (may be shortened).
Nicene Creed.
Recessional: Hymn.

In order that hymns may be wisely chosen and regularly taught, leading to the service in the church, a selection is made and posted for reference. The following regulations accompany these lists:

Hymns on list for each grade are all new to the scholars.
Children are supposed to know the hymns on lists below their present grade.
New hymns and tunes should be taught by the church organist, or one appointed by him, whenever possible.
A new hymn might be introduced in grades 3, 2, and 1, junior, every Sunday.
A record should be kept of the hymns used each Sunday.
Those in charge of rooms are to choose the hymns to be sung each Sunday from the lists provided. This should be done for the month, in advance.

The purpose is to secure for the child knowledge and familiarity with the grand old hymns and tunes of the church, which may be useful to him in after-life. It is felt that it would be unwise to teach the scholars hymns which they are most unlikely to hear or use later on. This lesson has been learned at the cost of a great deal of time and effort, and it explains why hymns have been chosen which may seem unsuitable for children of such tender years.

ADMINISTRATION OF AN INSTITUTIONAL CHURCH

HYMNS TO BE TAUGHT AND USED IN GRADE
PRIMARY

- 16^2 The Day is Past and Over
- 196 Our Fathers' God
- 516^1 Onward, Christian Soldiers
- 526 Jesu, from Thy Throne
- 534 Jesus, Tender Shepherd
- 544 There is a Green Hill
- 550 Jesus, High in Glory
- 553 There's a Friend for Little Children
- 562 I Think When I Read
- 567^1 Jesus, Meek and Gentle
- 577 In the Vineyard
- 616 He Leadeth Me

HYMNS TO BE TAUGHT AND USED IN GRADES
JUNIOR I. AND II.

- 7 The Day is Gently
- 8^2 The Radiant Moon
- 10^1 The Sun is Sinking
- 18^1 All Praise to Thee
- 44^1 On Jordan's Bank
- 66^3 Brightest and Best
- 68^1 O One with God the Father
- 80^1 Awhile in Spirit
- 86 O Thou That Hear'st
- 88^1 Lord in This
- 91 Ride On
- 110^1 Come, Ye Faithful
- 132 Our Lord is Risen from the Dead
- 176 For All the Saints
- 177 O King of Saints
- 179^2 Hark! the Sound of Holy
- 253^2 Fling Out
- 265^1 Arm of the Lord
- 306 Eternal Father
- 313 Lord of all Being
- 324^1 Joy to the World
- 340^1 In the Hour
- 368^2 Alleluia, Sing
- 374^1 Crown Him
- 385 Holy, Holy, Holy, Lord
- 394^1 O Paradise
- 416 (Ein feste Burg) A Tower of Strength
- 431 O Love that Casts
- 458^2 Praise, My Soul
- 460^1 O God of Abraham
- 464 The Spacious Firmament
- 490^1 Glorious Things
- 491 The Church's One
- 496 Lord of Life
- 503 Awake, My Soul
- 507^2 The Son of God
- 512^1 Rise, My Soul
- 519^2 Saviour Blessed
- 624^2 My God, I Thank Thee
- 642^2 Tarry with Me
- 646^1 Thro' the Day
- 678^1 There is a Land

HYMNS TO BE TAUGHT AND USED IN GRADE
JUNIOR III.

- 12^1 Abide with Me
- 63 Earth Has Many a Noble
- 72^1 Not by Thy Mighty Hand
- 109 Welcome, Happy Morning
- 127 Christ Our King
- 377^1 Come, Holy Spirit
- 409^1 The Roseate Hues
- 412^1 The King of Love
- 418 O God Our Help
- 432 Love Divine
- 454 Lift Up Your Heads
- 522^2 On Our Way

RELIGIOUS INSTRUCTION OF THE YOUTH

379¹	Come, Gracious Spirit	538³	All My Heart this Night
398¹	Hark! Hark My Soul	542	Saw You Never
584¹	Go Labor On	553²	There's a Friend
101	When I Survey	568	Hushed Was the Evening Hymn
548	God Almighty, in Thy Temple	656¹	Breast the Wave
284¹	O Word of God	504¹	My Soul, Be on Thy Guard
311¹	Ancient of Days	610	O Holy Saviour
336	Rock of Ages	312¹	Christ, Whose Glory
387¹	Round the Lord	318	Jesus Came
397	Oh, What the Joy		

HYMNS TO BE TAUGHT AND USED IN GRADE JUNIOR IV.

11¹	Sun of My Soul	450¹	All Hail the Power
13	Softly Now	344¹	Nearer, My God
15¹	The Shadows	345¹	My Faith Looks
17²	Saviour, Breathe	359¹	In the Cross of Christ
48¹	Come Thou, Long Expected	363¹	O Lamb of God
65	As with Gladness	386	Holy Father
76³	Gracious Spirit	388	Come, Thou Almighty King
79	Forty Days	389	Three in One
89¹	Saviour! When in Dust	396	Ten Thousand Times
249	O Zion Haste	402¹	Jerusalem, My Happy
252	The Morning Light	533	Come, Praise Your Lord
254	From Greenland's	540	Once in Royal David's City
339¹	O Thou to Whose	545³	Golden Harps

HYMNS TO BE TAUGHT AND USED IN GRADE JUNIOR V.

73¹	Alleluia! Songs of	434	Jesu, the Very Thought
130	Look, Ye Saints	444²	O Saviour, Precious Saviour
143	Jesus Calls Us	452¹	Children of the Heavenly
194	God of Our Fathers	466¹	Now Thank We All
199¹	O God of Love	506³	Oft in Danger
331	Watchman, Tell Us	531²	Jesus, King of Glory
335¹	Jesus, Lover	535¹	Now the Day is Over
383	Holy, Holy, Holy! Lord God	558	When, His Salvation
58	O Little Town	582	Stand Up
403¹	O Mother Dear	583	Work, for the Night
433¹	How Sweet the Name	602	I Need Thee

6. Lessons.

The lessons are arranged according to the age and

understanding of the learners. A scholar, on entering the school, is put in a class with others of the same standing in the public school. After that he works his way through. If the work of the winter warrants the belief that he can take a somewhat harder course, he is promoted on the recommendation of his teacher. He is marked according to the effort made rather than according to the results. Promotion is the only reward given in the school.

The following conspectus shows the course of study. Lesson-books for this course may be had on application to the Sunday-school Commission of the Diocese of New York, at 29 Lafayette Place, New York City. These lessons have been prepared by a committee of experienced Sunday-school workers, assisted by an eminent specialist in pedagogics. The plan is to have all scholars over nine years of age systematically write answers to a series of questions on the lesson for the day. In order to answer these questions, it is necessary to read extended passages of the Bible. The replies thus sought are commonly in regard to matters of fact, the theological and ethical explanations and applications being left to the teacher.

CURRICULUM
THE BIBLE

KINDERGARTEN—Ages, 3–6 years
Lessons arranged by teacher.

PRIMARY—Ages, 6–8 years
Bible stories from Old and New Testament; arranged in groups to illustrate certain ethical principles.

JUNIOR
Grade 5—Old Testament stories to time of Saul.—Ages, 8–9 years.

RELIGIOUS INSTRUCTION OF THE YOUTH

Grade 4—Old Testament stories from time of Saul.—Ages, 9-10 years.
Grade 3—Life of Jesus (events and acts), written answers.—Ages, 10-11 years.
Grade 2—Teachings of Jesus (parables, etc.), written answers.—Ages, 11-12 years.
Grade 1—Lessons on Acts, written answers.—Ages, 12-13 years.

SENIOR

Senior 5—Old Testament biographies.—Ages, 13-14 years.
Senior 4—Life of Jesus.—Ages, 14-15 years.
Senior 3—Teachings of Jesus.—Ages, 15-16 years.
Senior 2—Paul.—Ages, 16-17 years.
Senior 1—Church history: Christ the Main Factor in Modern Civilization.—Ages, 17-18 years.

BIBLE CLASS—Ages, 18 and over

Special subjects.

THE PRAYER-BOOK

JUNIOR GRADE—Ages, 10 years and over

Every Sunday in the year, fifteen minutes on Morning Prayer, with prayer-books (the clergy).

SENIOR

Every Sunday morning. Instruction in worship in all the services of the church (the Rector or his assistant).

CATECHISM

CHILDREN—Ages, 8-14 years

Are taught at the catechism service every Sunday afternoon, except during the summer months.

CHILDREN—Ages, 14 years and over

Catechism classes are held on Sunday afternoons for two months before the formation of the Confirmation classes. A certificate of knowledge of the catechism is necessary to obtain admittance to the Confirmation classes.

Communicants

Communicants' classes for instruction on the Holy Communion are held on Wednesday night before the first Sunday in the month.

Special Subjects of Instruction

Such subjects as lives of great men, of missionaries, church leaders, church history, hymnology, books of the Bible, etc., etc., are taken up in the summer for five months, and lectures given by some of the teachers from the platform.

As a result of this grading of the school, there has been developed a natural class organization. Each class has a president, vice-president, secretary, and historian, and holds its commencement exercises in the Parish House. At these exercises each graduate is presented by the Rector with a certificate. A list is printed of the names of the class, and is given to each member. Commonly the class is photographed, with the Rector, the staff, and the officers of the school. Thus the instruction of the school has a definite ending as well as a definite beginning.

After graduation, all are free to leave. Some leave, some remain to teach, some join classes for post-graduate study. A radical change is made in the theme and method of these classes from the undergraduate courses. These students take up Church history, comparative religion, Christian biography, modern problems. Sometimes a group of young people spend a winter in the reading and discussion of a recent book.

7. Teachers.

The teachers are chosen rather for their personality than for their technical skill. The purpose is to secure men and women of good judgment, of strong character, who are interested in human beings, and whose example will be as effective as their precept. They are commonly communicants, though the rule is not an invariable one. Occasionally it seems wise to enlist upon the staff of teachers an earnest man or woman who is not at the moment a communicant.

Each teacher is responsible for a small group of children, usually ten. These children are to be kept in place, Sunday after Sunday, regularly and punctually. The initial duty of the teacher is to get a good hold of their respect and affection, and keep it. In some of the departments the teachers are required to visit the scholars in their homes; and in all departments the value and importance of such visitation is emphasized.

The teachers meet for a study of the lesson; though where a teacher has been for several years giving instruction in the same course, this is not a required exercise. Twice in the year there is a teachers' conference. The first conference is held at the beginning of the winter's work, when the Rector invites an eminent scholar to address the meeting upon some large aspect of religious education. The second conference occurs in the middle of the winter, and is a practical and definite discussion of the immediate problems by the officers and teachers, with a summing up by the Rector. At each of these conferences a supper is served. Thus the teachers are brought into better acquaintance, and the spirit of the school is maintained.

Certain teachers from each department, together with the clergy, the deaconesses, and the school officers, compose a council. All matters affecting the welfare of the school are considered by the council. Changes of organization, plans of lessons, orders of service, selections of hymns, and other such arrangements are within its province. The council is advisory, not legislative; submitting all its recommendations to the Rector. Thus the traditions of the school are continued. A new superintendent, a new member of the clerical staff, finds here a group of persons by whom the whole conduct of the school is intelligently understood. No experiments have to be made twice. Nothing is changed without the careful consideration of responsible and representative teachers.

A blank such as follows is used to summon the members of the council and to inform them as to the business of the meeting.

ST. GEORGE'S SUNDAY-SCHOOL
207 EAST 16TH ST.

New York, ... 190

M ....

A regular meeting of the Sunday-school Council will be held in the office of the secretary of the school, on .... *evening,* .... *at eight o'clock. Please come prepared to discuss*

....
....
....
....

....
Superintendent.
....
Secretary.

RELIGIOUS INSTRUCTION OF THE YOUTH

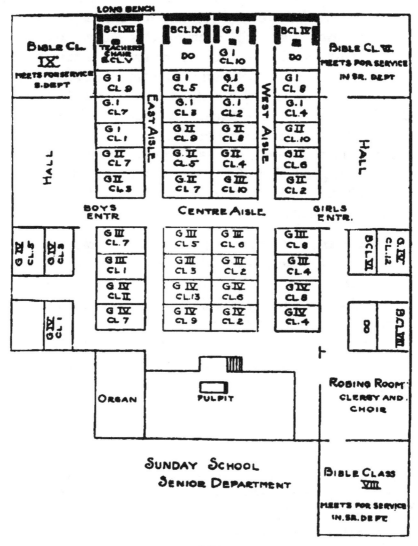

The plan of the school-room, shown on the preceding page, indicates the division of classes. Each class has one long bench and two short ones, and a seat for the teacher. The teacher faces the long bench, and has the short ones on either hand. When it is desired to use the room for other purposes, the two short benches and teacher's chair put together are just the length of the long one, making convenient rows of seats. By means of removable standards and rods, each class is curtained off by itself during the lesson. The primary department and the lowest grade of the junior department have their own rooms. There they are divided, indeed, into classes, but the function of the teacher is mainly to keep order. The teaching is done from the platforms.

The following minutes of an annual Teachers' conference give a good idea of the spirit and of the method of the teachers. The teachers were summoned by the following invitation:

The teachers and officers of the Sunday-school are invited to the last conference of the season on Wednesday, March 7th, at 8 P.M. The evening will be spent in discussing Sunday-school problems, in which discussion every teacher is invited to take part.

Early notice of the date of this meeting is given to enable teachers to keep this particular evening free from all other engagements.

....
Refreshments.   *Superintendent.*

Note.—When the scholar comes up from the junior department, he is put in Senior V., which is in the south gallery, apart from the main floor. After he has passed a year there he is moved downstairs to Senior IV., and on that floor each grade moves back, keeping the younger scholars in front.

RELIGIOUS INSTRUCTION OF THE YOUTH

The meeting was opened by the Rector with a hymn and a prayer. Then the meeting was conducted by the superintendent as follows:

He called upon the teachers of the various grades to describe their way of teaching the scholar, beginning with the child four years old entering the kindergarten, passing through the twelve grades, and thus to graduation.

Miss M—— explained her work in the kindergarten and primary department as follows:

We teach only the Bible in the primary grades. It is taught in story form in both primary and kindergarten classes, and there is no home study required of the children. The only memory work we ask of them is to learn their hymns. In order that a grown person may gauge the difficulties of a tiny child in the way of learning, it is not only necessary to try to see things with the child's eyes, but you should sit on the floor awhile and watch the passing show from an elevation of three feet. The teacher looks very big and busy to the kindergarten baby of four years old until she sits down on one of the little chairs beside him. Then he can see her face well; and a little child learns more from the face than from any words, for words are very big things at four years old and have to be explained. So much explanation and practice in pronunciation is necessary that it is with difficulty he learns to sing a few hymns and to say "Our Father." He does not know quite what it all means, but he associates it with the pictures his teacher gives him to paste in his scrap-book. The teacher tells in easy words the subject of the picture, and the child points out the objects she asks about. It is easier for him than to find words to answer. In this way he takes his part in the story; but as soon as he begins to know enough to be a help in the class to the teacher, it is time to promote him, so he comes into the primary class. Here the work is very much the same, only the stories are longer and harder, and there are more hymns to be learned. He has to take his own part in the story-telling here, for the method is by question and answer. Questions of home or natural surroundings that the child can answer and that bear on the topic are asked him till the climax of the story is reached, when he finds that he has told a good deal of it himself.

From the primary department the child goes to the junior department. The superintendent called on Miss H——, representing two grades, V. and IV, to tell what is taught in these two grades:

Junior V. and IV. are preparatory for the higher junior grades, where written work is done. The children come with some knowledge of Bible stories, but in this course they learn the use of the Bible for study and reference. The books used are *Stories in the Old Testament*, First Year and Second Year, and the lesson consists of a Golden Text, review questions on the lesson of the previous Sunday, and a Bible story told by the teacher. Written work is not required, and no mark is given for it in the class roll-book; but as a matter of fact, many of the children do it, receiving more or less help from their home people. Immediately after the opening exercises the teacher hears the class recite the Golden Text, asks the review questions, and then in the most graphic manner possible tells the story for the day. The children then tell it, either all speaking together, or one taking it up where another leaves off, until they are quite familiar with it. In preparation for the mid-year examination, there is a review of all the stories learned in the half-year, told in turn by the teachers of the room, illustrated by stereopticon pictures. A similar review will be given for the spring examination. Special drill in the practice of finding references in the Bible is given during the school year in Junior V. and IV.

The superintendent stated that next in the curriculum come the lessons on the "Life of Jesus," for Junior III., II., and I. These lessons treat of the words and acts of Jesus, followed in the fourth year by "Christian Ethics," and in the fifth year by the course on "The Early Church," a simple history of the Acts of the Apostles.

He then called upon Mrs. H—— to report on Junior III., II., and I.

The children have now reached the age when they can think and act for themselves, past the age of picture-books and toys, thinking of becoming soldiers or sailors —in fact, anything that has life or action. Their imagination needs to be directed. When they do their homework, a test—which consists of memorizing the Golden Text, ten review questions and written answers—is made. By this method the teacher soon learns the result of her labor. But to the teacher the lesson is not all; she gives to the children the very best that is in her, gaining their confidence by her earnestness, and in this way she gets back more than she gives.

The secretary of the junior department then reported as follows:

I have only one word to add, and that is on the necessity of every teacher keeping up the standard of the school. We are all only too ready to lower our standards, and where a teacher has rested content with careless and slovenly work on the part of a scholar, marked it perfect, and recommended the scholar for promotion, it is almost an impossibility for the teacher of the next grade to get the scholar to aim for a better standard of work. In a graded school there is also another reason for insisting on as good work as the scholar is capable of doing. Each year's work is not isolated from the work of the previous and subsequent years, but just part of one definite plan, and weak work in one year will result in poor work years afterwards, when the advanced work on the same subject is taken up.

The superintendent said:
You have seen a child taken at four years of age, and watched the progress of teaching, from the primary department to the junior department, with its various grades. The child is now between thirteen and fourteen years of age, and ready to be promoted to the senior department. Upon the faithfulness of the work done in these years by the teachers of the junior department depends much of the success of the teachers in the senior department. Upon the insistence and persistence of the teachers in Junior III., where the first written home-work is required, and the habits then formed, depends the effectiveness of the work in the two following years. Now, when we come to the senior department, the problems confronting the school become more complicated. The scholars consider themselves no longer children, not even at the age of fourteen. Most of them are working. The habit to study, gained in the public school, is soon lost, and the Sunday-school is the next thing they wish to give up. The Bible has been opened at the beginning of each year for five years, and a sense of weariness in relation to it is beginning to be felt. In

short, the scholar is tired of the programme. This necessitates sharp contrasts being made between the junior department and senior department—the sharper the better. We shall now consider what is being done in the senior department, and possibly what may be done in the future in the way of mending what is clearly evident, a condition known to the superintendent but not likely to be realized by the teacher. Before hearing the reports, I will say that the courses of instruction provided are built upon what has gone before. Senior V., "Old Testament History," deals with the great names and characters told about in story in Junior IV. and III. Senior IV., studying the "Life of Jesus" (senior text-book), has as a basis what has been taught several years before in Junior III.; the following year the teachings of Jesus, founded on these three previous courses on the Gospels. So it is with the course on "St. Paul," a broader treatment than that of the "Early Church." All of which goes to show the effort made to build on what has gone before, and save time and effort and wear and tear on teachers.

Mr. H—— will make his report.

At what age should boys be made to figure out things for themselves? This is a question which has been in my mind for some time, and which I have solved as far as it concerns my class. They are now at that age. They are fourteen. In the last year their judgment seems to have matured greatly. An individual desire to take part in each lesson has manifested itself. We devote about half of our time to the lesson. The balance of the time is used in having each boy give some experience or talk about some beneficial subject which has been given him to think over the Sunday before. His subject he always studies over, for he knows he can count on no one to help him, but must know it himself. We now and then read, study, and memorize certain proverbs. The minute a boy feels that he is a part of the class and that he is responsible for part of the morning's programme, he responds.

Remarks by the superintendent:

We must now consider the scholar having done five years of work in the senior department, passed the courses of study provided by the curriculum, and that he has graduated. It is necessary for us now to demonstrate what occurs at this period. The scholar has received an honorable discharge, same as a college graduate. Does he drop us? No. What follows? I shall call upon the teachers of the Bible classes, or post-graduate classes, to state what they are doing, and I would commend to the attention of the teachers whose classes graduate in May next. Not five per cent. of the class will discontinue active membership in the school; they are all too interested and will wish to continue. There are ten classes, of about one hundred and fifty scholars. What are you going to do after graduation? What course of study are you going to adopt? You will perhaps ask the Rector to tell you or provide a course. I don't believe he will. He will say to you, you better decide this for yourselves, in consultation with your scholars. He will be glad to confer and counsel with you, but you must be provided with alternatives. You will have to determine this in the next three months, before we break up for the summer; hence your interest in what follows.

Mr. W—— thereupon reported:

RELIGIOUS INSTRUCTION OF THE YOUTH

My boys range from seventeen to nineteen years of age, and vary greatly in natural capacity and education. The difficulty, obviously, is to find a common ground of interest. Our text-book is *The Teachings of Jesus*. The majority of our class took offence at the simplicity of the questions; refused to write down obvious answers, or do oral work of the same character. In consequence we have used the lesson passages as a background, and I have tried to make the class do some thinking for themselves. The Gospel narrative and its application to present-day living, its relation to modern life, what working-rules of conduct can be drawn from the lesson incidents, are discussed, leading often to astonishing difference in point of view, but usually to awakened interest and some enthusiasm. Taking Christianity as something for individual investigation, as a new thing and not as a matter of course, the boys ask questions for themselves. Some of them do outside reading. Christ's attitude towards work, wealth, sin, His life and its application to theirs; numerous questions of this nature are suggested by the lesson passages to the boys themselves. An incident in the lesson passage, if given in another Gospel, is looked up, not infrequently outside the class, and commented upon. My own work is little enough, beyond explanations of local manners, customs, and historical points, to make the Judaic setting less strange. Practically, the boys run the class, think and work for themselves. The result, while always crude, is not always wholly unsatisfactory.

Miss T——, who has a class of girls of eighteen to nineteen years of age, reported:

When the time came to choose a course of study for my Bible class this year, I found that the girls wanted something new. They had been over the established courses until they were tired of them. At the same time they professed and manifested an unlimited ignorance of the Old Testament, and said that they would like some sort of course to relieve that condition. I therefore suggested a study of the prophetical literature, beginning with the writing prophets.

We began the year with Amos, and different girls prepared papers on his life, the historical situation of his time, and different aspects of his teaching, using, as reference works, Kent's *History of the Hebrew People* and George Adam Smith's *Book of the Twelve Prophets*. Passages from the book of Amos were memorized, and while we did not attempt any exhaustive study of the text itself, at the same time I think it is safe to say that most of our girls have a fairly definite idea of who Amos was, and what he tried to teach. In much the same way we studied Hosea, and are now starting out on Isaiah, which will probably last us the rest of the year.

Miss U——, teacher of a class of young men who graduated under her instruction last year, spoke as follows:

We decided in my class this year to take up "The Life of Jesus," as illustrated by men of modern times. After canvassing various names, we decided to start with the life of Abraham Lincoln. It was hard at first to get the boys to write papers and read them. My class, which I had had five years, had been added to by another class, and as I did not know these boys as well, it made the work more difficult. We also were hampered by not having a room to ourselves. All the boys are working, and many of them have had night-work, and some go to night-school, so they have little time to write. We have prepared a scrap-book on the life of Abraham Lincoln. We divided it into the "Boyhood," "Youth," "Life as a Lawyer," etc. Under each head we have the "events" and "character." We had several papers written by the boys on the different periods of Lincoln's life, and views as to his character. The names of those who write papers are put on the first page of the scrap-book as "authors." The Sundays when we had no papers, we read aloud from a life of Lincoln, and some boy acted as "reporter," writing in the book the gist of what was said. We also discussed the different views of his character, etc. Besides this, the boys brought anything of interest they could find in the way of articles in papers and magazines, and pictures. All of these were pasted in the book in the class. We were fortunate this year, as there was an unusual interest in his life, in the way of articles, etc. February 11th, the Sunday before Lincoln's birthday, we made a special effort.

Miss Y——, having a class of young men of twenty to twenty-five years, reported:

The work that I have been doing in my Bible class of young men this winter has been a simple course in Christian ethics—an attempt to apply the principles of Jesus to the problems of modern daily life. We have had very animated, and, I trust, fruitful discussions on such topics as, "If you had a million dollars to spend on the moral and social betterment of New York, how would you use it?" "What are some of the *ideas* at the root of our civilization?" etc. I have been able to find no very satisfactory text-books on these or kindred subjects, but have in each case used the parables or other teachings of Jesus as the basis of our very informal discussions.

Mrs. S——, who has a class of twenty-five young men, whose ages range from nineteen to twenty-seven years, reported:

About three years ago an experiment, founded on the need of an advanced or post-graduate course, was inaugurated by Bible Class IX. The young men of the class, after spending many years in the study of the Old and New Testaments, decided it would be well to learn something of the lives and characters of men of modern times who were imbued with the spirit which was in Jesus, and in that spirit acknowledged Him as Lord and Master. Accordingly, they took up Livingstone, Robert Morrison, and Henry Drummond, including all the latter's essays. This class was run entirely by the members, the teacher, or leader, acting merely as chairman. Each Sunday one or two of the young men were responsible for the lesson, and the results have far exceeded our expectations. Young men who had never before written a paper or spoken in public, now write interesting essays, and have become self-possessed speakers. One of the chief inspirations for our work was the hope that we might evolve something not only for our own edification, but which might prove of value to the Sunday-school. We now have three courses of study mapped out, and are prepared, with the other Bible classes, to give a reason for the faith that is in us.

The superintendent said:

The next subject is the class organizations in the senior department. Although these have been inaugurated now for three years, there are many teachers who cannot quite understand their purpose. Some even look askance at this, some are ready to condemn, but by far the larger number, especially those whose classes organized themselves three years ago, graduating in 1906, and also the teachers of 1907, the next largest organized, are unanimous in commending them.

Class Organizations were then discussed. The chairman quoted from the St. George's *Herald:*

Every class has its officers, which they elect themselves. The teachers, of course, are in evidence, to the degree of directing and advising when necessary. The benefit that will accrue from this plan of systemized organization can be readily perceived. In the first place, the fundamental principle of the idea is to bring the scholars into personal contact with one another; secondly, to form a bond of friendship between the scholars, which will not only last while attending Sunday-school, but continue thereafter; thirdly and lastly, with such a gathering as in a few years will compose the alumni, what cannot be accomplished? Zest and interest will be continually diffused through the school, and the whole atmosphere will be pervaded with life and activity, which will make St. George's Sunday-school a closely knit band of young people, filled with the spirit of Christian brotherhood.

The boys and girls of the class of 1906, two Sunday afternoons out of every month, make visits to "the Island." Two or three of the teachers go over with the young people to help them with their songs and their talks. These young people not only take old papers and magazines for distribution among the inmates, but they take bright faces, friendly smiles, and kind words to those poor creatures who have long since forgotten the meaning of the words "sympathy" and "love." The class of 1907 endeavor to collect enough money among its teachers and scholars to endow a bed in Dr. Wilson's hospital up in the coal-mine district of Nova Scotia. Each class has also undertaken to keep up the attendance in the class, and to look after those whose attendance is irregular.

These organizations tend to attach the scholars to the school more firmly than any other interest, making of it not a collection of individual groups of teachers and scholars, isolated and having no interests in common, but a united Sunday-school, having common friends, and work, and interests—like a small college, where friendships are formed which last through life, where ideals and ambitions are gained which influence whole careers. Already we have the class graduations and the giving of diplomas; why should we employ the *forms* of college work and not expect the substance?

The superintendent said:

Of course we mean by all this that the class organizations are aids, not ends in themselves. The main aid to the school is that they help very materially the teachers to hold the boys and girls over fifteen in the school. The teacher is the great holding power.

The next subject is the "Teachers' Reference Library," and Miss L—— will tell what her committee is doing to help the busy men and women who fill our ranks of teachers.

Miss L—— reported:

The teachers of the class of 1907, which is studying the course on "St. Paul and the First Christian Missionaries," will remember finding in their class-books each Sunday, the early part of the winter, a printed sheet of references for the lesson of the following Sunday. These references were all to books to be found in the Teachers' Reference Library.

This will show what these reference sheets are like:

RELIGIOUS INSTRUCTION OF THE YOUTH

ST. PAUL AND THE FIRST CHRISTIAN MISSIONARIES

References for Chapter XXI.
(Defence before Sanhedrin)

AUTHOR	TITLE OF BOOK	PAGES
Bosworth,	*Studies in the Acts and Epistles*	208–209
	Cambridge Bible, "Commentary on Acts"	311–316
McGiffert,	*Apostolic Age*	350 (note 4)
Peloubet,	*Teachers' Commentary on Acts*	310–316
Purves,	*Apostolic Age*	232–233
Ramsay,	*St. Paul the Traveller and Roman Citizen*	(no reference)
Renan,	*St. Paul*	308–309
Stalker,	*Life of St. Paul*	(no reference)
Hastings,	*Bible Dictionary.* Articles on:	
	"Sanhedrin." Vol. IV., 400: (4) and 401–402: (VI.).	
	"Pharisees," Vol. III.	825–826
	"Sadducees," Vol. IV.	351 (*b*)

In preparing these references I have tried to keep before my mind this question: What references are going to be of most use to the teachers in preparing their lessons? I have tried to answer it by asking myself what would help me most, and therefore have sometimes given what I may call indirect references. For instance: In the course on "St. Paul," etc., Lesson XVIII. (Farewell to the Ephesians), begins with Acts, xx., 17, while the previous lesson (XVII.), ("Three Years at Ephesus"), ends with Acts, xix., 41. I have included references for Acts, xx., 1–16, in order to connect the two lessons. Also, at the head of this lesson (XVIII.) there is an extract from the Epistle to the Ephesians (vi., 10–24) which is a paraphrase from the Twentieth Century New Testament. I have therefore referred to the article on that Epistle in Hastings' *Bible Dictionary*.

For Lesson XX. ("Defence from Castle Stairs"), I have

given, in Hastings' *Bible Dictionary*, articles on "The Egyptian" (for whom Paul was taken by the Roman officer), and "Roman" (a good article on Roman citizenship).

For Lesson XXVIII. ("Paul a Prisoner at Rome"), I have included references to the end of Paul's life (for example, in Purves's *Apostolic Age*, a chapter on "The Last Years of Paul").

For Lesson XXIX. ("St. Paul's Companions"), I have given any helpful references I could find to Barnabas, Silas, Timothy, and Luke. For instance, in the Cambridge Bible (Acts), and in Peloubet's *Commentary on Acts*, I have given the introductions, which treat of the authorship of Acts, as references for Luke.

In the course on "The Teachings of Jesus," for Lesson XVI. ("Service as a Test of Greatness"), I have given, in Stock's *Lessons on the Life of Our Lord*, besides references to the lesson passages (John, xiii., 1–17, and Mark, x., 35–45), the lesson called "Some Mistakes Corrected," which treats of Mark, ix., 33–37, but bears directly on the teaching in this lesson.

The Rector then summed up the meeting. After prayer the teachers stayed for a half-hour longer. Simple refreshments were served, and the formal conference was informally continued in little groups.

8. Scholars.

Recruits for the school come from the families of the parish, from new families who bring letters of transfer, and from visitation. At times house-to-house visiting is done by the clergy, the deaconesses, the King's Daughters, the Girls' Friendly Society, the Married Women's Society, and the older scholars, inviting all children who do not attend other schools.

RELIGIOUS INSTRUCTION OF THE YOUTH

In order to know whether this invitation is accepted or not, the visitor gives the prospective scholar a card to present when he comes to the school.

To the Superintendent of
St. George's Sunday-school.

The bearer.............................
living at.............................
is..........years of age and wishes to join our Sunday-school.
Permission of parents..................
Date of visit.........................
Name of visitor.......................
Organization ....

The children are easily kept in the school, not only by its own attractions, but by the various parochial organizations. The youngest as well as the oldest scholars are thus laid hold of in many ways. In case of absence, they are looked up. This is done by the teacher; or, in case the teacher cannot do it, by the senior class organization, through its visiting committee. No name is crossed off the school list without the consideration of the staff. Every year, before the winter begins, the secretary makes out a list of persistent absentees, and the deaconesses endeavor by a final effort to bring them back.

The school gives no prizes and no presents, except at Christmas a box of candy and two oranges, and at Easter a plant in a pot. The teachers are not allowed to give personal gifts to their classes. The five grades of the senior department are each organized into the

"Class of 19—," whatever is the year, as in a college. These classes have social meetings, dances, entertainments, and picnics. The school outings are described in connection with the Fresh Air work.

The problem of the children of the well-to-do is confronting many large parishes on account of a notable increase of what may be called sanitary sensitiveness. Parents are afraid that their children may catch some contagious disease. They hesitate for that reason to send them into the perils of a large school. Social considerations enter but little into this reluctance; the difficulty is an honest anxiety concerning health. The fact that the dangers are for the most part imaginary makes little difference. The Sunday-school has not proved in experience to be a menace to physical welfare. But the possibility cannot be denied. Thus appears the problem.

The solution at St. George's is a branch Sunday-school up-town. Two large rooms are used in the building of a private school. A curate, a deaconess, and a kindergartner are in charge. The children meet at half-past three for a short service, in the course of which they are taught psalms and hymns. They are then divided into their classes for a half-hour of study of the lesson. At the end of that time they reassemble for the offering and a closing hymn.

II.—THE CONFIRMATION CLASSES

The work of instructing the Confirmation Classes is divided between the clergy and the deaconesses. The Rector has a class of men and women meeting at half-past three on Sunday afternoons. The deaconesses divide among themselves the girl candidates, and meet them in the Deaconess House on Tuesday evenings. On the same evening, in the Parish House, the clergy in their various studies meet the boys in groups.

The visitation of the Bishop takes place every year on Palm-Sunday, thus making it possible to order the times of instruction in the same way from year to year. At Epiphany the following letter is sent to every teacher in the Sunday-school:

The Confirmation Classes for the year begin on the evening of Wednesday, January 10th, at eight o'clock, in the church. Please make a canvass of your class and urge any members of it who have not been confirmed to attend the classes this year. You can help us especially by doing this, as you know your boys or girls better than we can know them, and your influence over them can mean a great deal just at this time. We shall be glad to help you with any individuals you may call to our attention.

Faithfully yours,

..............,

Epiphany, 19—. *Rector.*

About the same time the list of the unconfirmed is consulted as it is shown in the parish register, and to each such person of proper age the Rector mails a letter:

ST. GEORGE'S RECTORY
209 EAST 16TH ST.

DEAR FRIEND:

Again I want to remind you that the Bishop of this Diocese will administer the rite of confirmation in St. George's Church on Palm-Sunday, ..., at 8 P.M.

As you appear on the parish book as not having been confirmed, I take this opportunity of reminding you of our annual service.

I ask you to give confirmation your serious thought.

ADMINISTRATION OF AN INSTITUTIONAL CHURCH

When you have decided whether you will be confirmed or not, kindly let me know of your decision.
Your Friend and Rector,
....

CONFIRMATION CLASSES

For boys and young men, by the assistant clergy, Tuesdays at 8 p.m., beginning January 7th.
For girls and young women, by the deaconesses, Tuesdays at 8 p.m., beginning January 7th.
The Rector's class for men and women, Sunday afternoons at 3.30 o'clock, beginning February 9th.

In selecting candidates for confirmation, a certain amount of solicitation is used by the clergy and deaconesses to bring special, designated individuals into the classes, but the responsibility is made to rest for the most part upon the teachers.

The course of instruction for the younger members of the class extends over a period of twelve weeks. A lecture is given on baptism, another on confirmation, and another on the creed, but most of the time is spent in teaching the meaning of the commandments, one by one, and of the Communion Service, with reference to its spiritual use by the communicant. During the course of instruction a careful written examination in the catechism is required to be passed by every candidate.

Before the day of confirmation the clergyman or deaconess in charge of each division of the class has a personal conference with each candidate. An endeavor is made at this time to impress the children with a strong sense of friendliness and confidence, so that in any after trouble or difficulty they will turn naturally to their confirmation teacher.

The Rector's class has its meetings in a large room of the Parish House. The course of instruction is more brief than that appointed for the children. It deals with large questions of faith and duty. Many attend these lectures who have already been confirmed, and some who have no present intention to be confirmed. A letter such as follows is sent to summon persons to this class.

**ST. GEORGE'S RECTORY
209 EAST 16TH ST.**

The Rector's Confirmation Class will meet on Sunday afternoon, March 5th, at half-past three o'clock.

I shall be glad to have those who have not been confirmed and are interested in the subject attend this class, whether they purpose being confirmed this year or not. Please try to come promptly and regularly.

Faithfully yours,

March 1, 19—.   *Rector.*

On the Sunday before the confirmation, each approved candidate receives a card which admits him to the reserved portion of the church, and another card admitting his parents.

St. George's Church

Confirmation, 19—

PALM-SUNDAY, AT 8 P.M.

Name........................ Age....

Address....................................

W. S. RAINSFORD

Candidates to be in church at 7.45 P.M.

```
┌─────────────────────────────────────┐
│              19—                    │
│                                     │
│      CONFIRMATION SERVICE           │
│      ─────────────                  │
│                                     │
│         PARENTS' TICKET             │
│                                     │
│            Admit Two                │
│      ─────────────                  │
│                                     │
│   ENTRANCE AT THE REAR DOOR OF THE  │
│        CHURCH UNTIL 7.10 P.M.       │
│                                     │
└─────────────────────────────────────┘
```

Each candidate receives a prayer-book from the Rector before the service, and after the service a certificate of confirmation.

St. George's Parish
NEW YORK

Ye are the Temple of God, and the Spirit of God dwelleth in you.
  1 Cor., iii., 16.

Grieve not the Holy Spirit of God whereby ye are sealed to the day of Redemption.
  Eph. iv., 30.

.... *received the Apostolic rite of laying on of hands at a Confirmation holden in St. George's Church, by the Right Reverend Father in God, Dr......................... by divine permission Bishop of New York, on...................*
....

He that hath begun a good work in you will perform it until the day of Jesus Christ.—Phil., i., 6.

RELIGIOUS INSTRUCTION OF THE YOUTH

Communicants' classes.

The new communicants are gathered together on each Wednesday evening before the first Sunday of the month —the girls in the church, the boys in the Parish House— for a short service and instruction. The attendance at these communicants' classes is maintained by postal-cards which are sent each month as a reminder. These cards are brought with them when they come and serve as an account of their regularity.

Once a year a card showing a picture of the church is mailed to all the young communicants to remind them of the eight-o'clock communion on the morning of the first Sunday of each month. This service is intended especially for these young people, with their teachers, associates, supervisors, and leaders. "This is to remind you," says the back of the card, "of the communion service held the first Sunday of each month at 8 A.M., at which we hope to meet you. Please put the card where you will see it."

In this space is printed the picture and title of the church	Xmas Communion at 7 A.M., and Easter Communion at the same hour. January 7th February 4th March 4th April 1st May 6th June 3d July 1st August 5th September 2d October 7th November 4th December 2d [OVER]

For all teachers and scholars who have not time to go home between this service and the opening of the Sunday-school at half-past nine, a breakfast of rolls and coffee is served in the Parish House.

III.—THE LIBRARY

For the further edification of the youth, there are two libraries, one for general use, the other for the aid of the teachers. The library is in charge of a paid librarian, and is assisted by a member of the Deaconess House staff, and members of the parish to aid the children in selecting books. The applicant for permission to take books from the general library fills out a form of request. Upon acceptance of his application he is assigned a number. This he signs upon his card, with his name and address, whenever he returns or takes out a book.

**ST. GEORGE'S
FREE CIRCULATING LIBRARY**

Name...................... No........

Address.................................

Name of society of which you are member

....

Name of referee..........................

Fill out this and send in to St. George's Library, 207 East 16th Street

```
┌─────────────────────────────────────────┐
│  ⎧ NUMBER ⎫                             │
│  ⎨        ⎬ Returns ................   │
│  ⎩        ⎭                             │
│  ....................................   │
│          Wants one of the following:    │
│                                         │
│  ....................................   │
│  ....................................   │
│  ....................................   │
│  ....................................   │
│  ....................................   │
│  Name............  Address........      │
└─────────────────────────────────────────┘
```

The library is open every Monday, Wednesday, and Friday evening from 7.30 to 9.30; and on Sundays from 4.30 to 5.30. The usual card catalogues are provided.

Persons desiring to take out books from the teachers' library fill out such a card as follows:

```
┌─────────────────────────────────────────┐
│          St. George's Sunday-school     │
│         TEACHERS' REFERENCE LIBRARY     │
│                                         │
│  Author ............................    │
│                                         │
│  Title .............................    │
│  Please fill out this card if book is taken from the library │
│                                         │
│       Teacher's name ..............     │
└─────────────────────────────────────────┘
```

VI

WORK WITH BOYS

I. The Trade-school—II. The Battalion Club.

I.—THE TRADE-SCHOOL

THE trade-school is a growth from the Boys' Club. The boys were gathered together to get them off the street. At first, the sole effort was to amuse them. They were a rough lot, and the club was unpopular in the neighborhood. Quiet people did not like it. Gradually, with much patience, some order was introduced into the confusion. The boys became dimly aware that the young men who were in charge of the club had no motive but that of simple interest and friendship.

At first, in the initial process of organization, the note of betterment was pitched ideally high. There were five rules: to be loving and lovable; to be pure in heart, mind, and body; to pity and help the poor and weak; to be kind to dumb creatures; to hate sham, meanness, and dishonesty. These were admirable—for the saints. All the boys promised, readily enough, to keep them; in token whereof each boy received a knot of golden cord. If he broke one of the rules, he was to take off this badge and put it away till he had asked God to forgive him. At the meetings there was a service taken from the Sermon on the Mount, an address on one of the rules of the society, and several lantern views "illustrating some-

ST. GEORGE'S EVENING TRADE-SCHOOL
505 East 16th Street

thing from Holy Scripture." The lantern was the only feature which differentiated these assemblies from the chapter-meetings of a monastery. A merciful human touch was added, however, in a one-cent weekly assessment, the sum of which was to be expended in July for clam chowder.

The next start was made in the Sunday-school. Boys were invited to meet one of the clergy and some other gentlemen on a week-day evening to consider the starting of a boys' club. A good number accepted the invitation. The first speaker was a young man, a member of the church, an athlete who had won notable medals. He spoke of in-door and out-door sports, with no immediate reference to the beatitudes. That pleased the boys. Names of members of a club were enrolled then and there. A room was assigned to the club, and the boys were told that it would be open three evenings in each week. Each boy received a medal with the inscription "St. George's Boys' Club," and a number such as stood beside his name on the list. There was no provision for dues, and no record was kept of attendance. A number of gentlemen were found to undertake in turn the maintenance of order and the arrangements for entertainment. Games of bagatelle and crokinole were provided. Air-gun practice and donkey-parties were held, with prizes consisting of five-cent packages of chocolate.

This experiment worked better than the society of the golden cord, the Little Brothers of the Bowery. Gradually the men in charge learned what the boys needed. A house was taken. The first floor was open to all comers, and they who came had free access to games and books. The second floor was reserved for boys who had earned special tickets of admission. On this floor classes were held and some teaching was done. Presently, of their own accord, the up-stairs boys organized a debating society. But the classes were the great attraction, especially the class in printing.

Thus, by natural development and survival of the fittest, came the trade-school. At first the trade-classes were a small and tentative part of a club, formed mainly for recreation; gradually the mere recreation became the minor feature. There were still various entertainments for the boys; on Saturday mornings they were admitted to the gymnasium and shower-baths, under the supervision of one of the clergy and the director of the gymnasium; in the spring of the year there were walking-parties in the country. But the trade-school had taken the place of the Boys' Club.

The trade-school, like everything else at St. George's, began in a small way, proved its practical efficiency, and on that basis was given better facilities. Every considerable community has men of means in it who are willing to do much for any useful institution which has first demonstrated its usefulness. At first there was a carpenter's shop, a drawing class, a school of telegraphy with ten instruments, and a printing-office. The printing-office was too poor to have a press, and the business of setting type without printing anything was pretty dull. But a beginning was made, and presently there came into being the equipped building which we have described.

The trade-school has a board of directors, a superintendent, a corps of supervisors, and a faculty of trained and salaried mechanics. The directors are one clergyman and eight laymen, who manage the affairs of the school. All the details are in their hands. The work is therefore, to a great extent, independent of the superintendent. It is not carried on by any one man. There are some thirty supervisors to about three hundred boys.

WORK WITH BOYS

Their duty is to keep in close acquaintance with the lads, to visit them when they are absent from the school, to know their parents, to confer with the boys in regard to employment when they have learned their trade. They also arrange entertainments for them, give excursions at all times of the year, take charge of the trade-school camp in the summer, and in every way act as their friends. It is the supervisor who makes possible the development of those two sides of the boy, which is the object aimed at—love for trade, and a healthy body with a clear head. It is not so much the actual work done by the supervisor as his influence and example which guides the boy.

The following is the curriculum of the school:

WOOD-WORKING DEPARTMENT
CARPENTRY AND JOINERY   CABINET-MAKING
PATTERN-MAKING AND WOOD-TURNING

MECHANICAL-DRAWING DEPARTMENT
GEOMETRICAL DRAWING   ARCHITECTURAL DRAWING
WORKING DRAWINGS AND MACHINE DESIGN

PRINTING DEPARTMENT
TYPE-SETTING   PRESS-WORK   JOB-WORK

PLUMBING DEPARTMENT
PLUMBING   STEAM-FITTING   GAS-FITTING

MANUAL-TRAINING DEPARTMENT
DRAWING   CARD-BOARD DEVELOPMENTS   FRET-SAW WORK

FREE-HAND DRAWING DEPARTMENT
DRAWING FROM CAST   PERSPECTIVE
WOOD-BURNING AND DECORATING

For example: Albert Bruder is a lad of ten. He has just joined St. George's Sunday-school. In September his older brother Adolph, who is a member of the Sunday-school, received an English and German notice from the superintendent stating the objects of the trade-school and the trades taught, and directing all former members of the school to report on a specified evening for assignment to classes. New boys were to present themselves on the evening following. This notice was also given out in Sunday-school. On the designated evening Albert appears. He fills out a blank application. (See page 171.) This he presents to the superintendent, who assigns him to the third class in manual training. He is told to report on the following Wednesday, and to bring with him his month's dues of two cents. In the interval his application is verified by the secretary of the Sunday-school.

Albert's class meets once a week, and he is taught very simple mechanical drawing and card-board work, consisting of plane figures. One day he is absent, and his supervisor calls and finds that he is ill. In April his work is so good that he is promoted to the second class. Now he comes twice a week, and pays five cents a month. When he graduates from the manual-training department he knows his rule to the sixteenth of an inch, can handle correctly his toy square and triangle, is familiar with simple geometrical figures, and has a true appreciation of a plane figure and some perception of a solid. He has also acquired some skill with the scroll-saw, and can fit together the parts of simple furniture in models. He is thus prepared to enter intelligently upon the work of another department.

Albert's name is entered, on his entrance into the school, upon a blue card, on which his progress is noted.

> ### ST. GEORGE'S EVENING TRADE-SCHOOL
> 505 EAST 16TH STREET
> NEW YORK CITY
>
> #### APPLICATION
>
> No...*359*..   Date..*Sept. 27, 1905*......   Age..*10*...
> Name..*Bruder, Albert*.......................
> Address..*520 East 16th Street*....................
> Parent's name..*George*.........................
> P. S...*No. 40—Class 4A*.......................
> S. S. or Church..*St. George's Junior III., Class 1*......
> Former Class in Trade-school..*None*................
> Wishes to join..*Manual Training*..................
>
> ---
>
> #### REPORT
>
> *Sept. 28, 1905.—O. K.*
>   *Attendance fair.*
>
>   *Secretary of the Sunday-school.*
>
> ---
>
> #### DISPOSITION
>
> Date..*Sept. 29, 1905*....
> Dept..*Manual Training*....   Class..*III*............
> Remarks......................................

His attendance record is kept on white cards, which are renewed as he passes from one class to another. (See page 172.)

ADMINISTRATION OF AN INSTITUTIONAL CHURCH

```
No. 359.
Name, Bruder, Albert.                    Parent's name, George.
Address, 520 East 16 St.
Enrolled, Sept. 29, '05.        Left, April 3, 1909.
Age, 10   S. S., Jr. III., Class I.   * P. S., No. 40—4A.  Work,—
Class, Sept. 29, '05.  M. T. III. | Oct. 6, '07.  Carpt. II.
       April 2, '06.   M. T. II.  | Oct. 7, '08.  Carpt. I.
       May 1, '06.     M. T. I.
       Jan. 10, '07.   Carpt. III.
Remarks
```

* P. S. stands for Public School, and the dash after Work means the scholar does not work for livelihood.

CLASS CARD

Date, *April 2, '06.*   Dept., *M. T.*   Class, *II.*
Name, *Bruder, Albert.*   No., *359*

ATTENDANCE

OCT.	NOV.	DEC.	JAN.	FEB.	MAR.	APRIL

Remarks

WORK WITH BOYS

Every evening each instructor hands in a report of attendance like the following:

St. George's Evening Trade-school
505 East 16th Street
New York City

Date.. *November 5,.. 1905.*

REPORT OF

III........Class in.. *Manual Training*..............

No. on Roll.. *24*............

No. Absent.. *3*.............

NAMES OF ABSENTEES

..*Bruder, Albert*........   ....

..*Schmidt, Harry*.......   ....

..*Koener, John*.........   ....

....

....

REMARKS

Signed........................
                    Instructor.

These reports are entered in the record-book. The following table shows the schedule of classes:

SCHEDULE OF CLASSES, YEAR 1905-1906 (7.30 TO 9.00 P.M.)				
MONDAY	TUESDAY	WEDNESD'Y	THURSDAY	FRIDAY
Carpentry II. (16 boys)	Carpentry I. (16 boys)	Carpentry III. (16 boys)	Carpentry II.	Carpentry I.
Mechanical Drawing II. (16 boys)	Mechanical Drawing I. (16 boys)	Drawing for Carpentry I. and II.	Mechanical Drawing II.	Mechanical Drawing I.
Plumbing I. (16 boys)	Plumbing II. (16 boys)	Plumbing I.	Plumbing II.	Plumbing I.
Printing I. (14 boys)	Printing II. (14 boys)	Printing I.	Printing II.	Printing I.
Manual Training II. (24 boys)	Manual Training I. (24 boys)	Manual Train. III. (24 boys)	Manual Training II.	Manual Training I.
Metal Work (12 boys)	Design Class (12 boys)	Metal Work	Design Class	Drawing for Carpentry III.

II.—THE BATTALION CLUB

The Boys' Club, before it was merged into the trade-school, provided only for boys under fifteen years of age. Only boys over eighteen could join the Men's Club. This left those between fifteen and eighteen years of age, the most critical period in a boy's life, uncared for. For this reason the Battalion Club was started.

Any boy between the ages of fourteen and eighteen, connected with St. George's Sunday-school, is eligible for membership.

Applications for enrolment in the Battalion Club are made on such a form as is here shown:

> New York,............190
>
> ### St. George's Battalion Club
>
> APPLICATION FOR MEMBERSHIP
>
> TO BE FILLED UP BY THE APPLICANT
>
> *Name*...
> *Address*...
> *Age (must be between 14 and 18)*....................
> *Member of St. George's S. S.*.......................
> *Is name on book of St. George's Church?*............
> *Proposed by*......................................
> *Seconded by*......................................
> *Signature of one of Committee*.....................
>
> *This application must be accompanied by a half-year's dues ($1.00 for boys over 16, $0.50 for boys under that age), which will be refunded if applicant is not accepted.*

When a boy becomes enrolled in the battalion, he is assigned a rifle, belt, and uniform, all these three plainly marked with his company number, and he must keep them cleaned, brushed, and polished. He is encouraged in every way to take a personal pride in the condition of his equipment, and every facility is given him to do this, in a room which is assigned to the battalion as gun-room.

Each boy has his own locker for his equipment, and the things necessary for keeping it in order.

Of this equipment a record is kept in the name of each boy. (See page 176.)

St. George's Cadet Battalion ....Company

Record of..............................

Address...............................

Date of birth..................Date of enlistment..................

EQUIPMENT CHARGES						PINES			REMARKS
LOCKER	COAT	TROU-SERS	HAT	CROSS GUNS	EXTRA	DATE	CHARGES OR COMPLAINT	PAID	
Date Dr. When given out									
Date Cr. When returned									

NOTE I.—Under Equipment charges the following marks must be used:
* New.
G Good condition.
P Poor.
M Property of member.

NOTE II. This record must be kept up to date by first sergeant of each company, and the uniform and discipline committees must report to him at once on all matters relating thereto.

When the cadet has received his equipment he gives receipt in the following form:

St. George's Cadet Battalion

HEADQUARTERS 207 EAST 16TH STREET

UNIFORM MEMORANDUM

New York,.............*190*

Name..

Address..

Received—Pants   *Coat*

Signed...

There are two departments of the Battalion Club, the military and the athletic. These departments are not exclusive of each other. Each boy in the military department may also belong to the athletic department, and *vice versa*. The two departments are inevitably closely associated, as they have for their common meeting-place the battalion club-rooms.

The battalion club-rooms and club life, as such, are under the direction of the house committee. On this committee there are officers elected by the boys themselves, who represent both the military and athletic departments. The controlling influence and directive touch come, however, from the clergyman and instructors who have special charge of these two departments, and who are also members of this committee. (Compare constitution for the organization of Battalion Club, section on the house committee.)

The social life in the club is similar to that of all boys' clubs. The rooms are closed on Thursday night, which is reserved especially for the athletic department, and on Saturday night, which is set apart for the weekly drill of the battalion.

The athletic department is under the control and direction of the gymnasium instructor, who has charge of the athletic work of the St. George's organizations. He is assisted by the athletic captain, who is appointed from the athletic department of the Battalion Club by the Rector. This department is the only athletic organization of St. George's for boys of the age likely to compete in games and athletic events with other organizations. All such matters necessarily come under its direction.

The real problem, and one of the most difficult to solve, is the establishment on a firm basis of a successful military organization in connection with the club. It was only by learning from many failures that a system of organization for the battalion has been evolved that promises to be reliable as a working basis. First, to insure any length of life to the battalion, there must be an element of permanency in its system and management. This is gained by the board of directors, men who are interested either in boys or in military matters, who will act as advisers on all matters relating to the battalion. Thus the battalion depends for its success not on one man, but on a number of men, all interested in different ways and in different departments of the work, and the work takes care of itself.

The board of directors of St. George's Battalion at present comprises five members. Three of them have at some time served in the Seventh or Twelfth regiments of New York. They are men interested in church work, interested in boys, interested in military life. The military instructor is appointed by the Rector. He must be a man interested in boys and thoroughly conversant with military affairs. He should preferably be a man directly connected with some recognized military organization.

The battalion is divided into two companies—a senior and a junior, depending upon the size and age of the boys. There is also a drum, fife, and bugle corps in charge of a paid instructor.

The system used is that of the Seventh Regiment. This is introduced as far as it is practicable, even to details. The armories for the equipment of the battalion are in the Memorial Building, but the use of the Sixty-Ninth Regiment Armory hall is courteously extended to the battalion for drill purposes.

A unique feature of the work is a rifle-range in the Parish House basement, where the boys shoot regularly and with much enthusiasm, qualifying as marksmen, sharp-shooters, and experts, and paying enough to make the range self-supporting. The range is fifty feet long, and rifles of twenty-two caliber are used. The younger boys pay one cent for five shots and the others pay two cents. All the shooting is controlled by a rifle committee having representatives from the senior and junior companies, and drum, fife, and bugle corps. Each member of the battalion has one hour each week at the range. The targets are the same proportional size as are used by the National Guard.

To become a marksman, a boy must make a score of over thirty-five out of a possible fifty points three different times. Afterwards a score of forty-two must be made three more times to get a silver sharp-shooter's medal, and the expert score is forty-six or better. Thus it takes at least nine weeks to qualify as an expert.

This range-shooting is of great benefit to the members of the battalion. It teaches them self-control and patience, it accustoms them to the careful and proper use of a loaded weapon, and it produces a well-trained eye and a steady nerve, besides furnishing a healthful and exciting sport.

The rifle-range is fifty feet long, and is in the basement of the parish building. (See page 181.)

A marks the rifle-target, on two stands; it is about three and a half feet wide and seven and a half feet long. The front is made of boards, then comes a layer of endwood, and behind that a sheet of iron.

From the buttresses (B and C) to the rifle-target (A) runs a trolley system, as marked from a to b and from c to d. At point a is a large wooden pulley, and at point b a small iron pulley; both pulleys are connected by a belt-rope. Between the points c and d is fastened a stationary wire-rope. The wooden stick e is fastened to the rope on its left side, and on the right side of the stick is a loop through which the stationary wire passes. From the stick e hang the target-cards, suspended by wires (f, f, and g), the lower target-card for expert shooting. The wooden pulley (a) has a crank by which the target-cards can be drawn flat against the rifle-target (A), and, after the firing, pulled up again towards the buttresses for examination. The letter h marks the board from which the firing is done. Three men can shoot here at one time, one man to the right, another to the left, and the third in the middle, from mark e, on his stomach, for expert shooting. The guns are fastened by chains to the board, so that it is impossible to bring them to such a position as would render careless shooting dangerous. The letters i, i, i mark the lights for the upper target-cards, and are covered with a reflector,

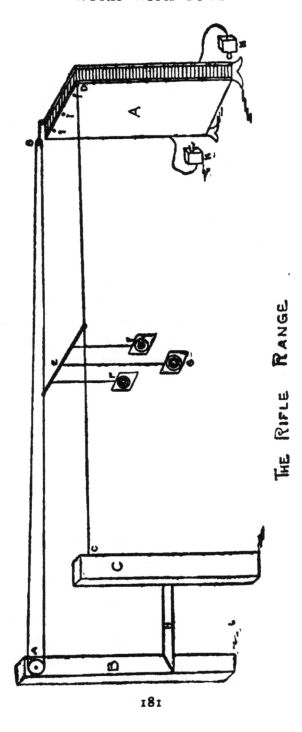

and the letters *k, k* mark the lights for the lower target-card.

In a space near at hand is a locker where the rifles, cartridges, target-cards, oil, and cleaning-rods are kept.

The cost of putting up such a range amounts to about twenty dollars. The rifles are an extra expense. A small charge is made to pay for the shooting expenses.

The success of the Battalion Club depends upon the amount of actual work done by the boys in connection with the military and athletic departments. Every member of the club must report regularly for military or athletic work. Continued unexcused absence is punished by expulsion. Every absence must be accounted for by the cadet personally appearing before the discipline committee; and absence unaccounted for either by business or sickness entails a ten-cent fine or an hour's work.

Every year the battalion goes into camp for two weeks. Notice of this event is conveyed to the members by a circular letter.

ST. GEORGE'S CADET BATTALION
HEADQUARTERS, 207 EAST 16TH STREET
NEW YORK CITY

To the Members of the Battalion, their Parents, and Employers:

The battalion will go to camp on Saturday, July —, 19—, at Eaton's Neck, Northport Harbor, Long Island, and return Monday, July —, 19—. Members will report at headquarters, Saturday, July —, at 11 o'clock.

The boys will live in tents, and a regular cook will accompany the battalion. The food will be plain and wholesome. One of the clergy (Mr. ———) and Mr. ——— will have personal supervision of the camp, also a doctor will be in attendance. Any member who disobeys regulations will be sent home.

Our aim is to give the boys plenty of exercise, plenty to eat, and plenty of sleep, and to bring them back feeling better for their week's camp.

We need the presence of every member of the battalion at camp, and we hope that the parents and employers of our boys will allow them all to have the benefit of a week or two of out-door life.

The battalion will go to camp in uniform, campaign hats and leggings, black shoes, and each boy will provide himself with a warm gray blanket, which will be carried, rolled, over his shoulder; if it is impossible to get a gray blanket, gray cloth covers will be furnished at ten cents each.

Each boy will get a canvas bag on Tuesday evening, July —, at the Memorial Building. Each bag should contain the following: old coat, pants, extra stockings or socks, two towels, handkerchiefs, white gloves, soap, comb, and tooth-brush. The senior company and the larger boys of the junior company, and drum, fife, and bugle corps must bring suits for bathing; the smaller boys can bring tights. All bags must be brought, all filled, to the Memorial Building on Wednesday night, July —, at which time they will be packed in barrels and sent away. Only guns and blankets can be carried to camp. Campaign hats can be obtained of ...., at one dollar, by members of this battalion, or second-hand ones can be bought at ...., Broadway, and other places.

Members of the senior company, and drum, fife, and bugle corps, will pay $3.75, and the junior company $2.75, for the camp. Each boy must pay for camp on Tuesday evening, July —, when he receives his bag. Address mail to Northport, Long Island, care of St. George's Battalion.

The camp is situated about three and one-half miles from

Northport by land and about three miles by water. Friends are cordially invited to visit the cadets at the camp. Members of the battalion staying only over Sunday, July — or —, can leave Sunday night by train. The charge for staying over Sunday, including boat excursion ticket (obtained from Mr. ———), will be $1.25.

Yours truly,
(Signed) ————————
Clergyman in charge.

Address all communications to
————————
207 East 16th Street,
New York City.

Shortly before going to camp, the following letter is sent to each member of the battalion:

ST. GEORGE'S CADET BATTALION
HEADQUARTERS, 207 EAST 16TH STREET
NEW YORK CITY

(General Orders No. 4.)

July —, 19—.

The battalion will leave for camp at Northport, Long Island, on Saturday, July —, 19—. Drill call at 12.15 P.M. Assembly at 12.20 P.M. Uniform — campaign hats and leggings. Don't fail to bring white gloves and wear a good strong pair of black shoes.

The camp is situated on Eaton's Neck, about three and one-half miles from Northport railroad station, and about the same distance from Northport village. Railroad excursion ticket, $2. Visitors coming to camp on Sundays can leave East 34th Street at 8.50 A.M.; take the electric car to Northport village, and, unless weather is stormy, *a yacht or launch will meet them there to take them to the camp. Return same way about four o'clock. On weekdays the yacht will meet the electric car which connects with the 9 A.M. train from East 34th Street. Other ways to get to the camp: (1) Take electric car to Monument, and walk two and one-half miles. (2) Hire a rig in Northport. Members of the battalion staying over Sundays only will be charged $1.25.*

The battalion will leave for camp at foot of East 24th Street, Recreation Pier, at 1 P.M. sharp. The battalion will arrive in New York (24th Street Recreation Pier) on Monday, July —, at about 3.30 P.M.

Address all letters care of St. George's Cadet Battalion, Northport, L. I.

By order of
H—— S——,
Commanding Officer.
E—— R——,
Adjutant.

The battalion goes into camp on the first or second Saturday in July. About ten days before, a committee, composed of three or more officers, overhaul the camp stuff and pass in a requisition for necessary new and additional material to the military instructor.

Two months or more before camping-time, arrangements are made to secure a proper site, and to provide for the transportation of the cadets and their supplies. This is attended to by the military instructor and a committee of the cadets. The camp is located as far away from civilization as possible, where the noise and play of the boys will disturb nobody, and where the camping-party will have to depend on its own resources for its amusement and pleasures.

Any boy in the battalion who is in good standing, and who has paid his dues to the Battalion Club, is eligible for camp. The senior company men pay $3.75, and the junior company $2.75. This money is paid on a definite evening to the military instructor a few days before the cadets leave for camp. Upon the receipt of the same each boy is given a canvas bag, two feet by one and a half, in which to put what things are necessary for the time which he is in camp—an extra suit of under-clothing, night-clothes, socks, one pair of trousers, toilet articles, and bathing-suit.

These bags are returned on a stated night, and packed and shipped with the rest of the camp stuff, under the direction of one of the older cadets, who assumes the duties of quartermaster.

The day before the battalion leaves for camp, a pioneer squad, composed of the military instructor, the cook, and four or five of the stronger fellows, arrive on the camp scene with all baggage and supplies and put everything to rights. The tents are put up in military form, straw is procured for the sleeping-bags, and all necessary arrangements for a sanitary and healthful camp are properly looked after.

By special arrangement with a steamboat company, cadets are carried to and from camp for one dollar each, round trip, making no charge for baggage. The battalion meets at headquarters on the day set for going to camp, and marches in regular military formation to the boat.

On arrival in camp they stand at attention in company-front formation, and are told briefly by the military instructor about the programme and régime of the camp for the coming week. They are then assigned their respective tents. The companies are assigned tents as follows:

Imagine a long street. In the middle of this street, at one end, is the tent for the military instructor and staff, here they can easily overlook the entire street. On one side are the tents of the Senior company and its commissioned officer; on the other side the tents of the Juniors, and officers. The tent of the commissary department is placed at some distance from this street. There is also a guard tent. In each tent there are seven or eight men and a cadet-officer in charge of them, a sergeant or corporal. As soon as the boys are sent to their tents they stack their guns by the rear pole, and select their places, filling their sleeping-bags with straw. They are then ready for the camp programme.

CAMP PROGRAMME

	A.M.
Reveille	6
Call to fall in	6.05
Roll-call	6.10
Mess	7
Inspection	8
Sick call	9
Company drills	9 to 10
Swimming	11 to 12
Mess	12

	P.M.
Swimming	4 to 5
Dress-parade	5.15
Mess	6
Call to turn in	10.15
Taps	10.30

Every boy must take part of the life and work of the camp. There are different details to which boys are assigned—*i. e.*, a detail to get water, wood, supplies from the village, etc. If a boy fails to comply willingly with the understood regulations of camp, he is placed on police-duty or extra guard-duty, and if the case is a serious one he may be asked to go home. If he is placed on police-duty, he must help pick up all scraps of paper or refuse in and about camp, scrub down the table where the staff and commissioned officers eat, assist the cook, etc. If he is placed on guard-duty, he patrols his beat, two hours on and two hours off, from 8 P.M. to 4 A.M.

The duty of a man on guard is to challenge all strangers who approach the camp after dark, to see that order is preserved in the tents and absolute quiet maintained after taps, to watch the boats on the shore, to guard against a raid on the commissary department, and to take the names and report all those of the cadets who come in late to the camp.

The menu of the camp is simple but wholesome and hearty. Plenty of stewed fruit and vegetables, with fresh meat once every day, forms the background of it. The milk and meat come from the city every day, and the launch brings over ice every morning from the village, which keeps them fresh. For an ice-chest, a military-chest is sunk into the sand under some bushes near by the cook's tent.

In the morning and afternoon, as well as in the evening, there is time not arranged for in the schedule given. To get the most out of the week, one day is set apart for athletic games, swimming and boating races; and one afternoon is given over to a competitive baseball game. The row-boats are secured from a near-by picnic-ground at two dollars per week, and the launch for transporting supplies from the village was run by the boys at a cost of twelve dollars. The competitive events come towards the end of camp-time, and the idle moments are taken up in getting ready for them. They do not interfere with the daily schedule. On Sundays, either a simple praise service is held in the open air and a brief talk given to the boys by the clergyman who is interested in the organization, or they march to some neighboring village and attend church in a body.

The discipline of the camp is in the hands of the military instructor and the commissioned and non-commissioned officers, who form a council and pass judgment on all offenders.

A camp for fifty costs about $425 for ten days. Of this amount, $150 is furnished by the boys. The other $275 is raised by subscription from those interested in the boys' outing, or else taken out of the annual appropriation for the battalion provided by the church.

The general itemized account is as follows:

RUNNING EXPENSES

Transportation	$50
Wages for cook	33
Groceries and meat	125
Milk, butter, and eggs	33
Straw, bread, ice, fresh vegetables, etc.	25
Launch and boat hire	35
Expressage	5
Cartage and transfer	20
Sundries	40
	$366
To this should be added an annual allowance for repairs on tents	30
And for refurnishing and new equipment	30
Total cost	**$426**

The constitution of the battalion follows:

CONSTITUTION

ARTICLE I
NAME AND OBJECTS

SEC. 1. This organization shall be known as the St. George's Battalion Club, and shall have two departments: (1) Military, and (2) Athletic.

SEC. 2. The objects of the club shall be as follows:
(1) To support St. George's Church in all its work.
(2) To promote true manliness among its members.
(3) To cherish good-fellowship and friendship.

ARTICLE II
MEMBERSHIP

SEC. 1. All boys between the ages of fourteen and eighteen, inclusive, who are connected with St. George's Sunday-school, shall be eligible to membership. Any member ceasing to be connected with the church may be dropped by the house committee.

ARTICLE III
MEETINGS

SEC. 1. The club shall hold meetings the third Wednesday of each month in the club-room, at 8 P.M. If the meeting comes on a legal holiday, then it shall be held on the following Monday.

A special meeting may be called by the president, or must be called on the written request of ten members.

ARTICLE IV
OFFICERS

SEC. 1. The civil officers of the club shall consist of a president, a vice-president, a secretary, and a treasurer.

SEC. 2. The president, vice-president, and secretary shall be elected by the club, semi-annually, at the February and October meetings. The treasurer shall be appointed by the Rector.

The club shall elect officers at the meeting when this amended constitution shall be voted upon, to serve until the February meeting.

ARTICLE V

HOUSE COMMITTEE

Sec. 1. The house committee shall consist of a clergyman of St. George's Church, who shall be the chairman; a counsellor, the military instructor, the athletic instructor, the chairman of the athletic department—all to be appointed by the Rector; the president, the vice-president, the secretary, the treasurer, the athletic captain, the commanding officers of the two military companies, the sergeant-at-arms, and the first sergeant of the drum, fife, and bugle corps.

ARTICLE VI

DUTIES OF HOUSE COMMITTEE

Sec. 1. The duties of the house committee shall be as follows:

(1) To act on all business that concerns the club.

(2) To inspect the books and reports of the secretary and treasurer at any time.

(3) To fill any vacancy among the elected officers of the club by a vote of the majority of those present, the person so appointed to hold office until the next regular election.

(4) To have jurisdiction of all questions of discipline, and to have the power to fine, suspend, drop, or expel any member or members for conduct prejudicial to the club, or non-payment of dues, after an opportunity to be heard is given the said member or members. Also to delegate the power of suspension for a period of not more than one week to such person or committee as they may see fit.

(5) To engage and discharge a superintendent to take charge of the club-rooms.

(6) To make purchases and contracts for the club.

ARTICLE VII

MEMBERSHIP COMMITTEE

Sec. 1. The president shall appoint two members of the club at each semi-annual election, who, together with the chairman of the house committee, shall compose the membership committee.

Sec. 2. This committee shall investigate all applicants for membership, and enter the names of those it elects in the club roll. It shall also have the power to receive and accept resignations (which should be written), provided the member resigning shall be in good standing.

ARTICLE VIII

Sec. 1. A quorum of the club shall consist of twelve members.

Sec. 2. A quorum of the house committee shall consist of five members.

ARTICLE IX

AMENDMENTS

Sec. 1. This constitution may be amended by a vote of the members of the club present at any meeting, provided the proposed amendments shall be approved by the house committee, and be posted in the club-rooms at least one week before the meeting at which the amendments are to be considered.

BY-LAWS

ARTICLE I

DUES

The dues shall be as follows:

(1) For members under sixteen years of age, one dollar per year.

(2) For members sixteen years old and over, two dollars per year.

All dues are to be paid to the superintendent semi-annually, in advance, on or before the first days of October and April. If not then paid, the house committee will suspend members until their dues are paid, or it may drop any member in arrears of dues for one month.

ARTICLE II

The treasurer shall render a report at each meeting of the club, and whenever called on to do so by the house committee. He shall also make a yearly report from April to April to the house committee. This report must be audited by two members of St. George's parish, appointed by the chairman of the house committee. The treasurer's books shall be kept in three divisions: Military, Athletic, and Social, the third being used exclusively for the expenses of the club. Each division shall have an equal share of the dues.

ARTICLE III

APPLICATION FOR MEMBERSHIP

All proposals for membership must be signed by two members and a member of the membership committee, and be accompanied by six months' dues. Such applications must be handed to the superintendent of the club-room and posted on the bulletin-board for one week before action can be taken.

ARTICLE IV

Special meetings of the house committee may be called by its chairman, or must be called at the written request of three of its members.

ARTICLE V

The secretary shall keep a record of the proceedings of the Battalion Club and the house committee, and shall read a report of the business transacted by the house committee at each meeting of the club. Also the minutes of each club meeting shall be read at the following meeting of the house committee.

ARTICLE VI

The military instructor shall have charge of the military department. Saturday night shall be reserved for the military department.

ARTICLE VII

The chairman of the athletic department and the athletic instructor shall have charge of the athletic department. Thursday night shall be reserved for the athletic department.

ARTICLE VIII

The heads of the various departments shall plan the work and arrange the organization of their several departments, subject to the approval of the house committee.

ARTICLE IX

All entertainments of this club, of whatever department, must be first authorized by the house committee.

ARTICLE X

Order of business at meetings of the club:
1. Call to order.
2. Call of roll.
3. Reading the minutes.
4. Report by the secretary of business transacted by the house committee since the last meeting of the club.

5. Treasurer's report.
6. Reports of committees and officers.
7. New business.
8. Adjournment.

ARTICLE XI

These By-laws may be amended by a vote of the majority of the members of the club present at any meeting.

VII

WORK WITH GIRLS

I. The Girls' Friendly Society—II. The King's Daughters—III. The Sewing-school.

I.—THE GIRLS' FRIENDLY SOCIETY

THE initial conditions which were encountered by the workers among the boys, confronted also the workers among the girls. With the young women of the parish as a nucleus, a branch of the Girls' Friendly Society was started, with the special intention of drawing into its ranks, and so within the influence of the church, the girls living in the neighborhood, and also those working in the shops and factories of the district.

Their response was immediate, and while at first they cared only for play and amusement, gradually, through the uplifting agencies of organization and friendship, the tone of the meetings improved, new members with higher standards sought admission, and, through the system of grading finally adopted, the branch became a great transforming agency in the lives of girls; so that the roughest who now join in the younger grades yield surely and quickly to the friendly pressure towards betterment, physical, mental, and spiritual, which is the atmosphere of the weekly meetings.

The following conspectus, which is posted in large type in the girls' hallway of the Parish House, shows in general the various activities and opportunities, industrial and social, which we propose now to describe in detail.

GIRLS' FRIENDLY SOCIETY—CLASSES AND MEETINGS

SUNDAY	G. F. S. A. Corporate Communion. First Sunday in November at 8 A.M.	G. F. S. Communion. First Sunday of each month, at 8 A.M.	G. F. S. Diocesan Service. Second Sunday after Easter, 4 P.M.	Club-room open, 3 P.M. to 6 P.M. Tea, 4 to 5 P.M.
MONDAY	Social Evenings. 8 to 9.30 P.M. Dues, 10 cents a month.	Entertainment. First Monday in month, 9 P.M.	Question Box. Questions dropped in box, answered by one of the clergy. 8.10 to 8.20 P.M.	Missionary Work. 8.20 to 9.15 P.M.
TUESDAY	Members' Classes: 8 to 9.30 P.M. Annual fee, 25 cts.; dues, 10 cts. a month. All are required to be present at opening service.	Calisthenics: 1st Div., 8.15 to 8.50; 2d Div., 8.30 to 9.30 P.M. Basketry and Cooking. Charge made for materials.	Drawn-work—Dressmaking—Embroidery—Millinery. Members provide their own material.	Gymnasium. 2d Div., 8.10 to 8.50 P.M. 1st Div., 8.50 to 9.30 P.M.
TUESDAY AFTERNOON	Candidates' Class. Dues, one cent each Tuesday. (Girls under 14 years.)	Games: 3.30 to 3.50 P.M. Service: 3.50 to 4 P.M. Classes: 4 to 5 P.M.	First Department: (10 to 14 yrs.) Calisthenics. Cooking. Embroidery.	Second Department: (under 10 yrs.) Kitchen-garden.
THURSDAY	Junior Probationers' Classes. Dues, 3 cents an evening. (14 to 16 years.)	Service: 7.30 P.M.	Calisthenics—Cooking—Basketry—Embroidery. Materials provided.	
FRIDAY	Members' Classes: 8 to 9.30 P.M. Annual fee, 25 cts.; dues, 10 cts. a month. All are expected to be present at opening service.	Calisthenics: 8.10 to 9.30 P.M.	Cooking. Charge made for materials.	Dressmaking—Drawn-work—Embroidery—Millinery. Members provide their own materials.
SATURDAY	Baths: 7.30 to 9 P.M.			
BUSINESS MEETINGS	Branch Helpers. Business meetings: 1st Monday in January, April, July, October. 8 to 9.30 P.M.	First Tuesday each month, October to June, 8 P.M.	First Friday each month, October to June, 8 P.M.	
ENTERTAINMENTS	Shirt-waist-Dance. November 8th, 8 to 11 P.M.	Quarterly Entertainments. November 23d, 8 P.M. Play by Recreation Com. Members owing dues not admitted.	Quarterly Entertainment. January 10th, 8 P.M. Members who owe dues not admitted.	Quarterly Entertainment. May 9th, 8 P.M. Members who owe dues not admitted.
	Annual Neighborhood Meeting. Wed., May 16th, 8 to 11 P.M.	For the G. F. S., in the parishes of Grace, St. Mark's, Calvary, St. George's.		

WORK WITH GIRLS

Lydia Dorcas appears at the Parish House on the second Tuesday in November, that being the "first day." She has a penny in her hand—the weekly due—and she desires to join a candidates' class. She reaches the house at half-past three, leaves her hat in the cloak-room, and gives her name, her address, and her penny to the associate at the door. She is shown into the kitchen-garden room, in one end of which associates and small children—Lydia is aged five—are playing games. For half an hour one game follows another, taking in all new-comers. Then the girls fall into line and are marched to their seats for the service which precedes the classes.

CANDIDATES' SERVICE

True friends help each other,
  Gladly give and take;
Bear with one another
  For sweet friendship's sake,
Even when parted always,
  Love each other still;
Both in joy and sorrow,
  Sharing good and ill.

Happy home, where Jesus—
  Best and truest friend—
Waits for Christian pilgrims
  At their journey's end.
Where the meek and lowly
  Find at length their part,
And a special blessing
  Crowns the pure in heart.
    Onward, etc.

Onward in life's journey,
  Clasping hand and hand,
Thus they seek together
  Friendship's native land.

PURITY IS CLEANNESS OF THOUGHT, WORD, AND DEED

LET US PRAY

Our Father, who art in heaven, hallowed be Thy name, Thy kingdom come, Thy will be done on earth, as it is in heaven; give us this day our daily bread, and forgive us our trespasses, as we forgive those who trespass against us; and lead us not into temptation, but deliver us from evil; for Thine is the kingdom, the power, and the glory, forever and ever. AMEN.

O Lord, we beseech Thee to bless us, and all who belong to the Girls' Friendly Society. AMEN.

O Lord, make us and keep us pure and clean in word and in deed. AMEN.

As soon as the service is over, the work of the classes begins. The lesson is given from the platform by the kitchen-garden teacher, and two young associates at each table direct its application. At five o'clock the classes are dismissed. Lydia, as she goes home, carries a card which has the candidates' service printed on one side and certain rules on the other. This card she is to study with the aid of her parents, and bring back at the next meeting.

GIRLS' FRIENDLY SOCIETY
OF
St. George's Church

CANDIDATE'S CARD

I PROMISE TO TRY

I. To be clean in body and neat in dress.
II. To be pure and clean in all I say or do.
III. To be kind and friendly to others.
IV. To be truthful, honest, and polite in meetings, at work, and in my home.
V. To be regular at meetings and faithful at work.
VI. To go to church every Sunday.
VII. To do all this because I am God's child.

Name ....

Address. ....

When Lydia is aged ten, she is advanced to the next department, which meets on the same afternoon in other rooms. Here, too, games are played for half an hour, while the children are assembling, and at four the service is said as before, and the girls disperse to their classes. Lydia now learns either simple cooking, such as boiling and poaching eggs and baking potatoes, or cross-stitch and embroidery. At twelve years of age she enters the calisthenic class, being an advanced grade of the same department. Now, eight weeks of consecutive attendance and thorough learning of the promises, prayers, and hymns on the card entitle her to wear the candidates' button. This is inscribed: "St. George's G. F. S. Candidate," in blue letters on a white ground.

At fourteen, Lydia Dorcas, like many of the girls of her age, leaves school to earn her living. She is therefore no longer able to attend the afternoon class. Accordingly, she receives a transfer-card by which she is admitted to the Junior Probationers' meeting, on Thursday evenings at eight o'clock.

Purity is cleanness of thought, word, and deed

GIRLS' FRIENDLY SOCIETY
CANDIDATES

Admit..................................

Address..............................

TO THE
JUNIOR PROBATIONERS
ON

October.........190.., at 8 P.M.
207 EAST 16TH STREET

Bear ye one another's burdens

In these evening classes, talks are given by the associates in charge, and the tuition is more advanced. After eight consecutive weeks of attendance here, her candidates' button is exchanged for another, marked in red letters "Junior Probationers."

At sixteen, after two years in this department, she learns the Resolution by heart.

> **RESOLUTION TO BE SIGNED BY MEMBERS OF ST. GEORGE'S BRANCH**
>
> **Resolved:** That as a member of St. George's Branch of the Girls' Friendly Society, I will earnestly strive after personal purity, in thought, word, and action, and will try by my own conduct to use my influence for purity with other girls.
>
> That I will show myself kind and friendly to others, especially to the girls belonging to this Society.
>
> That I will try by my own truthfulness, honesty, and orderly conduct in meetings, at work, and in my daily life to uphold the name of the Society.
>
>   **Amen.**

She is now given a transfer-card, admitting her to membership in the Girls' Friendly Society. (See page 201.) On the back of this card an associate certifies that Lydia Dorcas is sixteen years of age, has been a member of St. George's G. F. S. Junior Probationers for two years, and can say the Resolution and Prayer of the society.

Girls of sixteen or over, who have not passed through this novitiate, have a separate probation of three months. Once a year all of these girls, with those who have regularly gone over the prescribed stages, are admitted by the Rector to membership in the society. This takes place at a service in the church, which all who belong to the Branch in the parish are expected to attend. The Rector makes an address, and gives each new member

WORK WITH GIRLS

Purity is cleanness of thought, word, and deed

GIRLS' FRIENDLY SOCIETY
JUNIOR PROBATIONERS

Admit..................................

Address..............................

TO

MEMBERSHIP IN THE GIRLS' FRIENDLY SOCIETY

ON

October......... 190.., at 8 P.M.

207 EAST 16TH STREET

Bear ye one another's burdens

---

the silver badge of the Girls' Friendly Society. The Resolution is formally signed, and a member's book and card received. The book and card are printed by the general society, and may be had at their office in the Church Missions House, 281 Fourth Avenue, New York City.

Lydia's opportunities are now very varied, as is readily seen in the list of meetings here displayed:

MEMBERS

MONDAYS—All the year. 8 to 9.15 P.M.

SOCIAL EVENING

Question-box   Talks by clergy
Missionary work   Library open

Entertainment first Monday in each month, 9 P.M.

TUESDAYS—All the year. 8 to 9.15 P.M.

* October 1st to June 1st.

CLASSES

Basket weaving	Drawn-work	Gymnasium
Cooking	Dress-making	Literature
Calisthenics	Embroidery	Penny-provident

> June 1st to October 1st.
>> Dancing and games.

> FRIDAYS—October 1st to June 1st. 8 to 9.15 P.M.
>> CLASSES
>>
>> | | |
>> |---|---|
>> | Basket weaving | Drawing |
>> | Cooking | Millinery |
>> | Calisthenics | Recreation |
>> | Dress-making | Library open |

ASSOCIATES

First Friday in each month, at 11 A.M., at St. George's Deaconess House.

BRANCH HELPERS

Members' own organization to discuss and aid Branch work. First Monday in January, April, and October, 8 P.M.

In the choice of these classes, and in all the perplexities of her life where she feels the need of guidance, she has the friendly aid of an associate, who meets her half-way with sympathy and affection.

Now she has an opportunity to undertake, in her turn, some work for others, arranged and managed by the girls themselves, under the name of the Branch Helpers.

CONSTITUTION
OF THE
BRANCH HELPERS OF ST. GEORGE'S GIRLS' FRIENDLY SOCIETY

ARTICLE I
NAME

The name of this association shall be the Branch Helpers.

ARTICLE II
OBJECT

The object of this association shall be to further the interest and progress of the Girls' Friendly Society.

ARTICLE III
OFFICERS

The officers of this association shall be a president, vice-president, and secretary. They shall be members of St. George's parish.

ARTICLE IV
PRESIDENT

The president, or in her absence the vice-president, shall preside at the meetings of the association and of the council.

ARTICLE V
SECRETARY

The secretary shall keep the minutes of the meetings; she shall conduct the correspondence and keep the records of the association.

ARTICLE VI
MEETINGS

Meetings shall be held quarterly.

ARTICLE VII
ELECTIONS

Once in two years, commencing in 1899, the officers of this association shall be elected at the meeting held the second Monday in January; on nominations presented from each class in the Girls' Friendly Society, one member of each class shall also be elected and shall, with the officers, constitute the council, to hold office for two years.

ARTICLE VIII
COUNCIL

The council shall have general charge of the affairs of the association, and shall have full power; it shall be their duty to carry out the purposes of the association according to its constitution. Members of the council shall have been members of the Girls' Friendly Society for two years or more. The Branch secretary shall be *ex-officio* a member of the council.

ARTICLE IX
MEMBERSHIP

Any member of the Girls' Friendly Society shall be eligible to membership in this association.

ARTICLE X

This constitution may be amended at any quarterly meeting

of this association, provided such amendment shall have been posted in the Girls' Friendly Society rooms by unanimous consent of the council, one month previous to such meeting.

Each evening group or class elects a delegate to represent the class at meetings of the Branch Helpers council. There she makes such reports as are indicated in the following rules:

RULES FOR CLASS DELEGATES

I. To be present at all meetings of the class or council, and also at all quarterly meetings of the Branch Helpers.
II. To report the action of the council and quarterly meetings to the class.
III. To get the vote of the class on any subject referred to it by the council.
IV. To collect money at Christmas and during Lent; to give out the missionary work and see that it is returned finished, and to keep a record in the book provided for that purpose.
V. To call the roll, in the absence of the Associate.
VI. To report at the council and quarterly meetings, the average attendance of her class, the amounts collected at Christmas and during Lent; to give account of missionary work done, and to report any dissatisfaction or increased interest shown by the members in the work of the society.
VII. (And most important) To always smile and wear her badge.

COUNCIL MEETINGS

First Thursday of each month, at 8 P.M.

QUARTERLY MEETINGS

First Monday in January, April, and September, at 8 P.M.

The blanks on which these monthly reports are made show the names of the members of the class, the contribution of each to missionary work, the amount of work given out and finished, and her standing as to dues.

WORK WITH GIRLS

DRESS-MAKING CLASS—DECEMBER

NAME	CLASS DONATION		WORK GIVEN OUT				WORK FINISHED				DUES
	$	Cents	5	12	19	26	5	12	19	26	
Jane Allen		10	1		1					2	paid
Annie Brauer		15		2						2	"
Sarah Cross		10	1			1				1	"
Agnes Schloss		5	1							1	"
Lizzie Schmidt		10	1							1	"
Barbara Todd		15	1		1					2	"
Blanche Tuttle		25	1		1			1		1	"
Alma Tuttle		10									
Bessie Uhlmann		5	1					1			"
Minnie Vetters											
Kate Witte		10	1					1			paid
Bertha Waite		25		1							"
Mary Wessling		5	1								"
Mary Young		10		1	1					2	"
Associate		45									
	$2	00									

MONTHLY REPORT		REMARKS
Number in class	14	Two dollars given towards Christmas-box sent to Spring Hill Mines Hospital, N. S.
Average attendance	10	
Work given out	18	
Work finished	15	
Donations	2.00	
Number who owe dues	one	

Beside these provisions for work, there are also opportunities for play. Entertainments are held quarterly, on the third Wednesday in January, April, and October, with an excursion in July. These are open only to those whose dues are fully paid. There are dances in May and November, and during the year two plays. Every Monday there is a social meeting, at which the clergy answer questions put in a box, on religious, historical, and social current topics. The girls meet on this evening in groups, each of which has a special missionary object to further, under the guidance of an associate, who makes a study of the object chosen by her girls.

Each group in turn is assigned one month when it can claim the interest and work of all the other groups. At the first meeting of the month, the class-delegate of the group whose turn it is, rises after the opening service, explains the work in which she wishes to enlist the co-operation of all the others, and tells the special part her own group undertakes. Sewing for this special object is then taken up—the material is supplied by the members' and associates' dues—and at the close of the month the garments made during the interval are counted, given to the group, and the evening closes with a missionary entertainment illustrative of the field worked for.

To instil thrift, there is a station of the Penny-Provident Fund, receiving money on deposit in amounts from one cent to one dollar. For the sick there is a sick-benefit fund: those who pay twenty cents a month receive three dollars a week when sick; those who pay thirty-five cents receive five dollars. Finally, there is the Diocesan Vacation House, at Huntington, Long Island, open from the middle of June to the middle of September, where board may be had by members and associates for three dollars a week.

After Lydia has belonged to the Friday evening classes for three years, she is admitted to the privileges of the classes which meet on Tuesday evenings. Here both her privileges and her responsibilities are enlarged, for from these groups are taken the girls who work on the various committees, and who teach the Thursday evening classes of Junior Probationers.

Careful records are made of the attendance at all the classes. These are kept in class-books. After an absence of two weeks, a post-card is sent to every absentee.

G. F. S.

.... EVENING

You have been absent ....weeks. If you do not wish to lose your place in your class........and forfeit your class fee, please send or bring your excuse to Miss ....on................evening.

207 East 16th Street.

At the end of each month the attendance noted in all the class-books is entered in a general-attendance book, by the committee on books, who hand to the Branch secretary a list of all members who have not attended for a month. The name and address of each of these absentees is then written on a special report form, and is given by the Branch secretary at the next associates' meeting to that member's associate. She fills up the report, and returns it to the secretary, who files it with the member's record in the permanent card-catalogue. (See page 208.)

The leaf from an associate's book (given on page 209), which is provided by the general society, shows how carefully the records are kept.

In case a girl moves to some other part of the city or country, a letter of transfer, on an official blank form, insures her a friendly reception and good influences in her new home.

When she marries, a marriage-card is given her (see page 210), and she is commended to the Young Married Women's Society, where she further increases her skill in the art of housewifery, and in whose kindergarten her children may grow up, till the little girls begin to come around on a Tuesday afternoon and join the candidates' class, as their mothers did before them.

The associates are first tried in work with the candidates classes, and then with the Thursday evening classes. Those who pass this novitiate well are admitted at a service at which girls are received, receive the badge of the society, a list of girls specially committed to their care, and a statement of duties. The associate is expected, in her evening class or group, to discuss the work with the teacher for the sake of progress and interest, to be punctual at the opening service, to call the roll of the class, to inquire especially about the absent, and

ADMINISTRATION OF AN INSTITUTIONAL CHURCH

**ST. GEORGE'S MEMORIAL HOUSE
207 EAST 16TH STREET, N. Y.**

ABSENCE AND DUES REPORT

Name..
Address...
Absent..
Class............... *Night*....................
Dues owed........... *Paid*.....................

Please visit her home and fill out and return as soon as possible this report form.

.....................190..

Name..
Address...
Work............... *Wages*....................
Reason for { *Absence*..............................
{ *Owing dues*............................
....
....
....
....

When will she { *Return*..............................
{ *Pay*.................................
Associate's name......................................
Date filed....................

WORK WITH GIRLS

LEAF FROM AN ASSOCIATE'S BOOK

Name and home address of member: *Lydia Dorcas, 400 Av. A.*

Date of birth, *April 10, 1885.*

Baptized? *Yes.*   Confirmed? *Yes.*

Admitted by *Rev. W. S. Rainsford, D.D.*

Date, *January 10, 1903.*

Member's present address and employer's name, *John Wanamaker.*

Church, *St. George's.*

Employment and date of entering it, *Saleswoman—1901.*

Visits made,   *October 10.   Jan. 15.   March 14.   May 6.*

Visits received,   *Nov. 8.   Dec. 27.   March 4, 11, 18, 25.*

Letters written,   *June 5.   July 8.   Aug. 10.   Sept. 9.*

Magazines, *Girls' Friendly Society Magazine.*

Class attended, *Basketry on Tuesday evenings. (Class delegate.)*

Commended to,

Branch and Diocese,

Date of Commendation,

PAYMENTS

YEAR	JAN.	APRIL	JULY	OCT.	TOTAL
1903	*.15*	*.15*	*.15*	*.15*	*.60*
1904	*.15*	*.15*	*.15*	*.15*	*.60*

FURTHER PARTICULARS

Lydia has belonged to the G. F. S. ever since she joined as a candidate at five years of age.

She is a regular attendant on Friday evenings, and attended my Lenten evenings last March without missing one. She meets me regularly at Communion, the first Sunday in each month, and has taken up her new G. F. S. responsibilities very earnestly.

ADMINISTRATION OF AN INSTITUTIONAL CHURCH

MARRIAGE CARD (see page 207).

Presented to
.... Years Member of the Girls Friendly Society.

Prov. XII XXXI

A virtuous woman is a crown to her husband: her price is far above rubies. The heart of her husband doth safely trust in her. She will do him good and not evil all the days of her life.

She worketh willingly with her hands. She stretcheth out her hand to the poor; yea She reacheth forth her hands to the needy.

Strength and honour are her clothing; and She shall rejoice in the time to come. She openeth her mouth with wisdom, and in her tongue is the law of kindness. She looketh well to her household, and eateth not the bread of idleness.

Favour is deceitful, and beauty is vain, but a woman that feareth the Lord, she shall be praised.

Bear ye one another's burdens

on her marriage .... 19......
To................................

Gal. VI. 2

.... Associate.
.... Branch Secretary.
.... Branch.

maintain regularity, to see that general conversation is kept up and new girls made to feel at home, to have the class delegate present her report for the discussion of the class, and in general to promote good social feeling, and to encourage the friendship and confidence of the girls. She makes the following promises:

WORK WITH GIRLS

AS AN ASSOCIATE OF ST. GEORGE'S G. F. S.

I PROMISE:

I. To see each of the members on my list—in their own homes if possible, or if not there, then in mine—at least twice during the winter.

II. To write to each of them at least once during the summer.

III. To write to each of them during September, reminding them that the classes open in October, and advising them which to select.

IV. To keep a careful record of each of them in my Associates' Book, and return it on May 1st and November 1st for the information of the council.

V. To try to make real to each of them the objects of the G. F. S., and the advantages of its wide extension.

VI. To consider my weekly evening engagement at the G. F. S. rooms as prior and superior to all other engagements.

VII. To invite personally or by note those who have been confirmed, to attend the 8 A.M. Communion Service the first Sunday of each month, and to meet and welcome them there, if possible.

VIII. To attend regularly and promptly the monthly associates' meeting, and when unable to do so to notify the Branch secretary to that effect, *before* the meeting.

[SIGNED] ....

DUES

Payable yearly, in January, in advance $3.00

FINES

For absence from associates' meeting 50
" lateness at " " 25

ASSOCIATES' MEETING

The first Friday of each month, at 4 P.M.

ADMINISTRATION OF AN INSTITUTIONAL CHURCH

II.—THE KING'S DAUGHTERS

The purpose of this society is "to deepen spiritual life and to stimulate Christian activity." It was started by the Rector in 1891 in order to keep together and help the girl communicants. The girls who were confirmed that year were divided into groups for mutual encouragement and work for Christ. These groups were made a part of the International Order of the King's Daughters. The central offices of this society are at 156 Fifth Avenue, New York City, where the constitution and other printed matter, and the badge, may be obtained.

The following is the service used at the admission of members:

HYMN.

COLLECTS.

O God, who didst teach the hearts of Thy faithful people, by sending to them the light of Thy Holy Spirit, grant us, by the same Spirit, to have a right judgment in all things, and evermore to rejoice in His holy comfort; through the merits of Christ Jesus, our Saviour, who liveth and reigneth with Thee, in the unity of the same Spirit, one God, world without end.—*Amen.*

Lord of all power and might, who art the author and giver of all good things, graft in our hearts the love of Thy name, increase in us true religion, nourish us with all goodness, and of Thy great mercy keep us in the same; through Jesus Christ, our Lord.—*Amen.*

THE LORD'S PRAYER.

Almighty God, who didst give such grace unto Thy Holy Apostle, St. Andrew, that he readily obeyed the calling of Thy Son, Jesus Christ, and followed Him without delay; grant unto us all, that we, being called by Thy holy word, may forthwith give up ourselves obediently to fulfil Thy holy commandments; through the same Jesus Christ, our Lord.—*Amen.*

WORK WITH GIRLS

Hymn.

Address.

Receiving of Crosses.

Minister.—Receive this cross in the name of Jesus Christ, Thy Saviour, and may it be unto thee a token of His undying love, and of thy promise to serve in His name.—*Amen.*

Minister.—Bless, O Lord, this Thy servant, and make her faithful unto her life's end.

Response.—We beseech Thee to hear us, good Lord.

Minister.—Let us pray.

Our help is in the name of the Lord.

Response.—Who hath made heaven and earth.

Minister.—Blessed be the name of the Lord.

Response.—Henceforth, world without end.

Minister. O Lord, hear our prayer.

Response.—And let our cry come unto Thee.

O God, our Father and our King, vouchsafe to (these Thy servants) such a measure of Thy heavenly grace that (they) may be mindful always whose (they are) and whom (they serve). Defend (them), we beseech Thee, so that (they) may continue Thine forever, and daily increase in Thy Holy Spirit more and more, until (they) come to Thine everlasting Kingdom.—*Amen.*

O God, who hast purchased to Thyself a universal church by the precious blood of Thy dear Son, mercifully look upon the same, and guide and govern with Thy Holy Spirit all who may be chosen for any kind of service therein. Especially we pray Thee to bless this parish and to sanctify the mission of Thy daughters for the spread of the Kingdom, both within and outside of its borders. We ask it "in His name," and for His sake, our Lord and Saviour Jesus Christ.—*Amen.*

Benediction.

Hymn.—*"Lead as We Go"* . . . Mary Lowe Dickinson.

Lead now, as forth we go,
     Master divine;
 On paths of joy or woe
     Let Thy face shine.
	Where winds of trouble blow,
	 Where tides of sorrow flow,
	 Fearless our steps shall go,
	     Close after Thine.

Ours be the willing hand
    Thy work to share;
Ours be the loving heart
    Thy cross to bear;
True Daughters of the King,
New songs our lips shall sing.
Faint hearts and sorrowing,—
    These are our care.

Lowly our tasks, or grand,
    Serve we the same.
Bring by Thine own right hand
    Praise from our shame,

If but some soul in pain
Look up and smile again.
No deed can be in vain,
    Wrought "IN HIS NAME."

Drawn by Thy Spirit now,
    Ourselves we bring;
On prayer, and song, and vow,
    Our souls take wing,
Forth from this blessed place.
Lead us to show Thy grace;
Write on each lifted face,
    "Child of a King."

Each group keeps its own record of attendance, the names being entered on a card-catalogue.

Bauerle, Annie		
79 Greenpoint Av.	Entered	
	Took the Cross	1901
	S. S.	
	F.	
Visited	C.	
	\	

S. S. means a member of the Sunday-school; F., of the Girls' Friendly Society; C, is a communicant.

III.—THE SEWING-SCHOOL

The school is in four departments: kindergarten, primary, senior, and boys. Children between the ages of four and seven enter the kindergarten. Thence the girls

WORK WITH GIRLS

are promoted into the primary, the boys into their own department.

In the primary department, children are taught to use the needle, and to take the more important stitches. In the lowest class the subject is basting. Having mastered the theory of the stitch and done work which satisfies the teacher, the child is sent with a sample of her proficiency to the work examiner, who passes on its quality. The sample is put on file, the child passes an oral examination on the stitch just learned, the name of the stitch is checked off on her course-card, and she passes into the stitching class.

For the purpose of filing, a box is provided with envelopes, one for every child in the department, marked with her name. In these envelopes are placed the course-cards and all samples accepted by the examiner. These are transferred to a book which, when the girl graduates, becomes her property, and serves as a com-

---

FIRST-YEAR COURSE

- Basting . . . . o
- Running . . . . o
- Stitching . . . . o
- Back-stitching . . . . o
- Combination-stitch . . . . o
- Overcasting . . . . o
- Overhanding . . . . o
- Folding Hems on Paper . . . . . . o
- Hemming on Cloth . . . . o
- Model, Bag . . . . o

plete record of her progress and attainments, and as a proof of her ability should she wish to earn her living by her needle.

In the boys' primary department, the lads learn to sew on buttons, mend their pockets, cane chairs, and cobble shoes.

SECOND-YEAR COURSE

- Weaving . . . . o
- Garment Bias (Paper) . . . . o
- True   "   "   . . . . o
- Skirt Opening or Placket . . . . o
- Gathering and Putting on Band . . . . o
- Model, Petticoat . . . . o
- Fell Seam . . . . o
- French Seam . . . . o
- Button-hole, Eyelets, and Loops . . . . o
- Sewing on Buttons . . . . o
- Model, Corset-waist . . . . o

THIRD-YEAR COURSE

- Catch-stitching . . . . o
- Stocking Darning . . . . o
- Cashmere . . . . o
- Darned on Patch . . . . o
- Hemmed   "   . . . . o
- Mending . . . . o
- Model, Drawers . . . . o

WORK WITH GIRLS

```
FOURTH-YEAR COURSE

Skirt Binding (Velvet Braid) . . . . .  o
Seam Binding . . . . . . . . .  o
Whalebone Casing . . . . . . . .  o
Putting in Whalebone . . . . . . .  o
Sewing on Hooks and Eyes . . . . .  o
Placket and Putting on Bands . . . .  o
Making Pockets . . . . . . . . .  o
Putting Pockets in Seam . . . . . .  o
Tailor Button-hole . . . . . . . .  o
```

The cards are of different colors, and each bears on the other side the name of the scholar and the name of the school. A mark in the space opposite each accomplishment indicates the progress of the scholar.

Every new scholar receives a card, which is here shown, front and back:

```
No. . . . . . . . . . . . . . . . . . . . . . . . . . . . . . .

. . . . . . . . . . . . . . . . . . . . . . . . . . . . .
          IS A MEMBER OF
        THE SEWING-SCHOOL
               OF
         ST. GEORGE'S CHURCH
```

NOV.				DEC.				JAN.			
4	11	18	25	2	9	16	23	30	6	13	20	27

> THE SCHOOL MEETS SATURDAY MORNING, AT
> TEN O'CLOCK
>
> Keep this card clean, bring it with you each Saturday, and present it as you enter.
>
> *P will be cut for punctual, L for late.*
>
> | FEB. | MAR. | APRIL |
> |---|---|---|
> | 3 \| 10 \| 17 \| 24 | 3 \| 10 \| 17 \| 24 \| 31 | 7 \| 14 \| 21 \| 28 |

On Saturday morning the child brings the card. If she is on time, the card is punched with a "P" at the date of that day, and the number is checked on a numerical sheet. If she is late, an "L" is punched in the card and recorded on the sheet. The sheet contains numbers up to 500, only a part of which is here shown:

	1	11	21	31	41	51	61	71	81	91
	2	12	22	32	42	52	62	72	82	92
	3	13	23	33	43	53	63	73	83	93
	4	14	24	34	44	54	64	74	84	94
	5	15	25	35	45	55	65	75	85	95
	6	16	26	36	46	56	66	76	86	96
	7	17	27	37	47	57	67	77	87	97
	8	18	28	38	48	58	68	78	88	98
	9	19	29	39	49	59	69	79	89	99
	10	20	30	40	50	60	70	80	90	100

Thus the attendance is rapidly taken without the calling of a roll. This record is transferred during the week to a roll-book.

When the girl leaves the sewing-school, she has passed through a practical course in sewing and is ready to work under a dress-maker and earn wages.

The teachers meet for conference on the second Saturday of each month. This is preceded and prepared for by a meeting of the council on the first Saturday. The council consists of a chairman, secretary, and treasurer, and four others.

There is a Penny-Provident Fund in connection with the school.

St. George's Church has a scholarship in Paskall's Institute, where higher branches in dress-making are taught. For this scholarship the girl who has been most faithful and done the best work in our school is chosen.

For the better maintenance of enthusiasm among the young people, to let the parents see what their children are actually accomplishing, and to display to those who have given financial encouragement the fruits of their generosity, there is held an annual exhibition. Every department is represented. All the societies bring forward their completed work. The trade-school offers for inspection its work in wood and iron. The battalion gives an exhibition drill. The gymnasium people show their medals and cups and banners, and give athletic performances. The children from the kindergarten point with pride to their colored papers. The girls of the sewing-school present their sample stitches and their finished garments; and the kitchen-gardeners and cooking-scholars keep a restaurant during the hours of the exhibition, stocked with their own productions. The dress-makers and the milliners, and the basket-makers and the embroiderers have each an assigned place for their work. The Girls' Friendly Society presents its calisthenic classes.

ADMINISTRATION OF AN INSTITUTIONAL CHURCH

There is even a sample missionary box, to show how such benefactions are constructed.

AN EXHIBITION
OF THE
WORK OF ST. GEORGE'S PARISH
WILL BE HELD AT
ST. GEORGE'S MEMORIAL HOUSE
207 EAST 16TH STREET
ON
WEDNESDAY AND THURSDAY, MARCH 23D AND 24TH
FROM 8 TO 10.30 P.M.
AND ON
THURSDAY, MARCH 24TH, FROM 3.30 TO 6 P.M.
ADMIT ONE
PLEASE PRESENT THIS CARD AT THE DOOR
NO CHILDREN ADMITTED ON THIS TICKET
GOOD FOR ONE VISIT ONLY

The parish exhibition and the Christmas decoration of the church are the two eminent social events to which the whole parish is invited. On these occasions rich and poor meet together.

At less frequent times, not more often than once in two or three years, a fair is held for some special object. Such sales are never under the charge of any single organization; they are made a general matter. Societies needing money in excess of the amount appropriated by the vestry and received from dues, get the aid of all the other societies: but a strong effort is made to keep all expenditure within the means of the organizations.

VIII

MEN AND WOMEN

I. The Men's Club—II. The Gymnasium—III. The Married Women's Society—IV. The Mothers' Meeting—V. The Happy-hour Club—VI. The Sunday-afternoon Club—VII. The Dramatic and Literary Society.

I.—THE MEN'S CLUB

In planning the Parish House, one entire floor was assigned to the Men's Club. As completed and furnished, these rooms comprise the library, where about five hundred books are on the shelves; the common room, where all the local daily and weekly papers of good standing are to be found, together with the leading monthly magazines, and where there are chess and checker tables and a piano; the billiard-room, and the gymnasium. Smoking is allowed in all these rooms except the gymnasium.

The rooms are open daily from eight o'clock in the morning until eleven at night; on Sundays, from one o'clock in the afternoon until eleven at night. Any attendant at St. George's who is over eighteen years of age is eligible to membership on the payment of three dollars a year, with an added fee of two dollars if he wishes to use the gymnasium.

A person desiring to join the club makes application for membership on a blank form like the following:

ADMINISTRATION OF AN INSTITUTIONAL CHURCH

APPLICATION FOR MEMBERSHIP

No..........   New York,..............190..

ST. GEORGE'S MEN'S CLUB

(TO BE FILLED UP BY THE APPLICANT)

Name in full...

Residence..

Age............ *Occupation*.........................

Business address..

Attendant of what church?..........................

Member of any parish organization?.............

Proposed by..

Seconded by...

Certified by...
              (One of the parish clergy)

....
           (Member of House Committee)

The dues are $3 per annum, payable quarterly in advance; $2 per annum additional for gymnasium privileges, payable half-yearly in advance, if use of gymnasium is desired.

This application must be accompanied by one quarter's dues (which will be refunded if the applicant is not admitted), and must be presented by the applicant to a member of the house committee any Monday evening, between 8 and 9 o'clock, at the club-rooms.

- -

RECORD OF MEN'S CLUB
FOR ENTRY IN THE PARISH REGISTER OF ST. GEORGE'S CHURCH

FAMILY NAME	RESIDENCE	CHRISTIAN NAMES	YEAR OF BIRTH	BAPTIZED?	CONFIRMED?	COMMUNICANT?

MEN AND WOMEN

This application having been received, the applicant's name is posted on the bulletin-board of the club for two weeks.

ST. GEORGE'S MEN'S CLUB

APPLICANT FOR MEMBERSHIP

Mr. ....
Address. ....
Proposer. ....
Seconder ....
    Date ....

An occasional inspection is made of the parish register to ascertain the names of men who belong to the parish but not to the club, and to these men the Rector sends a card making an appointment to consider the matter.

Dear Sir:

I would like to call your attention to our St. George's Men's Club, an organization numbering over five hundred members, and having rooms in the Memorial House. The membership I am anxious to increase from the men of our congregation. The expense is only $3 per year for dues, payable annually or quarterly in advance. There is no initiation fee.

Will you not meet me and the house committee in the club and inspect it, on Monday, December 7th, after 8.30 P.M.?

Sincerely yours,
[*Signed by the Rector.*]

ADMINISTRATION OF AN INSTITUTIONAL CHURCH

At the beginning of the organization there were eight committees. The house committee had general oversight of the rooms, except the gymnasium, which was in charge of the gymnasium committee. The committees on membership, finance, and rules drew up the provisions necessary for establishing the club on a sound basis. The committee on hospitality and entertainments received, introduced, and informed the members on public occasions, heard complaints and suggestions, and undertook to amuse the society. The library committee discharged the duties which were appropriate to its name. For twelve years these committees, thus charged with the affairs of the club, were mainly composed of men of more than average education and wealth, accustomed to clublife. They managed the association for the benefit of the great body of members for whom it was intended. But as the boys of the Sunday-school have grown into young men, passed through the trade-school and the battalion, and become eligible for membership in the Men's Club, they have become the life of the society. Their training has cultivated their sense of responsibility. To-day the committees are mostly made up of these men.

There are now two committees instead of eight: the house committee, governing the club in general, and the athletic committee, governing the gymnasium. Half of the house committee is appointed by the Rector; the club elects the other half at an annual meeting. This committee meets every Monday evening. A superintendent is in charge of the general club-rooms, and a competent instructor is on duty in the gymnasium. A provision is printed at the end of the by-laws, to the effect that any or all of them may be suspended at the will of the Rector.

MEN AND WOMEN

Due notice of election to membership is mailed to successful applicants by the secretary of the house committee:

**ST. GEORGE'S MEN'S CLUB
207 EAST 16TH STREET**

New York,..................19...

DEAR SIR:

I take pleasure in advising you that at a meeting of the house committee, held this evening, you were elected to membership in St. George's Men's Club.

Yours very truly,

....
Secretary.

Thereafter, at the beginning of each month, the new member receives a postal-card informing him as to coming events:

**ST. GEORGE'S MEN'S CLUB
207 EAST 16TH STREET**

May 5th, Friday.—Basket-ball in the gymnasium at 8 P.M., Xavier A. C. vs. St. George's A. C. Hat-checks, 15 cents. Proceeds to be used towards defraying expense of uniforms for St. George's baseball team.

May 10th, Wednesday.—Ladies' reception in large hall at 8 P.M. Dancing until 12 o'clock.

May 14th, Sunday.—Group picture of members of ten years' standing in the club will probably be taken on afternoon of this day. Definite notice will be sent by mail to all such members.

ADMINISTRATION OF AN INSTITUTIONAL CHURCH

May 14th, Sunday.—Cross-country walk. The details of this walk will be found on the bulletin-board.

May 26th and June 2d, Fridays.—Rector's Cup competition, in in-door all-around athletics, in the gymnasium at 8 P.M.

House Committee.

New York, May—, 19—.

The following copy of an annual programme gives an idea of the character and variety of the interests of the club:

PROGRAMME

19—

October 1, 19—, to January 15, 19—,—Measurement for Clergy Development Prizes.

October	25	First smoker at 8 P.M.
"	31	Wrestling competitions.
November	12	Concert and ladies' reception.
"	21	Wrestling competitions.
"	26	Thanksgiving Eve—Ladies' reception.
"	29	Smoker at 8 P.M.
December	6	General meeting of the club at 8 P.M.
"	12	Gymnastic competitions.
"	31	New Year's Eve—Gymnastic exhibition and ladies' reception.

19—

January	16	Gymnastic competitions.
"	28	Championship wrestling tournament of the Church Athletic League, at Grace A. C. Gymnasium.
"	31	Smoker at 8 P.M.
February	4	Ladies' reception.
"	13	Gymnastic competitions.
"	18	Concert and ladies' reception.
"	21	Smoker at 8 P.M.

April 18—Athletic games under the auspices of St. George's A. C. and Company I, Eighth Regiment, at Eighth Regiment armory.
" 22—Ladies' reception.
" 25—Lecture by Mr. W. L. Mason, "Around the Circle to Salt Lake" (illustrated).
" 29 and 30—Dramatic performance at Carnegie Lyceum, under the dual auspices of St. George's Dramatic and Literary Society and the Men's Club.
May 14—Lecture of Dr. J. N. Bishop, "The Land of the Midnight Sun" (illustrated).
June 12 and 19—Annual competitions for the Rector's Cup.

At the end of each quarter, the superintendent calls on the members by mail for the payment of their dues:

```
ST. GEORGE'S MEN'S CLUB
207 EAST 16TH ST.
                New York,................19...
Mr.........................
         To ST. GEORGE'S MEN'S CLUB, Dr.

For club dues.........Quarter ending......$.......
For gymnasium dues....Half-year ending....$.......
                                          _____
         Received payment,                $.......
                  ....................
                          Superintendent.
```

Members who do not pay with proper punctuality receive a reminder, as follows:

> **ST. GEORGE'S MEN'S CLUB**
> **207 EAST 16TH ST.**
>
> New York,................19...
>
> Mr........................
> ....
>
> DEAR SIR:
>
> We beg to inform you that you appear to be in arrears for dues to the Club for the last...................... quarters ending............................amounting to........................Dollars.
>
> Will you please note the following extracts from the By-laws of the Club:
>
> ARTICLE II., SEC. 7. A member in arrears for dues for two quarters shall, on the last day of the second quarter, thereby be debarred from all privileges of the club and gymnasium until full payment has been made of all such arrears and of dues since accrued; provided, however, that notice of such debarment shall have been given in writing to such member not less than ten days previous to such date.
>
> ARTICLE II., SEC. 8. A member in arrears for nine months shall be notified thereof, and if such arrears are not paid within thirty days after such notice, he shall thereby be dropped from the roll and his membership terminated.
>
> Yours truly,
> HOUSE COMMITTEE.
>
> **EXTRACT FROM MINUTES OF THE HOUSE COMMITTEE**
> March 7, 1904
>
> RESOLVED:—That notice be sent to all members in arrears, in accordance with Article II., Section 7, of the By-laws, and that after ten days the names of those who are debarred from the privileges of the club shall be posted upon the bulletin-board.

Individual accounts are kept on cards. (See page 229.)

The superintendent keeps the stub of each receipt for dues, and the book containing these stubs is examined annually by the treasurer. (See page 229.)

MEN AND WOMEN

		CLUB	GYM.	TOTAL	DATE		CLUB	GYM.	TOTAL
	NOV.					NOV.			
	FEB.					FEB.			
	MAY					MAY			
	AUG.					AUG.			
	NOV.					NOV.			
	FEB.					FEB.			
	MAY					MAY			
	AUG.					AUG.			

Date of election............
Name............
Residence............
Business Address............
Remarks............ Joined Gym............

No. .... Date.....19..

Name............

For Membership
Dues, 3d quarter, $.......

For Gymnasium
Dues, 3d quarter, $.......

$........

No. ....   New York,..........19..

ST. GEORGE'S MEN'S CLUB

Received from............
.... Dollars,

For Membership Dues,
3d quarter, ending............$........

For Gymnasium Dues
3d quarter, ending............$........

$........   ....
                   Superintendent.

Care is taken not to force religious services upon the men. The idea is that the club is their own, and that they are free to use it without interference. At the same time, the whole intention of the club is religious. It is a manifestation of the friendliness of the church towards the men, and they naturally respond in kind. Acquaintance with the clergy and other parish workers leads to interest in the matters which they have at heart. The men must be St. George's men in order to be admitted—that is, they must have taken the church as their religious home. Many of them have been confirmed before becoming members, and these influence the others. They are encouraged to join Bible classes. They act as ushers at church services. Every year a confirmation class is formed of members of the club.

II.—THE GYMNASIUM

The use of the gymnasium is not confined to any one organization. On Tuesday evening it is open to the Girls' Friendly Society; on Thursday evening to the battalion; on Saturday afternoons the younger boys have the freedom of it. At all other times it is used by the Men's Club.

The salaried instructor examines all new-comers, and puts them through such a series of exercises as will do them the most good.

The athletic committee of the Men's Club is in charge of the general interests of the gymnasium, under the house committee. The chairman of the athletic committee is a member of the house committee, and the members who serve under him are chosen subject to the house committee's approval.

Various competitions stimulate the athletic interest. The Rector gives four gold medals every year to the best all-around athlete of the Men's Club, of the battalion, of the trade-school, and to the champion swimmer of the Sunday-school. Four cups given by the Rector represent these four attainments, the names of the medallists being engraved upon them year by year. The clergy give two prizes, a gold and a silver medal, for the best all-around development made in the gymnasium by members of the Men's Club. This is called the Clergy Development Prize. The Men's Club gives a medal, called the Point Prize, to the member receiving the most points in outside competition.

The instructor keeps a careful account of the condition and progress of persons using the gymnasium. (See page 232.)

The following card shows that a residence in New York does not necessarily prohibit the joys of country life:

All members are cordially invited to the
NEXT CROSS-COUNTRY WALK
From.................to...............
On Sunday........190.. (weather permitting)
Leave................arrive at............
Returning, leave......due New York at......
BRING LUNCH
For further particulars see Mr. E. R.

III.—THE MARRIED WOMEN'S SOCIETY

The society includes two departments, junior and senior. Women who have been married more than four and less than fifteen years are admitted to the senior department; those who have been married less than four years belong to the junior department.

ST. GEORGE'S GYMNASIUM RECORDS

No..............

	EXAMINATION												NAME
DATE	MO.	DA.	HR.	MO.	DA.	HR.	MO.	DA.	HR.	MO.	DA.	HR.	
Age...............													
Weight............													
Height............													
Depth of Chest.....													
GIRTHS:													
Neck...............													
Chest contracted....													
Chest expanded....													
Waist..............													
Right forearm......													
Right up-arm down.													
Right up-arm up...													
Left forearm.......													
Left up-arm down..													
Left up-arm up.....													
Right thigh........													
Right calf.........													
Left thigh.........													
Left calf...........													
MUSCLES:													
Consistency, Arm.													
" Leg..													
Development, Arm.													
" Leg..													
Size, Arm.													
" Leg..													
Dip...............													
Pull-up............													

REMARKS:

MEN AND WOMEN

The two branches meet at the same time, on Thursday afternoon, from half-past two till five o'clock, and join in an opening service, after which they separate into classes. They meet again at the end of the afternoon for tea.

PRAYER

OF THE

MARRIED WOMEN'S SOCIETY

Almighty God, our Heavenly Father, who art the only source of light and life, grant unto us, and to all the members of this society, Thy life, that we may truly live. May we take into our homes Thy love, that in the light of it we may do well the small things, in the day of small things, and great labors if Thou summon us to any—rising and working, sitting still or suffering, according to Thy word. Help us with earnestness of purpose to guard and sanctify all that is good and beautiful in our homes, that in so doing we may further the Kingdom of God in our city and nation. Give us faithful hearts devoted to Thee and to the service of all men for Thy sake; that with a deep sense of our responsibilities, and a sure confidence in Thy ever-ready help, we may live and work in the light of the life of Thy son our Saviour Jesus Christ. *Amen.*

The mothers being unable to come without their children, a nursery and kindergarten are maintained in connection with the meetings. The babies are cared for by a nurse, and the older children by a kindergartner, in separate rooms.

The classes receive instruction in cooking, dress-making,

millinery, drawn-work, first aid to the injured, physical culture, and literature. The members of the literature class listen to reading sometimes by professional readers, sometimes by associates; there is also some discussion of current events.

Any married woman proposed by the clergy or the deaconesses is eligible for membership without any ecclesiastical test. The marriage register is annually examined for names of persons who should be brought into the society. To each such person the following card of invitation is sent:

M. W. S.

The Married Women's Society of St. George's Church meets every Thursday at 2.30 P.M., at 207 East 16th Street. After the opening service, classes for

First Aid	Physical Culture
Literature	Cooking
Dress-making	Millinery
	Drawn-work

and a Mothers' Class on the care and feeding of children are held, followed by tea and music. Dues, 75 cents.

If you wish to become a member of this society, will you kindly fill out the enclosed blank and return to Mrs. ———, President, ——— Street, and an invitation to join the society will be sent to you. New members are probationers for six weeks, during which time they must attend the weekly meetings of the society, or *send an excuse in writing* to the President—failing to do this they cannot become members of the society.

If the person desires to become a member of this society, she makes application in the following form:

```
┌─────────────────────────────────────────┐
│              M. W. S.                   │
│              RECORD                     │
│  Name..................................  │
│  Address...............................  │
│  Age...................................  │
│  Date of Marriage......................  │
│  Parish................................  │
│  Introduced by.........................  │
│  Fill out and return to                 │
│            Mrs. ............            │
│  .........Street,           New York    │
└─────────────────────────────────────────┘
```

On receipt of this application, the name comes before a committee on membership, and, being accepted, a card of formal invitation, such as follows, is sent to the applicant:

```
┌─────────────────────────────────────────┐
│      ST. GEORGE'S MEMORIAL HOUSE        │
│            207 EAST 16TH ST.            │
│                                         │
│       THE MARRIED WOMEN'S SOCIETY       │
│         OF ST. GEORGE'S CHURCH          │
│             CORDIALLY INVITE            │
│                                         │
│      ...............................    │
│       TO BECOME ONE OF ITS MEMBERS      │
│         MEETINGS ARE HELD EVERY         │
│          THURSDAY AT 2.30 P.M.          │
│      PLEASE BRING THIS CARD WITH YOU    │
└─────────────────────────────────────────┘
```

There is an annual service for the admission of members. This service, like similar initiations into other parochial organizations, is held in the church in order to impress upon the people the fact that the church is the heart of all the organized life of the parish.

The following is the order of this service:

Hymn 311: "Ancient of Days."
Grace be unto you and peace from God our Father, and from the Lord Jesus Christ.
Our Father.
Collect, Seventh Sunday after Trinity.
Psalm 121.
Hymn 660: "O for a Closer Walk."
During this hymn those to be admitted come forward.
Minister. Do you desire to become a member of the Married Women's Society of St. George's Church?
Answer. I do.
Minister. I receive you into the fellowship of the Married Women's Society. Take and wear this badge as a faithful member of the society.
All repeat together the prayer of the society.
Other prayers follow.
Merciful Father, bless, we beseech Thee, with all best blessings, both spiritual and temporal, all members of this society, whether present or absent. Bestow upon them, O God, such measure of earthly prosperity as may be good for them, and keep them if Thou wilt, in health and safety.

But far above all earthly blessings we ask Thee to make the members of this society to be one in Thy service. Let Thy Fatherly hand, we beseech Thee, ever be over them, let Thy Holy Spirit ever be with them. Unite them together in the bonds of holy love, that they may abide in Thee, and after being separated for a little here below, may be again united in that kingdom where they can be parted no more forever; through Jesus Christ our Lord. *Amen.*

Almighty God, our Heavenly Father, who settest the solitary in families, we commend to Thy continual care the homes in which Thy people dwell. Put far from them, we beseech Thee, every root of bitterness, the desires of vainglory and the pride of life. Fill them with faith, virtue, knowledge, temperance, patience, godliness. Knit together in constant affection those who in holy wedlock have been made one flesh; turn the hearts of the parents to the children, and the hearts of the children to the parents, and so kindle charity among us all, that we be kindly affected one to another with brotherly love, through Jesus Christ our Lord. *Amen.*

Hymn 238: "O Perfect Love."
Address.
General thanksgiving.
Benediction, from the Marriage Service.
Hymn 249: "O Zion Haste."

The new member then receives the following certificate:

```
                    M. W. S.
This is to certify that
.................................................
has been admitted to the membership of The
Married Women's Society of St. George's
Church
On.................................................
    President.....................................
    Associate.....................................
```

A Members' Guide is given her, containing a form of receipt for payments of dues (see page 238), and the following rules:

1. No woman who has been married over fifteen years can join the Married Women's Society. Those already members may remain so always.

2. Members are to pay seventy-five cents a year towards the running expenses of the society. Those refusing to pay their subscription, without good cause, lose their certificate.

3. Members are to make their payments semi-annually, presenting this book at the same time to the secretary, that the receipt-form may be signed by her. If not able to do this, they should send their payments in stamps, with this book, in a letter, which will be receipted and returned.

4. Members must let the secretary know at once if they change their address; and they must be careful always to keep the society certificate and guide-book in their possession.

5. Members leaving the society, from whatever cause, must return their certificate, guide-book, and badge to the secretary. The money for their badge will be refunded.

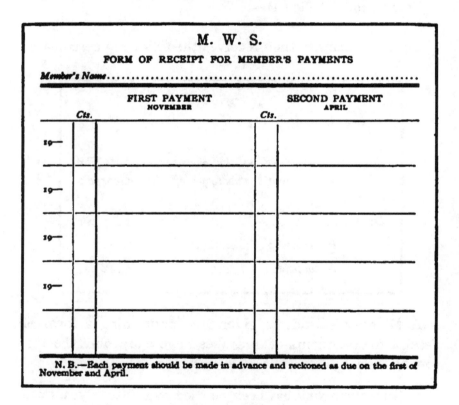

The badge is a circle of silver with wings, and the inscription, "Unity and Love."

The following is the constitution:

MEN AND WOMEN

CONSTITUTION

ARTICLE I

NAME

The organization existing under this constitution is the Married Women's Society of St. George's Church.

ARTICLE II

OBJECT

The object of this society shall be to promote the mutual well-being of its members by lectures, classes, etc.

ARTICLE III

MEMBERS

The members of this society shall be those married women whose names have been proposed by the clergy or deaconesses of St. George's Church, or by a member of this society, and approved by the president or executive committee.

ARTICLE IV

DEPARTMENTS

Women married less than fifteen years may join the senior department; those married less than four years may join the junior department. The two branches meet at the beginning of the session for the service, and at the end for tea.

ARTICLE V

ASSOCIATES

Associate members are appointed by the Rector to constitute the executive committee.

ARTICLE VI

EXECUTIVE COMMITTEE

The executive committee shall have charge of all business arrangements, and shall look to the general interests of the society.

ARTICLE VII

OFFICERS

The officers of this society shall be a president, vice-president, secretary, and treasurer, appointed annually by the Rector from the executive committee, and an assistant secretary elected annually from the members.

ARTICLE VIII
DUTIES OF OFFICERS

The duties of the president, vice-president, secretary, and assistant secretary shall be those commonly appertaining to those offices, the president *ex-officio* being a member of all committees. The treasurer shall receive the funds of the society and disburse them at the discretion of the president or executive committee.

ARTICLE IX
MEETINGS

The annual meeting of this society shall be held on the first Thursday in November of each year. At this meeting the executive committee shall submit the annual report. Special meetings shall be called by the president, or at the request of three or more members. One-fifth of the membership shall constitute a quorum.

ARTICLE X
AMENDMENTS

This constitution may be amended at an annual meeting by a two-thirds vote of the members present, provided due notice of such change shall have been given previously in writing.

BY-LAWS

ARTICLE I
DUES

1. *Members' Dues.* Every member of this society shall pay seventy-five cents annually, or semi-annually, in November or April, to defray the running expenses of the society.

2. *Associates' Dues.* Every associate member shall pay ten dollars annually, in November, to defray the running expenses.

ARTICLE II
COUNCIL

A council of ten members, elected annually from the society, shall consult from time to time with the president, in regard to the business of the society.

MEN AND WOMEN

ARTICLE III
MEETINGS

1. *Weekly Meetings.* Weekly meetings of the society shall be held, and consist of a short opening service, classes for instruction, followed by a half-hour of friendly intercourse.

2. *Executive Committee Meetings.* The executive committee shall meet monthly to transact the business of the society.

ARTICLE IV
DUTIES OF ASSOCIATES

1. Each associate of this society shall be responsible for four or more members whom she shall visit, and concerning whom she shall make a report at each executive committee meeting.

2. Every class shall have one or more associates in charge.

3. Five or more associates, forming a hospitality committee, shall take charge of the social half-hour at the weekly meetings.

ARTICLE V
HONORARY ASSOCIATES

Any person subscribing five dollars ($5) annually towards the expenses of the society, may become an honorary associate.

An honorary associate shall be entitled to attend all social meetings of the society.

The entertainments usually include dancing, and the husbands are invited.

The executive committee meets on the first Wednesday of each month, summoned by this reminder:

M. W. S.

The regular monthly meeting of the executive committee of the Married Women's Society of St. George's Church will be held on Wednesday,.................at 11 A.M., at 208 East 16th Street.

....
....
....
Secretary.

ADMINISTRATION OF AN INSTITUTIONAL CHURCH

Absent members are first looked after by post-card:

M. W. S.

In order to get the full benefit of the classes, it is most important that you should be regular in your attendance.

As you have now been absent for three weeks, please make an effort to attend the next meeting or send me an excuse.

....
Secretary.

When this fails, a letter is written to a member living in the neighborhood of the absentee, asking her to call. In this letter are enclosed slips of paper (as below) to be filled up

---

M. W. S.
To be Visited

Mrs. ....
Address. ....
By
Mrs. ....
Address. ....
Date ....

M. W. S.
Change of Address

Name ....
Old Address ....
New Address ....
Send to
Mrs. ...., Secretary
.... Street.

---

and returned to the secretary. On the reverse of the form containing the names of visitor and absentee, a report is to be made of the reason for absence.

IV.—THE MOTHERS' MEETINGS

The mothers' meetings are intended for the mothers of the neighborhood, to give them an hour's rest and refreshment once a week. Half of the time is taken up with a service and a religious instruction. This is sometimes conducted by one of the clergy, but more often by a deaconess or other lady of the parish. The other half-hour is given up to social enjoyment, which the ladies provide. The meetings open at the beginning of December and close at the end of May. The following invitations are sent to former members, and to women who seem to have no church associations:

**ST. GEORGE'S MEMORIAL HOUSE
207 EAST 16TH ST.**

The Mothers' Meetings will reopen on Thursday evening, December 5th, at eight o'clock. You are invited to attend. In connection with these meetings there is a Bible class held every Sunday afternoon at three o'clock, to which you are also heartily welcome.
Sincerely yours,

....
Deaconess.

At the door is a box into which the women may drop their offerings. The money thus collected is used for missions.

ADMINISTRATION OF AN INSTITUTIONAL CHURCH

V.—THE HAPPY-HOUR CLUB

This society is meant for the older mothers. Most of these come from the "Old Country," and many wear shawls over their heads, in the good old fashion. They have, to a limited extent, all that the other clubs enjoy—cooking lessons, talks, and entertainments.

VI.—THE SUNDAY-AFTERNOON CLUB

Those who know the conditions under which the tenement-house dwellers live, need not be told how impossible it is for the young people to meet and know each other in their own homes. Space is so contracted that the young girl cannot bring to her home her young man friend without seriously interfering with the comfort of the rest of the family, for some of the members have no doubt worked hard all day, and look forward to an evening of quiet, when they may dress according to their own ideas of comfort. Nothing is left to thousands but the parks, the low dance-halls, and the streets in which to do their courting. In order to overcome this want, and to enable the young people to meet in a social way, dances and entertainments were arranged. A Sunday-afternoon Club was started, at which the young girls and young men of the organizations could meet. The club is in charge of a deaconess, but all the members of the staff come in at their leisure. Tea and coffee are served at small tables placed around the room. Sometimes members of the parish give short musical entertainments or talks on travel. Any member of the parish over sixteen is eligible upon the payment of twenty-five cents. The club has few rules.

MEN AND WOMEN

VII.—THE DRAMATIC AND LITERARY SOCIETY

It was indirectly through the dances, entertainments, and short plays given that the Dramatic and Literary Society was organized. The social side developed into a new working organization.

St. George's Dramatic Society is limited to thirty members, fifteen men and fifteen women, organized under the following constitution:

CONSTITUTION
ARTICLE I
NAME AND OBJECT

SEC. 1. This society shall be known as the St. George's Dramatic and Literary Society.

SEC. 2. Its object is and shall be the mutual instruction and enjoyment of its members, through the medium of dramatic productions and the study of literature.

ARTICLE II
MEMBERSHIP

Sec. 1. There shall be dramatic, associate, and honorary members of the society. The dramatic membership shall be subdivided into active and advisory branches. The number of members of the active branch shall be limited to thirty—fifteen women and fifteen men.

SEC. 2. (a) The active branch of the dramatic membership shall consist of those who take part in the plays given by the society. (b) The advisory branch of the dramatic membership shall consist of those who assist the president in the preparation of a performance, either in coaching, costuming, or otherwise.

SEC. 3. Any enrolled member of St. George's parish, in good standing, shall be eligible to dramatic membership.

SEC. 4. Other persons may be appointed to the advisory branch by the executive committee, upon approval of the Rector.

SEC. 5. Persons may be elected associate or honorary members of the society, as hereinafter provided.

ARTICLE III
OFFICERS

SEC. 1. The officers of the society shall be an honorary president, president, vice-president, secretary, treasurer, and historian, all of whom shall be elected at a meeting of the society to be held on the second Tuesday evening after the fall production, or as hereinafter provided.

SEC. 2. Vacancies created from any cause whatsoever shall be filled by the society at its next regular meeting. Such election shall be by ballot.

ARTICLE IV

DUTIES OF OFFICERS

SEC. 1. The honorary president shall preside at all meetings of the society.

SEC. 2. The president shall preside at all meetings of the society when the honorary president is absent. He shall have charge of all rehearsals and productions and keep a general oversight on all other affairs of the society. He shall be at liberty to call to his aid, at any time, any person within or without the membership of the society; provided, however, that such person may be approved by the Rector or chairman of the executive committee. His decision on all matters of discipline or ability, at rehearsals, productions, or elsewhere, shall be final. The honorary president and president shall be members, *ex-officio*, of all committees.

SEC. 3. The vice-president shall, in the absence of the president, perform his duties.

SEC. 4. The secretary shall keep all the records of the society except the history. He shall give due notice of all meetings and rehearsals, inform persons by letter of their election, keep a list of the members of the society, conduct its correspondence, and discharge the ordinary duties of secretary. He shall also have charge of the press and printing.

SEC. 5. The treasurer shall have charge of the funds of the society, subject to the control of the executive committee. He shall take charge of the box-office returns on all productions, including the issuance of tickets and the counting up of the house. He shall make a statement of the financial condition of the society whenever called upon to do so, and shall keep such books as may be necessary to insure a full and detailed record of its transactions.

SEC. 6. The historian shall be the librarian of the society, and shall have charge of all the plays, books, music, and other literature. He shall keep a full account of all the productions of the society, and shall also gather and preserve the programmes of all productions and all press notices and criticisms.

ARTICLE V
COMMITTEES

SEC. 1. There shall be an executive committee, which shall consist of the president, vice-president, secretary, treasurer, historian, one of the assistant clergy, and four members of the active branch and two members of the advisory branch, to be elected at large.

SEC. 2. There shall be a committee on plays and books which shall consist of the historian, two members of the executive committee, and one member of each branch, to be elected at large.

SEC. 3. There shall be a committee on properties and costumes, which shall consist of four active and two advisory members, to be elected at large.

ARTICLE VI
DUTIES OF COMMITTEES

SEC. 1. The executive committee shall have general oversight of the affairs of the society, and shall pass upon the eligibility of all applicants for dramatic membership.

SEC. 2. The committee on plays and books shall investigate all plays and books before their study is taken up, and arrange for their purchase.

SEC. 3. The committee on properties and costumes shall gather together the properties required for the productions of the society, shall arrange for the costuming of all productions, and shall see to the care and preservation of the property of the society.

ARTICLE VII
MEETINGS

SEC. 1. There shall be an annual meeting of all the members of the society, which shall be held during the months of November or December, on a date to be fixed by the executive committee.

SEC. 2. There shall be a regular monthly meeting of the society for the transaction of business on the first Thursday of each month.

SEC. 3. Special meetings may be called by the president at any time, or on the request of three members of the society. At the meetings of this society, twelve (12) members shall constitute a quorum.

ARTICLE VIII
ELECTIONS

SEC. 1. The president of this society shall be appointed by the honorary president after consultation with the executive committee of the society. All other officers shall be elected at the regular November meeting of the society. No active member shall be eligible to hold office who has not taken part in at least one production of the society. Dramatic members only shall be entitled to vote.

Sec. 2. Applicants for dramatic membership shall be proposed and seconded by two dramatic members in good standing, and such proposal must be made to the executive committee in writing. The executive committee shall elect or reject such applicant at its next regular meeting, provided such applicant's name and address shall have been posted in the society's rooms for not less than two weeks.

Sec. 3. When the limit of membership hereinbefore named has been reached, applicants for membership who have been regularly proposed and seconded, whose applications have been affirmatively considered by the executive committee, shall have their names placed upon a waiting-list to be kept by the secretary, and shall be voted upon according to the precedence of proposal as vacancies occur.

Sec. 4. Applicants for associate membership shall be proposed and seconded by two dramatic or two associate members, and such proposal must be made to the executive committee, who may elect such applicants; provided, however, that such elections are reported to the society at the regular meeting next ensuing.

Sec. 5. Applicants for honorary membership shall be elected as set forth in section 4 of this article.

Sec. 6. Committees shall be nominated by the retiring executive committee, and such nominations shall be approved at the regular meeting after the annual meeting.

ARTICLE IX

DUES

Sec. 1. There shall be no dues for dramatic membership.
Sec. 2. The annual dues for associate membership shall be $2.

ARTICLE X

RETIREMENT AND EXPULSION

Sec. 1. An active member who shall be absent from three consecutive regular meetings of the society without written excuse, or who shall be unable without reasonable excuse to take an active part in at least one production per annum, if such part be cast to such member, shall cease to be a member of the society.

Sec. 2. A dramatic member may be expelled from the society by a two-thirds vote of the executive committee upon the recommendation of the president, provided that such member shall have first been notified in writing of such contemplated action at least two weeks previous to such meeting.

ARTICLE XI

AMENDMENTS

Sec. 1. This constitution may be amended at any regular meeting of the society by a two-thirds vote of the members present, provided that notice of such amendment shall have been given at the regular meeting next preceding, and that all members are notified in writing of such contemplated action when call for such meeting is made.

Application to join the club is made in the following form:

```
            New York..........190..
    Please propose my name for active member-
ship in
St. George's Dramatic and Literary Society.
   Name................................
      Address............................
```

At the regular monthly meeting the secretary makes a record of the attendance. Many attempts have been made at these meetings to develop the "literary side," but without success, for every member wanted to take part in a play. The interest in the dramatic side has always been very strong. These monthly meetings are important, as they keep the organization alive, dealing as they do with various interesting subjects.

The treasurer keeps a set of books, carefully classified,

minute in every detail. The following ledger headings will explain the system:

1. Costume account: Money expended for hired costumes.
2. House account: Money expended for keeping the club-room in order.
3. Orchestra account: Money expended for the orchestra (each play costing from $35 to $40).
4. Properties and cartage account: Any extras used in staging the play, which have been paid for.
5. Books and plays account: Money expended for books for the library on dramatic matters, and for plays being studied at the time.
6. Photograph account: Money expended for pictures of the performance taken on the night of the dress rehearsal—one set for the club-rooms, and additional sets sold to the members at cost.
7. Pin account: Pins with emblem sold to the club members.
8. Stationery account: Money expended for printing, stationery, stamps, aid in work.
9. Wigs and make-up account: Money expended for hire of wigs, and for the make-up man.
10. General play account: One side of the ledger shows the money received on T. W. Robertson's four-act comedy, "School," a two-night performance given at the Carnegie Lyceum in 1903, for the benefit of the Men's Club.

Received:

Tickets sold at box-office,	$ 16.50
Advance sale of tickets by dramatic society	708.00
" " " Men's Club	82.00
Tickets sold through other sources	6.00
Total	$812.50

(Prices: boxes, $6 and $10; tickets, 50 cents and $1.)

On the other side of this account are the amounts paid out:

MEN AND WOMEN

Expended:

Rental of theatre	$210.00
Property and cartage	28.93
Books	4.80
Printing, etc.	42.80
Wigs and make-up	36.00
Orchestra	73.00
Costumes	23.77
Photographs	44.80
Postage	10.66
Total	$474.76
Men's Club share of the net profits,	$168.87
Dramatic society's share of the net profits	168.87
	$812.50

When the society gives a play in one of the theatres, a lease in regular printed form is signed. If extras are required, a contract for these should also be signed. Under this heading are box-office attachés, head stage-carpenter, electrician, sufficient stage hands, door-keeper, ushers, cloak-room attendant, ladies'-room attendant, and footman, programmes, coupon tickets, admission tickets, pass-out checks, and carriage checks.

The cost of extras for one evening is about thirty dollars.

The society does not accumulate funds for its own use. The general expenses are paid out of the dues received from the associate members. If there is any balance, it is devoted to producing plays at the Parish House, for which no admission fee is charged. The cost of such a play amounts to from ninety to one hundred and twenty-five dollars.

IX

THE MINISTRATION OF RELIEF

I. The Rector's Fund—II. The General Poor Fund—III. The Grocery Department—IV. The Care of the Sick—V. The Women's Industrial Society—VI. The Fresh-air Work.

I.—THE RECTOR'S FUND

For use in the offering on Easter-Day, two envelopes are mailed to every member of the parish: one to contain money for the maintenance of the Fresh-air Work, the other for a contribution for the Rector's Fund. The amount thus received for the Rector's use is increased by occasional gifts of interested persons, and is disbursed by the Rector at his discretion. Thus relief is quietly given in such ways and to such persons as could not be ministered by the necessary process of public expenditure. Only the Rector knows in detail what good is done by means of this fund.

II.—THE GENERAL POOR FUND

A fund for general purposes of parochial charity is provided from various sources of supply. The communion alms, being the offerings taken on the first Sunday of each month, make up a large part of this sum. Additions are made by means of special collections; that is, the offerings taken on Ash-Wednesday, on Ascension Day, and at the Watch-Night Service. Further increase comes from donations, collected if the fund runs short, or coming in as voluntary contributions. Some money is obtained fro.n the earnings of the grocery department, and some from special cases, being the money subscribed to send a sick person to a sanatorium, or for the temporary support of a family, or for other considerable emergencies. These various sources of the relief fund are indicated at the top of the ruled columns of the book in which a deaconess keeps the accounts.

In the same book, the headings of other columns indicate the standard items of expenditure. Pensions are paid monthly to certain aged communicants of the parish. A monthly allowance is put in the hands of the trained nurse who cares for the sick in the parish. Every member of the staff, clergy and deaconesses, receives each month an allowance for use in worthy cases which come to their own notice. Certain wages are paid from this fund: as for a caretaker, one of the oldest communicants, to be in the church during the dinner-hour of the sexton's assistants, and also to see that prayer-books and hymnals are distributed in due proportion throughout the pews. Groceries, coal, and shoes are bought from this fund to be sold again to the poor at cost price. Rent is sometimes paid outright, and sometimes loaned. Two general items—sundries and special cases—complete the enumeration of expenditures.

III.—THE GROCERY DEPARTMENT

One of the staff of the Deaconess House buys groceries at wholesale, and a committee of volunteer workers put up the sugar, coffee, rice, oatmeal in half-pound, pound, and sometimes two or three pound packages, for the grocery-room cupboards. This department is open every

Wednesday afternoon, when the poor of the parish may come and buy good groceries at wholesale prices.

In necessary cases, these groceries are given to the poor without price; but it is found better in most instances to keep the transaction on a good, fair co-operative business basis.

The following table shows the transactions of this department for a summer month. The price-list is for the month of June. Sugar and flour have fluctuated considerably from time to time:

	CTS.
Coffee beans, per pound	16
Tea, per pound	20
Sugar, per pound	5
Rice, per pound	6
Oatmeal, per pound	3
Flour, per 3½ pounds	12
Cocoa, per pound	18
Soap, per bar	4
Milk, per can	9

Following is the amount of groceries sold and given away during the year:

	SOLD	GIVEN
Coffee, pounds	1047½	334½
Tea, pounds	596	245
Sugar, pounds	2338	570
Rice, pounds	113	515
Oatmeal, pounds	45	508
Flour, pounds	451	1666½
Cocoa, pounds	88	107
Milk, cans	84	311
Soap, bars	77	479

IV.—THE CARE OF THE SICK

This department is in charge of a trained nurse who lives at the Deaconess House. In the hall is a slate on which are daily set down the names of all sick persons in the parish. These names are collected in various ways. Sometimes a member of the family in which the sickness has occurred calls and reports it. Sometimes a visitor who has called for another purpose will mention the case of a neighbor who is ill. Each of the deaconesses, on her return from visits or meetings, reports such instances of illness as have come to her attention. The names are kept on the slate until the persons are convalescent.

The sick persons thus found are called upon by the parish nurse, and by the clergy, to whom a copy of the list is submitted every morning. The nurse keeps office hours daily from 9.30 to 10. A.M. The trained nurse is also in charge of the convalescent rooms of the Deaconess House.

The use of a hospital is encouraged wherever possible. The parish has a bed, endowed by the year, at the Presbyterian Hospital; and another, endowed by a fund, for incurables, at the Home of the Holy Comforter; and a third, perpetually endowed, for consumptives, in the Stony Wold Sanatorium.

The district nurse keeps her records in the following form:

```
Name of Patient............Address..........
Child or Adult..............Date of first visit...
Disease.....................................
............................................
Finale......................................
............................................
```

Many articles are loaned to the sick, as bed-pans, hot-water bags, air-cushions. These are accounted for as follows:

Date of Loan	Name of Patient	Address	Article Loaned	Date of Return	Good Condition	Bad Condition	REMARKS

V.—THE WOMEN'S INDUSTRIAL SOCIETY

The society has a salaried superintendent, and is divided into two departments, for home work and for workroom work.

The home-work department receives needy women, recommended by the deaconesses, and gives them sewing which they can take home and return the following week, and pays for it in money. In this department are made glass towels, roller towels, kitchen towels, maids' frocks, shirt-waists, aprons, bibs, butlers' aprons, sheets. The goods are purchased by a buying committee, checked off as they come in, and placed on labelled shelves in a set of closets. The selling committee sends a weekly report to the cutting committee, signifying what articles are needed. After the goods are cut out, they are placed on a separate set of shelves, in charge of the superintendent. From the superintendent, the applicants receive them on Thursday morning. When the completed articles are returned, they are stored in the stock closet, where there is a labelled compartment for each article. Thence the selling committee takes them to fill orders.

In the work-room work department, the superintendent's office and three rooms are open four days in the week, between the hours of eight and four. Three sewing-machines are continually in motion. In the experimental stages of this department it was the custom to ask the parishioners to send old clothing, which, on certain days, was given to the poor. But it was perceived that under these conditions the applicants were becoming both grasping and beggarly. A room was therefore opened where all the old clothes which came in were repaired, and where new ones were made. In this way it became possible to give fifteen women four days' work in the week, for six months in the year, at fair wages. The articles thus made or renovated were sold to the poor at reasonable prices. In one year twelve hundred dollars were thus earned by this department and paid out again in wages. Some of the women applying for honest work under these wise conditions belong to the class who had formerly asked for alms. Thus the department is made use of by the staff to meet the demands of the great number of unemployed who come to the door. Few of those who apply know much at first, about sewing, most of them having been shop-girls before marriage. The provision of garments which are easily put together often offers to such persons new possibilities, and they become fair needle-women, able to sew both for their own families and for their neighbors.

The work is varied, to cover the differences of ability. For those who are quite without experience there are rags to be cut and sewn or woven into rugs, garments to be ripped, buttons to be fastened, or errands to be done

ADMINISTRATION OF AN INSTITUTIONAL CHURCH

for the others. Thus all kinds of old garments are useful: those beyond repair being made into rag-carpet. After being repaired and sorted, the garments are put into the selling-room closets. The large garments are hung on hooks or laid on shelves. The smaller ones are put in stiff card-board boxes. Everything is plainly labelled. Wednesday afternoon is market-day, when both the grocery department and the industrial department are open for business.

There is also a department for ordered work. Here shirt-waists, maids' dresses, and simple frocks for little children are made, the material being sent with the order.

The following forms show the methods of keeping the transactions of these departments well in hand:

STOCK RECEIVED

DATE	Glass Towels, Per Doz.		Roll'r Tow., Each	Kitchen Towels, Per Doz.		Aprons, Each		Sheets, Each		Etc.
1905	$2.50	$3.00	$ .45	$1.50	$1.75	$ .30	$ .45	$ .70	$ .80	
October 1....	30	10	20	60	40	25	15	30	15	
" 8....	15	10	10	15	10	15	10	21	15	
" 15....	10	5	5	25	15	10	5	20	18	
" 22....	5	5	4	15	10	18	12	15	12	
" 29....	5		15	5	0	20	10	20	18	
November 4....	6	1	5	10	5	12	6	10	6	
Number of garments made..	71	31	59	130	80	100	58	116	84	
Number of garments sold...	36	16	31	55	34	45	32	34	22	
Number of garments on hand	35	15	28	75	46	55	26	82	62	

STOCK SOLD

DATE	Glass Towels, Per Doz.		Roll'r Tow., Each	Kitchen Towels, Per Doz.		Aprons, Each		Sheets, Each		Etc.
1905	$2.50	$3.00	$ .45	$1.50	$1.75	$ .30	$ .45	$ .70	$ .80	
October 5....	10	5	10	20	8	15		10	5	
" 12....	5	5	10	10	8	10	4	2	5	
" 19....	5	1	4	10	6		10	8	2	
" 26....	4	1	1	5	6	10	6	8	2	
November 2....	5	1	5	7	3		6	3	4	
" 9....	7	3	1	3	3	10	6	3	4	
	36	16	31	55	34	45	32	34	22	

For each woman who takes out sewing in the home-work department, a small blank-book is kept, bearing on the outside her number, name, and address; and within, the date, kind, and quantity of work, and whether paid for or not. Thus No. 28 takes away twelve towels to stitch. The fact is entered in the book in her presence. She receives the goods and a slip like this:

```
                        Mrs. E.
_____

12 towels, - - - - - - - - - - - 50 cents
_____

November 28th.
_____

Returned December 4th.
_____
```

She comes back with the towels on December 4th, is paid fifty cents, and "Pd." is written against that item in her book.

In the work-room department, the superintendent keeps the following record from which she makes her weekly pay-list:

	PAY-ROLL—WORK-ROOM WORK						
Week beginning October 31, 1905.							
NAMES	WORK DAYS				No. of Days at 75 cents	AMOUNT DUE	
	Mon.	Tues.	Wed.	Fri.		$	cts
Mrs. G. ——....	1	1	1	1	4	3	00
Mrs. F. ——....	1			1	2	1	50
Mary G. ——....	1	1			2	1	50
Alice P. ——....	1		1	1	3	2	25
Mrs. S. ——....	1				1		75
Mrs. ——	1	1	1	1	4	3	00
Miss ——		1	1		2	1	50
May G. ——....	1		1	1	3	2	25
					21	15	75

To draw from the treasurer the money to pay the women, the superintendent makes application in the following form:

No.......... New York,................190

To the Treasurer of St. George's
    Women's Industrial Society:

  Kindly let me have a check for the following:

Work-room Work

    ....women,.........days' work,
    at 75 cents per day . . . .|......

Home Work

    ....women at 50 cents per person ......|......

*Extras

    ....|......
    ....
    ....
    ....
                                              ......|......

The above is for the week ending....................

            Respectfully yours,

                    ....
                                  Superintendent.

  * Under Extras go such expenses as needles, thread, etc.

The figures are here shown which represent the prices received at sales for the articles made in the two departments:

THE MINISTRATION OF RELIEF

PRICE LIST OF HOME WORK

Glass towels	from $2.25 to $3.00 per dozen
Roller towels	45 cents each
Kitchen towels	from $1.55 to $1.75 per dozen
Linen scrim towels	$3.00 per dozen
Maids' frocks	from $1.25 to $1.95 each
Shirt-waists	50 cents each
Lawn aprons, with and without bibs,	35 cents to $1.75 each
Gingham aprons	25 to 40 cents each
Butlers' aprons	from 45 cents to $1.10 each
Sheets	30 to 85 cents each
Pillow-cases	35 cents pair
Sweeping covers	65 cents to $1.50 each

etc., etc.

PRICE-LIST OF WORK-ROOM GOODS

OLD CLOTHING

MEN'S CLOTHING

Suits	from $ .75 to $3.50
Trousers	" .15 " 1.25
Vests	" .05 " .20
Overcoats	" .75 " 3.00
Hats	" .05 " .20
Underwear	" .05 " .35
Shirts	2 for .05
Collars	.01
Hose	2 pairs for .05

BOYS' CLOTHING

Suits	from $ .15 to $1.00
Trousers	" .05 " .30
Overcoats	" .20 " 1.00
Underwear	" .05 " .15
Caps	.05 each

Other articles about same as above.

WOMEN'S CLOTHING

Suits	from $ .75	to $4.00
Wrappers	" .20	" 1.50
Waists	" .05	" 1.00
Coats	" .05	" 1.75
Skirts	" .20	" 1.25
Petticoats	" .05	" .30
Flannel	" .10	" .30
Underwear	" .05	" .30
Hats	" .15	" 1.00
Shoes	" .05	" .90
Hose	2 pairs for .05	

GIRLS' CLOTHING

Dresses	from $ .05	to $1.00
Coats	" .10	" 2.50
Skirts	" .10	" .60
Underwear	" .05	" .15
Flannel petticoats	" .10	" .25

SUNDRIES

Infants' dresses	from $ .05	to $ .75
Infants' coats	" .20	" 1.25
Infants' shirts	" .05	" .15
Caps	" .05	" .20
Afghans	" .20	" 2.00
Comforters	" .15	" .60
Curtains	" .05	" .20
Pillow-cases	" .05	" .12

The selling committee keeps such an account as follows, and turns the proceeds over to the treasurer every month:

THE MINISTRATION OF RELIEF

ORDER-BOOK

DATE	ORDER RECEIVED FROM		Description of Goods Ordered and How Much	Price Per Piece	Total Cost	Date of Goods Delivered	Paid
	Name	Address					

The money received from the proceeds of sales are turned over to the treasurer every week in this form. The following is a strong envelope, in which the superintendent places the amount according to the direction of the same:

```
           TO THE TREASURER
              OF THE
      WOMEN'S INDUSTRIAL SOCIETY
          ST. GEORGE'S CHURCH
               NEW YORK

          Date.................19..


              Enclosed please find
    $................Account Work-room Sales
    $...................do................
    $...................do................
    $................ Total

                  ......................
                        Superintendent

          Remarks:
```

The treasurer of the society is appointed by the Rector, and keeps a book like this:

THE MINISTRATION OF RELIEF

RECEIPTS							EXPENDITURES							
Date	Through Work-room	Through Home Work	Approp. by Church	Sundries	Balance	Amount	Date	Number of Check	Salary of Supt.	Wages Work-room	Wages Home Work	For New Material	Sundries	Amount

Members of the congregation are frequently urged on Sunday to send to the Industrial Society not only old clothing, but shoes and household articles, such as quilts, blankets, carpets, mattresses, pillows, and even furniture. All find purchasers.

VI.—THE FRESH-AIR WORK

The beneficiaries of this work are some of them guests for a day, and some guests for a week, at the Sea-side Cottage.

The daily guests come five days in the week, in number about two hundred. Thus, of a summer, there are some ten thousand who have a glimpse of the great deep. This, however, is a total amount, and includes many repetitions. Every poor person in the parish has a chance to go to the sea-shore four or five times during the summer.

The weekly guests are selected by the deaconesses. The lists are carefully prepared during the winter. Some weeks the house is filled with tired mothers and their children; then with young women; then with boys. All leave together, both daily and weekly guests, on Friday evening.

The daily excursions begin on the Friday before the Fourth of July, which is the time when the public schools close, and continue until Labor Day. Transportation, a bathing-suit, a towel, and a dressing-room are provided free of charge to everybody.

At the beginning of June the mailing-list is prepared from the records of the Day Kindergarten, Sunday-school, and Parish Record. A reply post-card, such as is printed on page 267, is mailed to all persons in the parish to whom such an excursion may be a privilege.

ST. GEORGE'S CHURCH COTTAGE
Rockaway Park, L. I.

THE MINISTRATION OF RELIEF

**ST. GEORGE'S MEMORIAL HOUSE
207 EAST 16TH ST.**

New York, June 15, 19..

DEAR FRIEND:

The Rockaway excursions will soon begin. If you want to be placed on the list for excursions, please fill out the attached card and return same to me at once. On the card put the names of the children who are in the Primary and Junior Departments of our Sunday-school, and those who are too young to go to Sunday-school. (Special excursions will be arranged for the members of the Senior Department.)

Sincerely yours,
....
Superintendent.

REPLY

Mrs. Anna Schultz, Address, 204 Ave. ———.

I would like to have my name placed on the list of Rockaway excursions this coming summer, and also those of my children, whose names and ages are below. I also agree to bring no children who are not my own, and give no tickets away to any one else.

John..........Age..13   Mary.........Age....8

Sam............Age..6   Lottie..........Age..1-2

The name of the applicant is entered on the record-card bearing the family name, the number of persons, and the names of the children, with an indication (P. D. for Primary Department) of their place in the Sunday-school. Upon this card are entered the dates of the excursions on which the family are taken. Thus this sample card shows that this family had the privilege of three daily excursions and one week in the house.

```
Schultz, Mrs. Anna, 204 Ave. ——        | 1+4

J. D.      J. D.     P. D.
John       Mary      Sam       Lottie
                                  Aug. 16, 1905

July 13, 1905
July 20, 1905
Aug.  1, 1905

Aug.  8, 1905, week.
```

When the time comes to make up the excursion, this post-card summons the guests:

Present this card on August 10, at 10.30 A.M., Memorial Building, 207 East 16th Street, to be exchanged for Rockaway tickets. Only one member of the family must bring this card.

....
Superintendent.

ST. GEORGE'S CHURCH COTTAGE
    Rockaway Park, L. I.

To Mrs. Anna Schultz, 204 Ave. ——.   1+4

Upon the presentation of this card a ticket like the following is given out, and the date is entered as above upon the record-card.

THE MINISTRATION OF RELIEF

ST. GEORGE'S CAR—PRIVATE

FROM LONG ISLAND CITY TO ROCKAWAY PARK
AND RETURN
FOR THIS DATE ONLY
Train Leaves Long Island City at 9.20 A.M.
WEDNESDAY, AUGUST 16, 1906

................., *Superintendent.*
Mrs. Schultz and 4—204 Ave. ——.

For the weekly guests, the rising bell rings at six, though most of them are up before that hour. Breakfast is served at seven, dinner at twelve, and supper at half-past five.

For breakfast there is bread and butter, a cereal (a different cereal each morning), tea, coffee, or milk.

The following are bills of fare for dinner:

Monday.	Beef soup, boiled ham, potatoes, tomatoes.
Tuesday.	Roast beef, potatoes, another vegetable, and dessert.
Wednesday.	Beef and mutton stew, made with potatoes, onions, and dumplings, and dessert.
Thursday.	Roast beef, potatoes, another vegetable, and dessert.
Friday.	Pea soup, fish, potatoes, another vegetable, and ice-cream.

Bread and tea or coffee, whichever is preferred, are served with the dinner. On Monday and Friday, when there is no gravy, butter is allowed.

This is the menu for supper.

Monday.	Cheese and fruit.
Tuesday.	Fruit and cake.
Wednesday.	Cold meat and cake.
Thursday.	Fruit and pot-cheese.

ADMINISTRATION OF AN INSTITUTIONAL CHURCH

SUMMER 190....

Month	Date	Cash Received	NAME	Ch'ck No.	Object	PAYMENTS											
						Plant	Refurnishing	Transportation	Wages	Provisions	Print'g and Stat'ry	Fuel and Ice	Medicine	Sundries	TOTAL

THE MINISTRATION OF RELIEF

STATISTICS

Date	Extra Meals Given			Inmates for a Week								Excursionists			Totals			Total Number Cared for a Day
	Male	Female	Total	W O 21	B 16-21	G 16-21	B 2-16	G 2-16	B U 2	G U 2	Total	Male	Female	Total	Adults	Children	Total	

Cold meat is always given in addition, when any is left. With supper there is, of course, bread and butter, with tea or milk. Everybody can have all they want to eat.

The only housework done by the guests is the making of their beds and the brushing-up of their rooms after breakfast.

After breakfast, until bathing-time, some walk along the beach, some fish from the docks, some rock themselves in big chairs on the pavilion, keeping time to the swing of the waves. The daily excursion arrives about half-past ten. Then begins the bathing in the sea. The excursionists bring their own lunches, but are provided with all the tea, coffee, and milk which they desire. The hot beverages are prepared in kettles holding twenty cups apiece. The clergy and deaconesses assist in the distribution. Everybody drinks from three to five cups.

The excursionists of the day depart at five. After supper the children play games on the pavilion, and the young people sing and dance to the music of an Aeolian. Prayers are said at nine, and then, to bed.

For those who would not be helped by the sea air, other resorts are provided. Also the battalion and trade-school, as we have said, have their own camp.

A leaf from the ledger shows how the accounts are kept. (See pages 270 and 271.)

X

THE FINANCES OF A FREE CHURCH

I. The Envelope System—II. The Maintenance of Institutional Work—III. The Maintenance of Missions, Foreign and Domestic—IV. The Endowment Fund—V. The Banking System—VI. The Corporation Treasurer.

I.—THE ENVELOPE SYSTEM

THE envelope system is brought to the immediate attention of every person who associates himself with St. George's Church. There was a time when a card on the back of every pew reminded the worshippers that the church was maintained by voluntary offerings; at the same time, the people were addressed upon the matter from the chancel. These methods have given way to individual communication. The matter is managed with entire frankness, and everybody is given to understand beyond mistake that he is expected to contribute to the support of the church. If the people believe in the free church the money must be regularly supplied, to carry on its work.

We have already noted the fact that the blank for the record of a family has on the back a statement regarding the envelope system. Following this statement is a form of subscription. This is put into the hands of every person who wishes to be accounted a member of St. George's. (See page 274).

ADMINISTRATION OF AN INSTITUTIONAL CHURCH

THE ENVELOPE SYSTEM

Those who find a church home in St. George's are invited to pledge themselves to make a free-will offering weekly, monthly, or yearly for its maintenance. When the subscription slip below is returned, a package of envelopes will be mailed, containing one for every Sunday or every month, as the case may be. The offering should be put in the envelope and placed upon the plate each Sunday, or, if absent one or more Sundays, the offerings and envelopes to correspond should be enclosed.

For further information an appointment should be made with the Rector's secretary, who will call and explain this system.

REMARKS:

St. George's Church
Stuyvesant Square, N. Y.

OFFERINGS FOR SUPPORT OF CHURCH AND CLERGY

Name (Mr., Mrs., or Miss)................................

Address...

Weekly offering..

Monthly   "   ....

Yearly   "   ....

Date from which offerings begin.........................

When filled in, mail to

THE RECTOR,
209 *East 16th Street.*

THE FINANCES OF A FREE CHURCH

For the further information of persons coming newly into the parish, the following explanation is printed. Whenever a family-record blank is mailed to be filled up, this circular goes with it:

St. George's Church
New York

THE ENVELOPE SYSTEM

For the benefit of those who do not understand the financial system by which St. George's Church is supported and its work carried on, we give a brief description.

The system is called "The Envelope System," and by it a church, with its pews free to all comers, known and unknown, is able to form an estimate of what financial support can be relied upon.

Those who find a church home in St. George's are invited to pledge themselves to make a free-will offering weekly. Upon application a card is sent to a subscriber, to be filled out with name, address, and amount of weekly pledge. When this is returned, a number is assigned, and a package of envelopes mailed, containing one dated for every Sunday in the year, and each one bearing this number. The offering should be put in the envelope, sealed, and placed upon the plate each Sunday, or, if absent one or more Sundays, the offerings and envelopes to correspond should be enclosed. Regular accounts are kept with each member, and amounts credited under the dates received. At the end of every quarter a memorandum is sent, showing amount due, if anything, and if there is a discrepancy it can then be adjusted.

All subscriptions are supposed to be for one year at least, and to continue thereafter until the treasurer is notified to the contrary.

Those who prefer to subscribe monthly or yearly are free to take this method. In the latter cases no envelopes are sent.

The sums pledged are considered confidential, and are known only to the Rector and those who have immediate charge of the system.

ADMINISTRATION OF AN INSTITUTIONAL CHURCH

In the case of families, not only the head of the family, but every member is asked to take envelopes.

Although subscribers are supposed to pledge themselves for a year, this is not to debar those whose residence is uncertain from subscribing weekly as long as they remain in New York. But residents of New York who spend the summer in the country should remember that the church's work goes on the same in summer as in winter, and they are supposed to continue their subscriptions during the summer months, making them up on their return to the city, the same as they would keep their seats in a church where pews were rented.

Into this plan of regular contributions are enlisted not only all who attach themselves to the parish by attendance at the services, but all who grow up in the parish, from the time of their confirmation. A letter such as these which follow is mailed to every member of the confirmation class:

ST. GEORGE'S RECTORY
209 EAST 16TH ST.

April 16, 19....

DEAR MR. ....:

I want all who will, who were confirmed this Easter, to take envelopes in St. George's Church. I don't care how small the sum may be, nor do I care whether they give once a month, or once a year, or once a Sunday. But it would help me very much if all joined the system. The only way I can keep my work together is by having the support of all my friends.

If you do not understand this system, please let me know, and my secretary will call at any time you may state and explain it.   Very sincerely yours,

W. S. RAINSFORD.

THE FINANCES OF A FREE CHURCH

ST. GEORGE'S RECTORY
209 EAST 16TH ST.

April 10, 19....

DEAR FRIEND:

I want all who will, who were confirmed this year, to take envelopes in St. George's Church.

You cannot give much money to help our church—I don't want you to give much money. If you can give one cent, two cents, three, or five cents, as the case may be, fall into line and take the envelopes.

Therefore, if you feel that you are able to give anything, even from one cent up, say so on the enclosed card. Upon return of this card to me, a package of envelopes will be mailed to you, containing one envelope for each Sunday. The offerings should be put in the envelope, sealed, and placed upon the plate each Sunday. Or, if you should be absent from the church for a number of Sundays, then when you next go to church you should put in all the envelopes of the Sundays you have missed, with each Sunday's offering in each. If you don't understand this plan, or if you wish it further explained to you, just say so on the card, and one of the committee will call and explain. If you cannot join this system, please say so under "Remarks" on the card and mail it to me.

Believe me always to be,
Your sincere friend and Rector,
W. S. RAINSFORD.

In the cases of persons who do not respond to these initial appeals, a further letter of reminder is mailed. The parish register is regularly inspected for the purposes of such an appeal, the names being noted of all persons who are not contributing.

ADMINISTRATION OF AN INSTITUTIONAL CHURCH

ST. GEORGE'S RECTORY
209 EAST 16TH ST.

I wish you could help me by joining my envelope system. I do not care how small a sum it is you give, nor do I care whether you give it once a week, a month, or a year. But the time has come in the parish when I must get those who want to help me to back up my plan. Everybody who joins this system does so. Won't you think of this?

If you do not understand this system, please let me know, and my secretary will call at any time you may state to explain it.   Very faithfully yours,

W. S. RAINSFORD.

With such letters a card, such as is here shown, is sent:

St. George's Church
Stuyvesant Square, New York

OFFERINGS FOR SUPPORT OF CHURCH AND CLERGY

Name..

Address..

Weekly Offering.................................

Monthly or Yearly...............................

Date from which offerings begin.................

When filled in, mail to the Rector,
209 East 16th Street.

THE FINANCES OF A FREE CHURCH

On receipt of the subscription, envelopes are mailed to each subscriber, a form of which is here printed:

No. 77

**St. George's Church
New York**

FEBRUARY 18, 19...

Put each week's offering in its own envelope and deposit in the plate of any collection. If absent one or more Sundays put entire amount due in one envelope and enclose the unused envelopes of past dates.

Offerings are expected to continue till the treasurer is notified to the contrary.

In the early stages of the envelope plan a special effort was made to reach those members of the parish whose narrow means seemed to exempt them from this payment. Not only was there a good response to this letter, but the theory was justified that the giving of even a very small amount every week to the church is an act of moral significance, and attaches such givers to the parish of which they feel themselves to be a part. The following card was sent out:

St. George's Church, N. Y.

OFFERINGS FOR SUPPORT OF CHURCH

*Name............... Address..............
Amount of Weekly Offering.................
Date from which Offerings begin..............*

ADMINISTRATION OF AN INSTITUTIONAL CHURCH

**ST. GEORGE'S RECTORY
209 EAST 16TH ST.**

March 10, 19....

MY FRIEND:

Over 4500 people, out of 7000 people connected with St. George's Church, live in tenement houses. More than 2500 of these live east of First Avenue; and to you, as one of these, I wish to address a few words.

The desire of my heart, since I came to New York, has been to make the people who live in tenement houses, young and old, feel that St. George's is meant for them. We would rather have them come to its services than any people in the whole city, rather have their children in our Sunday-school, their boys in our gymnasium, their girls in our "Girls' Friendly" and "King's Daughters," than any other class of people, however rich or well-to-do, in any part of the city. After I had been in St. George's for four years, there were only about 800 people east of First Avenue connected with the church. Now, as I say, that number has grown to 2500 and over.

You cannot give much money to help our church—I don't want you to give much money, but I do want you to give the little you can. Supposing you could give only one cent a Sunday—I think it is your duty to give that and to give it regularly. Of all the 2500 members of the church who are living east of First Avenue, there are only thirty-nine at present who give to the church through the weekly envelopes. If you can give one cent, two cents, three, five, or ten cents, as the case may be, fall into line and take one of these envelopes.

There is another reason why I wish you to do this besides the reason for supporting the church, which is a very important one. By a new law of our state, every male mem-

ber of the church who wants to cast his vote at the Advent Vestry election must be a regular contributor to the church. It does not matter how little he gives; he must give something and he must give it regularly.

Therefore, after you have read this letter, if you feel that you are able to give anything, even from one cent up, say so on the enclosed card. Upon return of this card to me, a package of envelopes will be mailed to you containing one envelope for each Sunday. The offerings should be put in the envelope, sealed, and placed upon the plate each Sunday. Or, if you should be absent from the church for a number of Sundays, then when you next go to church you should put in all the envelopes of the Sundays you have missed, with each Sunday's offering in each. If you don't understand this plan, or if you wish it further explained to you, just say so on the card, and one of the committee will call and explain. If you cannot join this system, please say so under "Remarks" on the card and mail it to me.

Believe me always to be,
Your sincere friend and Rector,
W. S. RAINSFORD.

When the Rector receives the card containing the name of the subscriber and the amount subscribed, he turns it over to the treasurer. The treasurer enters the items on two lists. One is the Numerical Record, showing number, name, address; the other is the Alphabetical Record, showing name, number. These are to facilitate reference. Then the number only is entered in the Envelope-Book, and accounts are kept with numbers, not with names. This is to keep the matter a confidential one between the Rector, the treasurer, and the giver.

A page of the Envelope-Book is here submitted. Arrears are brought forward every three months. Ruled spaces indicate the Sundays of the month. The amount for each Sunday is set down at the bottom of the page, and the total on the preceding page is brought forward and added. Thus, say, the first page shows the numbers from 1 to 59, and these persons, on the first Sunday in October, give $18.50; the numbers from 60 to 89 give $1.75. Under the $1.75, at the foot of the column, is set the $18.50, and the sum of $20.25 is carried forward. The check-marks against Subscriber No. 86 mean that he had made an advance payment up to and including November 10th. This is often done by those who leave in the spring to be gone all summer. In the case of Subscriber 86, it would probably mean that he expects to come back to town about the middle of November. A record of the offerings of all the Sundays is kept in the back of the book.

At the end of each quarter, the treasurer sends out a reminder to all subscribers who are in arrears for more than one month:

St. George's Church

Envelope No. 60 appeared to be in arrears $42.00 at the end of the Second Quarter of our fiscal year, September 30, 1905. If this is correct, will you kindly send in the amount? Please make checks payable to the order of St. George's Church.

Yours, etc.,
W. F.
Committee on Envelope Subscriptions,
No. 6 Bible House, New York.

THE FINANCES OF A FREE CHURCH

A pledge is not accounted as a legal obligation, and no attempt is made to enforce it. No name is taken off the list for non-payment until the subscriber signifies his desire to discontinue his subscription. The Rector's secretary calls personally upon persons who are seriously in arrears, endeavoring to make a right adjustment. Thus, a pledge is sometimes diminished which had been made too large, or subscriptions are paid which had been neglected.

II.—THE MAINTENANCE OF INSTITUTIONAL WORK

As the number of organizations increased the number of necessary appeals for financial support increased also. The confusion which ensued was reduced to order by the plan of setting apart two Sundays in the year when the offering should be for parish missions. It was provided that on those days the people should give whatever they could afford for the work in general, the whole amount to be divided among the various societies according to their needs.

This necessitated a second system of envelopes. In addition to the envelopes for the fifty-two Sundays of the year, already supplied to all the members of the church, others were sent for two Sundays, the second in March and in November. The fifty-two envelopes were for the support of church and clergy; the two additional envelopes were for the parish missions—that is, for the institutional work.

These two offerings are now prepared for by the mailing of the following letter to every parishioner, with a card for the subscription:

ADMINISTRATION OF AN INSTITUTIONAL CHURCH

Please read carefully.

**ST. GEORGE'S RECTORY
209 EAST 16TH ST.**

March 1, 19....

DEAR FRIENDS:

I want you carefully to consider your duty towards the various missionary objects of St. George's Church, which you, I feel sure, will agree with me are vitally necessary to the very life of the Church. Our Parish Missions are dependent on two semi-annual offerings taken up the second Sunday in March and second Sunday in November.

You give, through your Envelope Subscription (it may be once a year, or once a month, or once a week—it matters not), a sum of money to pay your Clergy's salaries, and to maintain the fabric and worship of the Church. This Envelope offering, as we call it, has first claim on you. But there are other claims. Below I give you a list of the most important of them. Have you thought how vitally important they are? Examine your Year-Book and see for yourself that the money spent on them is spent economically. What are you doing to support them?

Some to whom this letter goes cannot really afford to give more than their Envelope gift. This I know full well. I am not writing to them, but to the large number who do not understand our financial plan, and who, moreover, evidently do not realize that the very life of the Church depends upon the successful prosecution of these missionary works among the people of the neighborhood.

I do not now write to families, but to each of you, individuals in families. I would wish each one of you to consider his or her responsibility and liability. Giving, surely, is an important element in holy life.

Your friend and Rector,

W. S. RAINSFORD.

THE FINANCES OF A FREE CHURCH

These are the objects I want you to support:

Girls' Friendly Society	$1,100
Sewing-school	300
Women's Industrial Society	900
Sunday-school	1,500
Memorial Building (running expenses)	9,000
Battalion	575
Brotherhood	25
Gymnasium	600
Total cost for one year	$14,000

On November first a similar letter is mailed to the parishioners, but in condensed form, reminding them of the fact that the second half-yearly collection for Parish Missions will be taken up on the second Sunday in November.

To those who have already made a pledge, this card of reminder is sent, calling attention to the amount and to the approach of the Sunday:

St. George's Memorial House

207 EAST 16TH STREET

MEMORANDUM

As per pledge of.............your contribution for Parish Mission Collection Second Sunday in { March / November } is $...........

....
Secretary.

Please, make check payable to St. George's Church.

ADMINISTRATION OF AN INSTITUTIONAL CHURCH

To all, both old subscribers and new, these envelopes are sent:

St. George's Church

PARISH MISSIONS

Collections 2d Sundays in March and November

Name.....................................

Address..................................

Amount of offering.......................

1. Sunday-school. 2. Girls' Friendly Society. 3. Gymnasium. 4. Battalion. 5. Women's Industrial Society. 6. Sewing-school. 7. Memorial Building. Total cost, $14,000.

PLEDGE CARD

St. George's Church
Stuyvesant Square, New York

OFFERINGS FOR PARISH MISSIONS

Collections to be taken up Second Sunday in March and Second Sunday in November.

Name (Mr., Mrs., or Miss) ....

Address..................................

Amount due 2d Sunday in March ....

" " " " Nov.............

When filled in, mail to the Rector, 209 E. 16th St.

The accounts of these subscriptions are kept in the Alphabetical Book, a page of which is here shown:

THE FINANCES OF A FREE CHURCH

ST. GEORGE'S CHURCH. PARISH MISSIONS—(Alphabetical Book).

NAME	ADDRESS	DATE OF PLEDGE	AMT. PLEDGE MCH.	AMT. PLEDGE NOV.	PAID, 1902 MCH.	PAID, 1902 NOV.	PAID, 1903 MCH.	PAID, 1903 NOV.	PAID, 1904 MCH.	PAID, 1904 NOV.	PAID, 1905 MCH.	PAID, 1905 NOV.
Johnson, Mrs. J. R.	——	1890	25.00	25.00	25.00	25.00	25.00	25.00	25.00	25.00	25.00	25.00
Jones, Mr. James	——	1895	5.00	5.00	5.00	5.00	5.00	5.00	5.00	5.00	5.00	5.00
Jordan, Miss M.	——	1901	2.00	2.00	2.00	2.00	2.00	2.00	2.00	2.00	2.00	2.00
Jost, Mr. and Mrs. F. P.	——	1903	50.00		50.00		50.00		50.00		50.00	
Johnson, John T.	——					10.00	5.00		8.00		6.00	10.00

287

ADMINISTRATION OF AN INSTITUTIONAL CHURCH

The Christmas letter informs the congregation as to the object of the offering on that day. Commonly it is for the endowment fund, but sometimes, as appears below, for special purposes.

ST. GEORGE'S RECTORY
209 EAST 16TH ST.

DEAR FRIEND:

Will you not come to one or other of our services Xmas Day, 7 or 11? I ask your offering, for the changes that have been made in the church—our new doors—are beautiful. They were necessary. They are costly. All must give what they can, if the expense incurred is to be met. We need $24,000 (twenty-four thousand dollars).

God bless you and "lead you on forever."

Your grateful friend and Rector,

W. S. RAINSFORD.

Advent, 1904.

At the same time, this card is sent to certain persons on a special list, asking for contributions for Christmas expenses:

St. George's Rectory
209 EAST 16TH ST.

We want to try, as usual, to give a Merry Xmas to the 2000 children that attend our School. We no longer give prizes, but at the same time we think a little candy and fruit and a Xmas-tree cannot do the children any harm. We give dinners to some of our very poor, and decorate the church ourselves. The total cost of these three comes to about $1000. Please help me to give these.

W. S. RAINSFORD.

December 18, 1901.

THE FINANCES OF A FREE CHURCH

Two funds—for the Fresh-air Work and for the Rector's Private Charities—are maintained by the Easter offering. A letter such as the following is sent to every individual in the parish, other than young children. It is accompanied by two envelopes.

ST. GEORGE'S RECTORY
209 EAST 16TH ST.

MY DEAR FRIEND:

I must write to you what I would far sooner say by word of mouth. Come, please come, to the Lord's Table, Easter-Day.

Come seeking pardon for the past—seeking help for the days to come—whether they be few or many.

Try and be more forgiving to your enemies.

Try and be true to your friends.

Try and believe in all men, so that you can serve them.

Bring an offering to God, which costs you something.

I want to use your alms—to send the tired and sickly to the sea—and for my poor fund.

"Oh, while we have time, let us do good unto all men."

Your friend and Rector,

Lent, 1904.
Holy Communion, 7 A.M. and 10.30 A.M.
Easter-Day.

SEA-SIDE FUND	(Yellow Envelope) EASTER OFFERING Name....................................... Address.................................... Amount....................................

> | (White Envelope) |
> | RECTOR'S FUND | EASTER OFFERING |
> | Name.................................. |
> | Address................................ |
> | Amount................................ |

At the same time, this card is sent to a list of selected names asking for contributions for Easter plants:

> **St. George's Rectory**
> 209 EAST 16TH ST.
>
> *We are in need of 2500 growing plants to give our children at the Easter-Sunday Festival. Will you kindly contribute in money for that purpose? I shall need about $300.*
>
> *If you wish to give money towards decorating the Church on Easter-Day, please send it as soon as possible.*
>
> W. S. RAINSFORD.
>
> *April 5, 1897.*

In addition to the requests for money which are sent to the names on the Christmas List and on the Easter List, similar letters are sent to those whose names are on the Thanksgiving List. These careful memoranda protect the congregation against the overburdening of some givers and the overlooking of others.

THE FINANCES OF A FREE CHURCH

ST. GEORGE'S RECTORY
209 EAST 16TH ST.

DEAR FRIEND:

We want to give, as usual, dinners to some of our very poor on Thanksgiving Day. For this I need about $300. Please help me to give these.

Sincerely yours,

W. S. RAINSFORD.

November 20, 19—.

The Deaconess House is maintained not by offerings in the church, but by private subscriptions. New subscribers are asked to fill out the following card:

SUBSCRIPTION CARD

St. George's Deaconess House

208 AND 210 EAST 16TH STREET

My subscription towards the support of the Deaconess House of St. George's Church per year is..................................Dollars, and I will contribute the same amount annually, unless I notify you to the contrary.

Name..................................

Address..................................

State here when subscription is payable..........

When filled out, return to
Rev. W. S. RAINSFORD, Rector,
209 East 16th Street, N. Y.

ADMINISTRATION OF AN INSTITUTIONAL CHURCH

This subscription the Rector turns over to the treasurer, who enters it on the Alphabetical List and on an Annual List. The Alphabetical List shows the name and address. The Annual List shows for each month the name, address, and subscription of the persons whose subscriptions are due in that month, with ruled spaces for the years in which such subscriptions have been paid.

At the beginning of each month, the treasurer turns to the proper page, and sends the following notice to all persons whose names appear:

**207 EAST 16TH STREET
NEW YORK**

*Your annual subscription for.................
of $..................to St. George's Deaconess
House is now due.*

If this is correct, will you kindly send your check to me?

....
Treasurer.

To

M.............................

The treasurer pays such bills as for electric light, coal and gas and repairs, and every quarter provides the deaconess who acts as housekeeper with an amount sufficient to pay for wages, provisions, telephone, and other current expenses. A leaf of the Deaconess House fund is here shown:

THE FINANCES OF A FREE CHURCH

DEACONESS HOUSE FUND — YEAR 1905-1906

RECEIPTS

DATE 1905	Subscriptions	Donations	Interest	Missionary Society	Balance	TOTAL	
Forward......	$2414.00	$1270.00	$164.20	$736.00	$843.03	$5427	23

EXPENSES

DATE 1905	Deaconesses	Serv.	Ho'se	Elect. Current	Gas and Coal	Rep.	Taxes	Ins.	Hosp.	Sund.	TOTAL	
Forward	$400	$280	$600	$150	$200	$210	$31		$100	$41.89	$2012	89

III.—THE MAINTENANCE OF MISSIONS, FOREIGN AND DOMESTIC

St. George's parish is organized as a whole into a Missionary Society, of which each member of the church is considered a member by that fact. Various missionary organizations in the parish are branches of the general society. Of this general society, the Rector is the president; there are three vice-presidents, a treasurer, and an assistant treasurer, a recording secretary, and a corresponding secretary. The executive committee is composed of these officers and of two members each representing the following branches: the Clergy Branch, the Vestry Branch, the Deaconess Branch, the Women's Branch, the Girls' Friendly Branch, the King's Daughters' Branch, and the Sunday-school Branch.

Concerning the work of the St. George's Missionary Society, the Rector made the following statement in a letter to the parish:

The missionary work of the Protestant Episcopal Church in its corporate capacity, both in the United States and abroad, is carried on under the direction of a Board of Missions appointed by the General Convention, a body which is representative of all the dioceses, and, through the dioceses, of all the parishes in the country, including our own. Besides the work for which the Board of Missions makes itself financially responsible, many expenses in excess of the appropriations made by the Board of Missions, incidental to that work, are met, either in whole or in part, by offerings made direct to the missionaries in charge. There are thus two kinds of missionary work that appeal to us for support: (1) that for which the Church in its corporate capacity is directly responsible; and (2) that which is authorized through the action of missionaries enjoying the confidence of the Board of Missions, but for which this Board assumes no responsibility. As to missions of the first kind, the effort is made to meet the Board's financial responsibility by what is known as the Apportionment Plan. Missionary work of the second kind is supported by gifts made for the purpose, which are known as "Specials." This parish is asked to give its share under the Apportionment Plan; and it is also under pledge to give certain Specials, for missionary work not carried on under the financial responsibility of the Board of Missions. The Board of Missions estimates as carefully as it can the amount necessary to be spent each year for missionary work. This amount it also *authorizes* to be spent; for missionaries cannot be sent into the field and be supported there without a binding agreement to pay their stipends.

According to this understanding, all persons and societies in the parish who contribute in any way, by offerings for the general work or by gifts for special work in the mission field, are asked to make their contributions through the executive committee. It is further desired that every such gift should be made subject, first of all, to the right of the executive committee to make good out of any funds placed in its hands the sum needed from the parish for the general missionary work of the Church under the charge of the Board of Missions; and also the sum needed for specials, for diocesan and local missionary objects, for the support of which the parish is in the habit of contributing.

Donors may, if they prefer, specify the field, such as Foreign, Domestic, Indian, or Colored, for which they wish to give. The use to be made of any undesignated sum in excess of the minimum necessary for the general Foreign and Domestic missionary work of our Church will be determined by this committee, which represents all the missionary agencies of the parish.

All gifts confined to special objects only are of course forwarded by the society as designated.

The offerings for missions is taken on the second Sunday in January. It is prepared for by a letter which is sent to every parishioner, calling attention to the object of the offering, the date, and the amount needed, and adding the following explanation:

ADMINISTRATION OF AN INSTITUTIONAL CHURCH

EXPLANATION

The enclosed envelope is to be placed on the plate the second Sunday in January, at either the morning or evening service. If not placed there then, it may be put on the plate on any other Sunday, or sent to the treasurer. Undesignated Envelopes will go to the Apportionment as far as necessary.

If you wish to give to the Parish Apportionment, which has a first claim on the missionary giving of the parish, place amount of gift on line No. 1 on the envelope.

If you wish to give for such Missionary Work as the St. George's Missionary Society may decide, place the amount on line No. 2. The society urges generous gifts under this head, but holds itself free to make good out of such gifts any deficiency in the offering for the Parish Apportionment.

If you wish to give to the Women's Auxiliary Fund of the United States, place the amount on line No. 3.

If you wish to give for any special object, such as Philippine nurse, state the object or objects on lines No. 4, and place the amount for each on these lines.

Checks should be made payable to St. George's Church, New York.

St. George's Missionary Society

COLLECTION TO BE TAKEN UP SECOND SUNDAY
IN JANUARY, 1906

1. For the Parish Apportionment $..........
2. Missionary Work
   (See letter for explanation) $..........
3. Women's Auxiliary
   (See letter for explanation) $..........
4. Special Objects
   (See letter for explanation)

.... $..........

.... $..........

Name....................................

Address.................................

THE FINANCES OF A FREE CHURCH

The following list shows the various objects for which collections are made at St. George's in the course of the year. Of these, the offerings for the Endowment Fund, for Parish Missions, for Foreign and Domestic Missions, and for the Sea-side Work and Rector's Fund at Easter, are preceded by preparatory letters and special envelopes. The others are announced from the chancel only. Of course, alongside of all these go the regular envelopes Sunday by Sunday for the support of the church:

Endowment Fund	Christmas Day
For the Parish Poor .	{ First Sunday of each month Ash-Wednesday Ascension Day Watch-night Service }
Parish Missions . .	{ Second Sunday in March " " " November }
Midnight Missions, First Sunday in January (Evening)	
Missions — Foreign, Domestic, Indian, etc. .	Second Sunday in January
N. Y. City Missions . .	" " " June
N. Y. Bible Society . .	" " " July
Seamen's Mission . .	" " " September
Diocesan Missions . .	" " " October
Hospital Fund . . .	Last " " December
Colored People of the South	Good-Friday
Sea-side Work and Rector's Fund . .	Easter-Sunday
Widows and Orphans of Clergy .	Thanksgiving Day

Sometimes a special offering, for an unusual purpose, is preceded by a circular letter and envelope:

ST. GEORGE'S RECTORY
209 EAST 16TH ST.

May 7, 1902.

The Collection next Sunday will be applied to two objects: 1. After the many years of constant usage, the floors of the Kindergarten rooms and the floor of the Main Sunday-school room are worn out, and require to be renewed at once. For this I need $1100.

2. The furnishing of the Deaconess House is now complete, but I have not received an adequate amount to pay for it. I still need $800.

Will you help me to pay for these? If you are not going to be in Church next Sunday, will you kindly use the enclosed envelope, returning same to me at an early date?

W. S. RAINSFORD.

St. George's Church, N. Y.

SPECIAL COLLECTION,

SUNDAY, MAY 11, 1902.

OBJECTS: Necessary Repairs Memorial Building and Amount Owing on Furnishing of Deaconess House.

Name.....................................

Address..................................

Amount..................................

Occasionally a collection will be taken for a special object, after some week-day description of its purposes and needs.

DR. WILFRED T. GRENFELL will give an illustrated lecture on Work Among the Deep-Sea Fishermen off the Coast of Labrador and Newfoundland, at St. George's Church, Stuyvesant Square and Sixteenth Street, on Saturday evening, the eleventh of February, at half-past eight o'clock. The lecture will be given under the auspices of the St. George's Men's Club. The public is cordially invited. A collection will be taken at the close of the lecture for the support of Dr. Grenfell's work.

The lecture will be preceded at eight o'clock by an organ concert by Mr. Homer Norris.

THE FINANCES OF A FREE CHURCH

IV.—THE ENDOWMENT FUND

In order to maintain such a parish as St. George's, situated as it is in the midst of poor people and being made up in great part of such folk, there is needed not only the money which comes from the people themselves, in spite of all their generous giving, but also the considerable sums which come from the rich. In this respect St. George's has been abundantly blessed. The Memorial House, the Deaconess House, and the Trade-school have all been given to the parish. And much of the means of the church has come in large gifts; such gifts, however, are the most uncertain of all honest kinds of support. For the permanence of such a work in such a neighborhood, an endowment fund is necessary.

Accordingly, the Rector has brought the matter frequently to the attention of the parishioners. "The largest, strongest, and most beautiful churches of our cities should be situated," said Dr. Rainsford, "where they can be most accessible to the poor and middle classes. Where the conditions of life are dullest and hardest, there we need the best preaching, best music, and best embodiment in every way of Christian worship." And to this good end a moderate endowment is a great help.

Therefore, the offering on one day of the year, commonly on Christmas Day, is devoted to this purpose. As such a fund grows, even from small beginnings, it is increased by bequests.

FORMS OF BEQUEST

CHURCH

I hereby give and bequeath to the corporation known as The Rector, Church Wardens, and Vestrymen of St. George's Church, in the City of New York, for the purposes of the Endowment

*Fund, the sum of..
.... dollars;
and in case my personal property should be insufficient for the
payment of this legacy, I charge the payment of the same upon
my real property.*

DEACONESS HOUSE

*I hereby give and bequeath to the corporation known as The
Rector, Church Wardens, and Vestrymen of St. George's Church,
in the City of New York, for the purposes of the Endowment
Fund of its Deaconess House, the sum of....................
.... dollars;
and in case my personal property should be insufficient for
the payment of this legacy, I charge the payment of the same
upon my real property.*

V.—THE BANKING SYSTEM

Each organization has its own treasurer. Formerly, each of these officers deposited the funds of his society in any convenient bank, drawing on the account by individual check. This system, however, as the work increased, proved unsatisfactory. A meeting was therefore called by the Rector to represent the various societies in a discussion of the difficulty, and the treasurer of the corporation presented a plan which was adopted and has worked successfully. According to this plan, the church is the bank for all the different funds of the parish, and the corporation treasurer is the banker. Each depositor has his own pass-book and check-book, and deposits and draws money according to the usual bank customs.

Here, for example, are shown the deposit slip and pass-book in connection with the deposit of $1000 by the treasurer of the Sea-side Fund:

THE FINANCES OF A FREE CHURCH

```
                    DEPOSITED BY

                  SEA-SIDE FUND

                       WITH

                𝔖𝔱. 𝔊𝔢𝔬𝔯𝔤𝔢'𝔰 𝔆𝔥𝔲𝔯𝔠𝔥

                     New York, July 15th, 1905.


          Bills, . . . . .
          Specie, . . . .
          Checks, . . . .         1000
```

𝔖𝔱. 𝔊𝔢𝔬𝔯𝔤𝔢'𝔰 𝔆𝔥𝔲𝔯𝔠𝔥, 𝔑. 𝔜.,   IN ACCOUNT WITH SEA-SIDE FUND

Mch.	1	Balance............	87.83	July 31	30 Vouchers returned as per list	2076.50
May	5	Dep. W. F.........	500 ..		Balance............	511.33
June	3	W. F.........	1000 ..			
July	15	W. F.........	1000 ..			
			2587.83			2587.83
Aug.	1	Balance............	511.33			

The treasurer of the Sea-side Fund also enters the deposit in his check-book, and presently draws check No. 313 to the order of the Long Island Railroad, in payment for transportation. The railroad deposits the check in the usual way with its bank. The bank presents it to the treasurer of the church, who by accepting it makes it payable at the bank in which the funds of the church are kept. (See insert facing page 302.)

This is the way check No. 313 looks when it comes back to the treasurer of the Sea-side Fund, after his passbook has been balanced. (See insert facing page 302.)

The treasurer of the church, as banker for the organizations, keeps two books for this purpose. The first is called "Deposits." Here he enters from the depositing slips the amounts under the proper column. (See insert facing page 304.)

The other book is called "Checks Accepted." Here the checks are entered, as to number and date, by whom drawn and to whom made payable, and amount of check entered under the column to which it is charged. Thus the check so described would be entered in the Sea-side column. The totals of the various columns are posted at the end of each month, to the various accounts in the ledger, and the balance to the credit of each account is brought forward to the next month in red figures at the head of the column. Thus the condition of the account can be seen at a glance. (See insert facing-page 306.)

VI.—THE CORPORATION TREASURER

The corporation treasurer keeps a set of books in the usual business form, showing all cash transactions and the condition of the Endowment Fund. These books are kept in the office of the treasurer, open to inspection. They are also on hand at every meeting of the vestry.

The collections of each Sunday are counted after the evening service by the treasurer and the sexton, and memoranda are made according to the following form:

SEASIDE FUND

No.

Pay

Th

$ 3

THE FINANCES OF A FREE CHURCH

No..............

St. George's Church

COLLECTIONS, SUNDAY,........................190

	A.M.			P.M.	
For..........................			For..........................		
Bank Bills . $..............			Bank Bills . $..............		
COIN:			COIN:		
Gold . . . $..............			Gold . . . $..............		
Silver . $1.00..............			Silver . $1.00..............		
.50..............			.50..............		
.25..............			.25..............		
.10..............			.10..............		
Nickel . . .05..............			Nickel . . .05..............		
.01..............			.01..............		
Checks . . . $..............			Checks . . . $..............		

Total, $...................

(This is left in the book.)

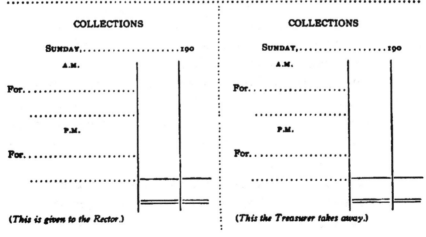

COLLECTIONS   COLLECTIONS

SUNDAY,...............190   SUNDAY,...............190

A.M.   A.M.

For.................   For.................

P.M.   P.M.

For.................   For.................

(This is given to the Rector.)   *(This the Treasurer takes away.)*

The money is then put by the treasurer into a bag which has two keys, one in his own possession, the other in possession of the bank. The bag is locked up over night in the safe in the Memorial House. On Monday morning the assistant sexton takes it to the bank.

At the annual meeting of the vestry, a Property Committee is elected. This committee has charge of all the property belonging to the corporation. No repairs, improvements, or alterations may be made without its approval. No employees are allowed to contract debts of any kind, or to purchase anything in the name of the church without first getting a requisition signed by a member of the committee.

The requisition-blank on page 305 is used by the secretary. He has charge of that department.

The sexton of the church, who is also the superintendent of the Parish House, uses a similar blank, which only differs in this respect, that he makes requisition for extra labor, small repairs, refurnishings, etc. Matters which appertain to the running of a building.

Annually, before the close of the fiscal year, the treasurer presents to the vestry a budget for the coming year, which has been prepared by the Property Committee for discussion and adoption. This shows the estimated income and expenses, based upon the receipts and expenditures of the previous year. (See page 306.)

At each meeting of the vestry the treasurer presents a statement of receipts and disbursements to date, showing the sources from which the various receipts have come and the payments made in accordance with the various appropriations adopted in the budget.

Annually, for the Year-Book, the treasurer prepares a general statement. It shows in detail the payments and receipts of a great parish. (See insert facing page 308.)

St. George's Church

REQUISITION ON TREASURER

..............................190..

For the month of..............................I will require the following:

	CASH	CREDIT
For Postage-stamps for Clergy .		
" Aid in Work		
" Mailing		
" Delivering		
" Printing		
" Stationery		
" Sundries		
....		
....		
....		

N. B.—An Itemized Statement of the above Expenditures must be rendered.

....
Member of Committee.

Approved,..................190

Received above amount,

....

ADMINISTRATION OF AN INSTITUTIONAL CHURCH

St. George's Church, N. Y.

BUDGET FOR YEAR 19— to 19—

ESTIMATED EXPENSES	CURRENT YEAR	PREVIOUS YEAR	ESTIMATED INCOME	CURRENT YEAR	PREVIOUS YEAR
Account Church			*From Endowment*		
Salaries			Rents, real estate		
Rector			Interest on bonds		
4 Assistant Clergy			Mortgage, Cash		
Secretary					
Organist			From plate collections		
Sexton			" Envelopes		
Asst. Sexton			" P. Mission Collec.		
Music			" Cash Bal. (say)		
Gas					
Elect. Current			Estimated income	$61,191.60	$55,046.60
Coal					
Print'g, Stat., St'ps.					
	$29,625.00	$28,176.26	Estimated income for		
Sundries			current year	$61,191.00	
Asst. to Treas.			Total appropriations	59,000.00	
Laundry, Wine, Adv.					
Decorations, Chancel care, care of clocks, etc.			Unappropriated Bal.	$2,191.00	
Fire insurance					
Taxes on Ch. and R.					
Rep. church					
Care organ & motor					
Total appropriation for church	$35,085.00	$32,168.26			
Milner Fund					
Anderson "					
Spencer "					
Diocesan "					
Episcopal "					
Special salary					
	$37,105.00	$34,138.26			
Account, Inc. fr. End.					
Taxes on real estate					
Rep. on real estate					
Run'g exp. of apartment-house					
	$41,305.00	$37,413.36			
Account Memorial Hse.					
Salaries					
Superintendent					
Janitor					
Engineer					
Librarian					
Gym. instructor					
Elevator boys					
Labor					
Coal and wood					
Gas					
Elect. light supplies					
Electric current					
Telephones					
Water tax					
Engine supplies					
Ordinary rep. bldg.					
Sundries					
New carpets					
Total Mem. House, $13,890.00	$55,195.00	$51,203.26			
Account Parish Miss.					
Wom. Ind. Soc.					
G. F. S.					
Sewing-school					
Sunday-school					
St. Andrew's B. H.					
Battalion					
	$59,000.00	$55,033.26			

XI

GENERAL PRINCIPLES

The St. George's plan, formed to meet the conditions of a crowded neighborhood in a great city, cannot profitably be taken without a good deal of modification into a country town. We hope, indeed, that many of the details which we have here described may be found suggestive. We have described them in that expectation. St. George's parish has no copyright on them. They are here put at the disposal of all good Christians. The best part of our work, however, will be found in the principles which underlie all of these details, and which have been the vital elements in them from first to last. With the mastery of these principles, the spiritual success of the institutional church is secured, no matter on what street it stands. To begin with the imitation of details is like trying to make trees out of boards: it works the other way about—first are trees, then boards for roofs and tables. A student who was asked to define the difference between Hume's theory of causation and the modern theory, replied that according to the modern theory the cause precedes the effect, but according to Hume's theory the effect precedes the cause. It is to be hoped that he was not preparing for the ministry. That is the hypothesis which has brought the institutional church into disrepute. First the spirit and then the life, first faith and then works, first the principles and then the details—this is the procedure whereby the institutional church and the inspirational church come to be the same—as they are in St. George's parish.

One of the general principles which these details reveal is that the substantial basis of permanent parochial life is to be laid in the Sunday-school. Dr. Rainsford perceived the strategic importance of the right instruction of the youth in the truths of the Christian religion, in the habits of a religious life, and in the devout ways of the Church. He had the foresight which looks long ahead and plans for future results; he had also the patience which makes cheerful waiting possible. Thus, out of the most discouraging conditions he brought a sound success, and this he did in that gradual fashion of which a pattern is set us in the slow procedure of nature. The ardent reformer who cried, "The trouble is that God isn't in a hurry, and I am," ought to have followed the confession with repentance and amendment. No great work is done in a hurry. Even in a small parish the best results grow into fruition slowly and quietly, like the leisurely processes of the plants. And the seed-plot is the Sunday-school. All the care which is put into the selection of lessons, the instruction of teachers, the ordering of departments, all the personal attention which brings the minister into friendly acquaintance with the boys and girls who are presently to be the men and women of the parish, all the endeavor and energy which goes to bring these young people into relation with the parish, and in a great variety of ways to keep them—all this is akin to the importance of the sermon and of the sacrament. When Dr. Rainsford came to St. George's he came to stay. Therefore he first asked himself, "What sort of parishioners do I wish to have about me twenty years from this day?" Then he asked,

GENERAL PRINCIPLES

"What shall I do with them now, in their tender youth, in order that they grow up to the measure of that stature?" The result of a definite asking and answering of these two questions is a parish built upon enduring foundations. The men and women who compose it have not been brought together by any temporary attraction. They have grown up in it. They have passed from the Sunday-school into the Battalion and the Men's Club, into the Married Women's Society and the Industrial Society, and into the communion of the church, well grounded in religion, able to give a reason for their faith, good Church folk, regarding the Church as they regard their own families, as a normal part of a good life.

Another principle which is revealed in the details of these parochial arrangements is the principle of co-operation. Everybody has a place in the parish. There is a constant endeavor on the part of the clergy and the deaconesses to bring people on from being visitors or guests to being members of the family. Attendance at the services is accounted as only an initial step. At that point people are recipients only, "hearers of the Word," as St. James says, but not yet "doers"—that is, not doers in union with the purposes of the parish. The desire of the Rector and his associates is to give these persons a home feeling, a sense of possession, a conviction that the church is their church, and that they have a part in all that goes forward in it. To this end, great emphasis is laid on the moral significance of money. It is interesting to see how the fact of contribution enters frankly into every organization, and is brought to the attention of every individual. The parishioner pays for what he gets. He does not pay the cost price in any case, being in that respect in the position of the student in the college: the cost price necessarily exceeds what the individual contributes. Indeed, for the most part, that which the individual receives is of such a nature as to be beyond all material computation. It cannot be paid for adequately. But the parishioner pays. He does the best he can. Thereby he is taken out of the ranks of passive beneficiaries and made a member of a co-operative fraternity. The state of mind of the man who is contributing to the support of an institution is wholly different from the state of mind of the man who is being supported by an institution. The act of giving has a moral, transforming, regenerating value. There are a number of men in St. George's parish who could easily pay all of the expenses. Nothing could be more unfortunate than such a misjudged kindness. There are parishes in which that thing has been done, where a rich rector pays his own salary, or a rich vestry make up the annual deficit on Easter-Monday out of their own pockets. But these are weak parishes, to which the parishioners are attached but loosely. According to the St. George's plan, the people are an integral part of the parish. It is a co-operative institution, like a factory in which every employee has a share in the business. And this is effected by the fact of contribution.

At the same time, according to the ideals at St. George's, this democracy is combined with a strong autocracy. This is the third principle which appears in the working of this parish. The people have their great part; everybody makes his contribution and has his vote; but over all are the corporation and the staff; and the head and ruler of the whole is the Rector. The provision in the constitution of one of the societies that the Rector may change its by-laws at his discretion is highly significant. It indicates a centralization of authority by which alone a parish can be made strong. Professor Harnach, in his account of the *Expansion of Christianity in the First Three Centuries*, attributes the spread of the new religion in great part to the combination of the centripetal and the centrifugal forces in the Church. That is, the Church was at the same time an autocratic and a democratic body. It was congregational and individualistic in the power which was exercised by the people of the parish. It was presbyterian in the supervision of that power by local assemblies of the clergy, to consult together, to determine the best ways of action, and then to act together. It was episcopal in the oversight of both the congregation and the clergy by a central officer, charged with responsibility for the general good, and given large powers of direction. Thus it was in every part instinct with life. A successful parish follows that ancient precedent. Parochial democracy by itself means disorder, and parochial aristocracy by itself means discord and dissent, but the two together make for strength and peace and progress. The Rector of St. George's is like a general manager of a mill: all the workers have each his own work, with wide discretion in the doing of it, and plenty of room for originality, but they all report to him and carry out his will.

In this central management of the parish, the greatest care is taken with details. This is a fourth principle of the St. George's plan. The minuteness with which we have been able to describe the work of the parish represents the attention to the least things which marks the ordering of it all. Nothing is left to chance. There are no loose ends. For example, the envelope system is carried on like a business; the accounts are kept with business punctuality and care; every contributor is looked after as if he were a customer, first interested and brought in, then kept informed, then held. Nobody who once makes himself known as connected with the parish is afterwards let go until every effort has proved vain. The child who stays away from Sunday-school is visited, and his name, once on the list, is not taken off until his schoolmates, his teacher, one of the officers of the school, one of the deaconesses, and one of the clergy, in succession, have called upon him. A like care is taken in all the other organizations. So it is with the contributors. Moreover, in regard to the collections, great pains are taken to inform the people as to the times and nature and amount of the offering needed. The parish makes continual use of the printer. The great amounts given by the congregation, out of all proportion to their apparent means, are the result of this sedulous care: they are the consequence of preparation. They do not fall down out of the trees. They are like the fruit of an orchard which has been planted, pruned, ploughed, and then picked. The same is true of all the parochial arrangements. Whether it is the hymns for Septuagesima Sunday, the bills of fare for luncheon at the Sea-side Cottage, the succession of stitches in the curriculum of the Sewing-school, the order of service at the admission of a King's Daughter, or the position of the clergy in the chancel on the occasion of a Confirmation, all is thought out, and arranged, and set down beforehand. And all this is recorded for the maintenance of traditions, and for help in doing better another year.

The combination of autocracy with democracy is essential to the life of a strong parish. Still more is it necessary to combine with all this organization the fervor of a religious spirit. Of all Dr. Rainsford's contributions to the parish, this is the most important and the most characteristic. He made an institutional church of which nobody has ever complained that the gymnasium is more conspicuous than the chancel. He kept the perspective true. He set forward the social mission of the church without minimizing its spiritual mission. Both the social and the spiritual are indeed included in the ideal of religion which He proclaimed who sent His disciples to preach the Gospel of the Kingdom and to heal the sick. They were to minister to the whole man, body and soul alike. The teacher in the Sewing-school is engaged in a religious occupation quite as valid as the teacher in the Sunday-school, and may thereby accomplish quite as much in the name and for the sake of God. But while in body man is akin to the animals, in soul he is akin to God. The soul is the man, not the body. Whatever changes, awakens, overjoys the soul makes a different man. From the point of view of the best progress the material is of interest and value because it affects the spiritual. It is also true that the spiritual dominates, determines, transforms the material. The most necessary amendment of social conditions, even in their most depressing phases, is not that which produces a better house, but that which produces a better man to live in the house. To this end all the material betterment is subordinate; in part, it contributes to spiritual betterment, and in part it depends upon it. Thus, Dr. Rainsford said that the best thing which can be done for the reformation of a bad neighborhood is to plant in the midst of it not a model tenement, not a school, but a church. With a good church, all other good things would logically follow. And by a good church he meant one which by its brotherly interest in the whole life of its neighbors gains their confidence and affection, and then, upon the basis of this gain, gains them. Such a church he organized. It was never a parish house with a church attached; nor was it a church with a parish house attached. It was a church, a place of religion, expressing itself in all these various ways. Thus, one notices that every organization is vitally connected with the church, as the branch to the tree. New members of the organizations are received by the initiation of a service of prayer in the church. The ultimate object of every organization is not to amuse, nor even to instruct, but to bind the members closer to the church. At the heart of all the parish arteries are devout men and women who are both working and praying, doing all that they do as Christian folk, for Christ's sake. Dr. Rainsford made St. George's what it is to-day, not only by his administrative ability, but by his religious fervor, by his zeal for God, by his concern for the salvation of the soul. Without that, the institutional church may be a foolish and complicated waste of time. With that, the institutional church even in the hardships of poverty, with crude machinery and incompetent workmen, will be a power for good. This is the significance of the St. George's plan.

On Friday, February 2, 1906, the vestry of St. George's accepted with profound reluctance their Rector's resignation, putting on record in the following words their "devout gratitude to God," as they said, "for the gift of such a pastorate":

"The Rev. William S. Rainsford became Rector of St. George's parish in 1883. He was then thirty-two years of age, of splendid physique, and in robust health. When he assumed his charge the church was practically without a congregation; with limited facilities for parish work; with small endowment, and with a reputation in the diocese that was little more than a tribute to a memorable past. He lays down his charge after twenty-two years of exhausting labor, impaired in health by the burden of a care of seven thousand souls; with the Endowment Fund increased by three hundred thousand dollars; with a parish building complete in accommodation and equipment, and which is a model of successful and useful operation; with a Deaconess House, a Trade-school, and a Sea-side Cottage; with an official force of twenty men and women; an army of volunteer workers unsurpassed in numbers, intelligence, and devotion; and with a reputation acquired for the parish as extended as American Christianity. His name is written large in the annals of our religious and civic life, and he will be followed in his retirement by the affectionate solicitude for his welfare of the congregation that he gathered, and by the respect of the many who profited by his teaching and by his personal ministration."

At the same meeting they chose as his successor one of his own spiritual sons, trained by his own hand, and filled with his spirit. This was on the Feast of the Presentation of Christ in the Temple, commemorating the consecration of the house of religion by the presence of the Lord of Life. To open the church doors wide for His blessed entrance had been the purpose of all of Dr. Rainsford's ministry. Christ, indeed, dwelt in his own heart. This was the open secret of all his splendid spiritual success.

INDEX ACCORDING TO SUBJECTS
THE ADMINISTRATION OF AN INSTITUTIONAL CHURCH

I.—GENERAL MANAGEMENT

I. THE CORPORATION: The legal title, 2; annual meeting of the parish, 2; qualifications of electors, 2; qualifications of wardens and vestrymen, 2; term of office of wardens, 2; term of office of vestrymen, 2; officers of the vestry, 2; committees of the vestry, 2; names of the present vestry (1905), 3.

II. THE STAFF: How composed, 3.
Assistant Ministers: How chosen, 3; assignment of duties, 3; form used by Rector to notify some members of the congregation when one of the clergy will make a personal call, 5; importance of the office of "clergyman on duty," 5.
Deaconesses: How chosen, 6; assignment of duties, 7.
Staff Meetings: Importance of the weekly, 8; how carried on, 8; how the week's work done is reported at the, 9; forms used to report the week's work, 10; secretary's note-book, showing how the interests of individual parishioners are studied, 8, 9; plan showing distribution of work, 7, 8.
General Conference of Workers: When held, 11; how carried on, 11.

II.—THE PLANT

I. THE CHURCH: When open, 13; Rector's box, purpose of, 13; what printed matter is kept here, 13; what remedies in case of illness, 14; closet for ushers' coats and hats, 14; floor-plan of church, facing 22; seating capacity, 14.
The Vestry-room: How the vestments of the clergy are taken care of, 14; what literature, blanks, and records are kept here, 14; duties of the chancel committee, 14; prayer used before the beginning of the processional hymn, 14, 15; fees for marriages, 15.
The Choir-room: How the vestments, prayer-books, hymn-books, and music are kept, 15.

II. THE MEMORIAL HOUSE: The need of a parish house, 16; order-of-work board, showing the days and hours of all parochial industries, 17; how the machinery of the Parish Memorial House, as to its parochial industries, is controlled through a system operated from the office of the secretary, 18–27; assignment of rooms to the various organizations, how made, 18; first floor plan, diagram of the, facing 22; explanation of the use of the first floor, 18; second floor plan, diagram of the, facing 22; explanation of the use of the second floor, 21; mezzanine-story plan, diagram of the, facing 22; explanation of the use of the mezzanine floor, 22; third floor plan, diagram of the, facing 22; explanation of the use of the third floor, 23; fourth floor plan, diagram of the, facing 22; explanation of the use of the fourth floor, 23; fifth floor plan, diagram of the, facing 22; explanation of the use of the fifth floor, 24; basement floor plan, diagram of the, facing 22; explanation of the use of the basement, 24; plan showing how each organization's claim on the largest room of the building for dances and special gatherings is taken care of, 24, 25; calendar to meet the demand for rooms, which have to be prepared as the need arises, and how operated, 26; duty of the superintendent of the building in charge of the arrangement of rooms, 27.

III. THE DEACONESS HOUSE: The need of a Deaconess House to supplement the work in the Parish House, 27; the need of trained women workers, 27; first floor plan, diagram of, 29; explanation of the use of the first floor, 28; second floor plan, diagram of, 30; explanation of the use of the second floor, 28; third floor plan, diagram of, 31; explanation of the use of the third floor, 32; fourth floor plan, diagram of, 33; explanation of the use of the fourth floor, 32; basement floor plan, diagram of, 34; explanation of the use of the basement floor, 32.

IV. THE TRADE-SCHOOL: First floor plan, diagram of, 35; explanation of the use of the first floor, 36; second floor plan, diagram of, 37; explanation of the use of the second floor, 38; third floor plan, diagram of, 39; explanation of the use of the third floor, 40; basement floor plan, diagram of, 41; explanation of the use of the basement floor, 42.

V. THE SEA-SIDE COTTAGE: Place and purpose of the cottage by the sea, 42; first floor plan, diagram of, 43; explanation of the use of the first floor, 44; second floor plan, diagram of, 45; explanation of the use of the second floor, 46; basement floor plan (under the pavilion), diagram of, 47; explanation of the use of the basement floor, 48.

III.—THE RECORDS

I. THE PARISH REGISTER: Blanks for entry on Parish Register, where kept, 49; specimen blank form, 50, 51; names of church publishers, where registers in conventional form may be bought, 49.

Name of Parish Register used in St. George's Church, 49; where bought, 49; specimen pages, 52, 53; explanation of its arrangement, 54; how changes of address are taken care of, 54; form of change-of-address pad, 54.

Baptism Record: Blank used for entry on, 55; baptism certificate, 56.

Confirmation Record: Blank used for entry on, 56.
Marriage Record: 57.
Burial Record: Blank used for entry on, 57.

II. RECORD OF STATISTICS: How statistics, as to parish membership, are recorded, 58; specimen page, showing the exact condition of the parish membership, 58.

III. THE MAILING-BOOK: Purpose of the same, 58; explanation of the use of the same, 59; specimen page, 60.

INDEX ACCORDING TO SUBJECTS

IV. RECORD OF SERVICES: Where kept, 59; when entry is made, 59; by whom, 59; specimen page, 61.

V. WHERE IS WHAT? System used to make it easy to find things, 62.

VI. THE PARISH CALENDAR: Purpose of the same, 63; specimen pages arranged in book form, 64, 65; specimen form arranged as card catalogue, 66.

VII. THE YEAR-BOOK: When published, 66; form of letter used to collect the reports from the officers of the various organizations, 67; arrangement of the Year-Book, 68; distribution of the Year-Books, 69; form of letter used in the same, 70; explaining how through it new names are added to the Parish Record, 70; explaining how through it new workers are procured, 70; explaining how through it new subscribers are procured, 71; importance of this letter, 72.

IV.—SERVICES AND SERMONS

I. THE CONGREGATION: How recruited through visiting and correspondence, 73; forms of letters used for the same, 73, 74; seating of the congregation, how taken care of, 75; instructions to ushers, 75.

II. THE SERVICES: Hours of service, 76; church decorations, 77.
Christmas Services: 78; Rector's letter to communicants inviting them to the, 78.
Watch-night Service, 79.
Lenten Services, 79.
Easter-Day Services, 82; Rector's letter to communicants, 83; admission by ticket at the 10.30 o'clock service, 83; form of ticket, 83; to whom sent, 84; how the parish is recruited through this ticket system, 84; how new-comers are invited to join the church, 84.

III. THE CHOIR: How composed, 85; graduation of choirs, 86; list of hymns with tunes used according to calendar days, 86.

IV. THE SERMONS: How the preaching is divided among the Rector and assistant clergy, 98; lectures in church on vital current topics, 98; form of letter used to one of the lectures for working-men, 99; what use of the press is made in advertising, 100.

V.—RELIGIOUS INSTRUCTION OF THE YOUTH

I. THE SUNDAY-SCHOOL:
Importance: What relation the school holds to the church, 101.
2. *Officers:* By whom appointed, 102; heads of departments, 102; duties of department secretaries, 103; rules for secretaries, 103.
3. *The Records:* How the school is divided, 103; method of receiving and placing a scholar, of marking his proficiency, and keeping the records, 103–120.
Forms, letters, records; rules used: Form used applying for admission to school, 104, 105; form showing how attendance is kept in the primary department, 107; rules printed in the class-books of the junior department, giving also suggestions to teachers, 107; specimen pages of class-book in junior department, 110, 111; form of letter used for information to parents, 112; form used in promoting scholars from junior to senior department, 113; certificate of

graduation, 114; specimen form from card catalogue of the whole school, alphabetically arranged, showing how entry is made, 115; specimen form, arranged according to department, grade, and class, 114; form used for gathering the attendance, 116; form used for transferring from grade to grade, 116; form used by graduates applying to join post-graduate courses, 117; Rector's letter to graduates, 117; how the standing of the scholars in the junior department is reported to the parents, 118; form in use for the same, 118; forms of letters used by the superintendent to teachers to procure information as to the scholars standing, 119; form used to notify parents that scholar is not entitled to promotion, 120.

4. *Accounts:* How the general expenses of the school are met, 120; how the collections are used, 120; method of collecting the money in the various departments, 120; form of envelope used in the junior department, 121; form of envelope used in the senior department, 121; where same can be purchased, 121; specimen pages from collection book, 122, 123; how Lenten offerings are taken care of, 124.

5. *Services:* How arranged, 124; service in use by primary department, 125; service in use by junior department, 126; service in use by senior department, 130; what stress is laid on choosing hymns, 133; list of hymns to be taught in the primary department, 134; list of hymns to be taught in the junior department, 135.

6. *Lessons:* How arranged, 136; where lesson books may be bought, 136; curriculum used, 136; catechism, when taught, 137; communicants classes, when held. 138; special subjects of instruction during summer, 138; class organization, 138; graduation, 138; interest of scholars, after graduation, how held, 138.

7. *Teachers:* How chosen, 138; responsibility, 139; teachers' meetings for the study of lessons, 139; teachers' conferences, when held and how often, 139; the council, how composed, 139; its duties, 139; how the council affects the stability of the school, 140; how the members of the council are summoned, 140; floor-plan, showing divisions of classes, 141; explaining same, 142; minutes of an annual teachers' conference, 142; how teachers were summoned, 142; how meeting was conducted, 143–156.

8. *Scholars:* How the school is recruited, 156; whose aid is required, 156; form used by the visitor to introduce the prospective scholar, 157; how scholars are held in school, 157; how absent scholars are cared for, 157; what is done about prizes and presents, outings and entertainments, 157, 158; the problem of the children of the well-to-do, the solution of at St. George's, 158.

II. CONFIRMATION CLASSES: How divided between the clergy and deaconesses, 158; when the classes meet, 158; when confirmation takes place, 159; how the Sunday-school teachers are called upon to assist the staff in getting candidates, 159; how the Parish Register is consulted to procure candidates, 159; Rector's letter to the unconfirmed, 159; Sunday-school teachers' responsibility in the selection of candidates, 160; courses of instruction, how arranged, 160; what written work is required, 160; personal conferences with candidates, 160; the Rector's class, how conducted, 160; how persons are summoned to this class, 161; form of admission card to the reserved portion of the church for the approved candidate, 161; form of admission card for the parent of the candidate, 162; form of certificate used, 162; how the young communicants are held through classes and notices, 163; eight o'clock communion, first

INDEX ACCORDING TO SUBJECTS

Sunday in month specially arranged for the young people and associates, 163; why breakfast is served afterwards, 164.

III. THE LIBRARY: When open, 164; form to take out a book from the library, 164, 165; teachers' library, 165.

VI.—WORK WITH BOYS

I. THE TRADE-SCHOOL: How a boys' club grew into, 166; the management of, 168; the curriculum of, 169; method of receiving and placing pupils, of marking their proficiency, and of keeping the records, 170–174; form of application for admission, 171; presentation of form by applicant, 170; placing of pupil in class, 170; payment of dues, 170; the new pupil at work and his promotion, 170; card catalogues, showing pupil's progress from date of entry to date of leaving, 172; form of report turned in by instructors, 173; schedule of classes, 174.

II. THE BATTALION CLUB: Why started, 174; eligibility for membership to, 174; form of application for membership, 175; how equipments are taken care of, 175; form used for recording equipments, 176; form used by cadet as receipt for same, 177; the club, how divided, 177; how governed, 177; how the social side is looked after, 178; how the athletic side is looked after, 178; how the military side is looked after, 178; qualifications of directors, 178; how divided into companies, 179; the use of the Sixty-ninth Regiment Armory, 179; the rifle-range, explanation of the use of, 179; plan of, 181; the camp, form of letter used for notifying the members, parents, and employers of the event, 182; form of letter used for giving instructions to the cadets, 184; what arrangements have to be made before going into camp, 185; assignment of tents in camp, 186; arrangement of the tents, 187; camp programme, 187; how discipline is maintained, 187; cost of running a camp, 189; constitution and by-laws of the Battalion Club, 190.

VII.—WORK WITH GIRLS

I. THE GIRLS' FRIENDLY SOCIETY: The problems of its early years, 195; conspectus showing classes and meetings for the year, 196; method of receiving and placing candidates and of keeping the records, 197–211; candidates' class, how to join the, 197; form of service in the, 197; what work is done in the, 198; rules governing the, 198; advancement in the, 198; what work is done in the advanced, 198; junior probationers' meeting, form of transfer from candidates class to, 199; what work done here, 199; full membership, form of resolution governing, 200; transfer from junior to, 200; form of transfer, 201; list of classes and meetings, 201; the branch helpers, 202; constitution of and rules for, 202; class-books, keeping of, 204; form showing how kept, 205; how the social side is looked after, 205; how missionary work is encouraged, 205; what opportunity given for saving, 206; what opportunity given for fresh air, 206; how absentees are looked after, 206; how prolonged absence is looked after, 207; form of absence and dues report, 208; form of a page from the associates book, 209; how transfers to other branches are made, 207; how provided for after marriage, 207; form of marriage card, 210; rules governing associates, 207, 211.

II. THE KING'S DAUGHTERS: Purpose of the society, 212; service of the society, 212; form of record for keeping attendance, 214.

III. THE SEWING-SCHOOL: How divided into departments, 214; scholars, how taught, 215; system of marking, 217; forms used for taking attendance, 217, 218; what chance the scholar has for advancement and for earning a livelihood after leaving, 219; the parish exhibition, purpose of, 219; form of admission to, 220.

VIII.—MEN AND WOMEN

I. THE MEN'S CLUB: Uses of club defined, 221; eligibility of applicants for membership, 221; form of application for membership, 222; form of card used for posting applicant's name, 223; how the club is recruited, 223; form of letter used, 223; a short history of the life of the club, 224; committees of, 224; officers of, 224; form of letter used notifying member of his election, 225; form of letter used notifying members of coming events, 225; list showing events for one year, 226; form of notification for payment of dues, 227; form of notification to delinquents, 228; card catalogue, form showing how membership record and individual accounts are kept, 229; form of receipt for dues, 229; how the religious side is approached, 229.

II. THE GYMNASIUM: How the use of is directed, 230; duty of the paid instructor, 230; duty of the athletic committee of the Men's Club, 230; how athletics are encouraged in the parish, 230; form of record kept by instructor to show condition and progress of the training athlete, 232; form of invitation to a cross-country walk, 231.

III. THE MARRIED WOMEN'S SOCIETY: How divided, 231; time of meeting, 233; form of prayer of the society, 233; how the children of the members are taken care of, 233; how the society is recruited annually, 234; form used in recruiting the society, 234; form used for making application to join the society, 235; form used by membership committee, 235; admission service, when, held, 235; order of, 236; form of certificate of membership, 237; what the membership guide contains, 237; form showing how dues are posted, 238; constitution and by-laws of, 239; form showing how the executive committee is summoned, 241; forms showing how absent members are looked after, 242.

IV. THE MOTHERS' MEETING: Purpose of, 243; programme of the evening, 243; form of invitation to join, 243.

V. THE HAPPY-HOUR CLUB: Purpose of the, 244; what work done at, 244.

VI. THE SUNDAY-AFTERNOON CLUB: Why started, 244; qualifications of applicants to, 244.

VII. THE DRAMATIC AND LITERARY SOCIETY: Constitution and by-laws of, 245; form of application to join the, 249; how regular meetings are conducted, 249.

IX.—THE MINISTRATION OF RELIEF

I. THE RECTOR'S FUND: Purpose of, 252; how funds are procured for, 252; how disbursed, 252.

INDEX ACCORDING TO SUBJECTS

II. The General Poor Fund: How funds are procured for, 252; how expended, 253.

III. The Grocery Department: Meetings, when held, 253; groceries, how dispensed, 254; price-list of groceries, 254.

IV. The Care of the Sick: Trained nurse in charge of the sick, 254; how the names of the sick are reported, 255; what care is given, 255; when hospitals are made use of, 255; form of record kept by the nurse, 255; how loaned articles are looked after, 256.

V. The Women's Industrial Society: Home-work department—how applicants are chosen to the, 256; what work is done by them, 256; how finished garments are taken care of, 256; how disposed of by sale, 256; work-room work department — work-rooms, when open, 257; what work done here, 257; by whom, 257; forms showing the methods of recording the stock, 258; forms and explanations showing system of giving out work and how payments are made, 259; form showing how the superintendent draws on the treasurer for funds, 260; prize lists, 261; form showing how selling committee keeps the order-book, 263; form showing how proceeds of sales are turned over to the treasurer, 264; form showing a page from the treasurer's record, 265.

VI. The Fresh-air Work: The Sea-side Cottage beneficiaries, how chosen, 266; the daily excursions, when begun, 266; how mailing-list is prepared, 266; form of "reply post-card" mailed to those invited, 267; explanation of how the mailing-list is kept, 267; sample-card from the mailing-list, 268; invitation to call for tickets, 268; form of ticket, 269; the weekly guests, house rules for, 269; bills of fare for, 269; what housework is expected from, 272; forms of pages from the record of accounts and statistics, 270, 271.

X.—THE FINANCES

I. The Envelope System: Importance of, 273; circular used explaining, 275; circular letters used, inviting parishioners to join, 276, 277, 278, 280; forms of subscription blanks used, 274, 278; forms of subscription envelopes used, 279; method of keeping accounts, 281–283; sample page of envelope book showing how amounts are posted, facing 282; form of notice of arrears, 282.

II. The Maintenance of Institutional Work: How supported through another system of envelopes, 283; collections, when taken up, 283; form of letter used, 284; form used to collect pledges due, 285; form of pay envelope, 286; form of pledge card, 286; sample page from subscription book, 287; list of regular collections for the year, 297; how funds for special purposes are collected, 288, 297, 298; how funds for the Christmas festival are collected, 288; how funds for Fresh-air Work are collected, 289; how funds for Rector's Fund are collected, 289; how funds for Easter festival are collected, 290; how funds for Thanksgiving dinners are collected, 291; Deaconess House, how funds are collected, 291; form of subscription-card, 291; subscriptions, how entered, 292; form used to collect pledges, 292; form of page from the treasurer's record, 293.

III. The Maintenance of Missions, Foreign and Domestic: The Missionary Society, how organized and methods of collecting money, 293.

IV. THE ENDOWMENT FUND: Importance of, 299; forms of bequest, 299.

V. THE BANKING SYSTEM: Method of keeping the funds of the various organization treasurers in one fund, through the banking system of the church, 300–302; a leaf from the check-book, facing 300; how deposits are made: form of depositing slip, 301; form of page from pass-book, 301; how the check looks, when it comes back to the organization treasurer, facing 302; sample page of the book called "Deposits," facing 304; sample page of the book called "Checks Accepted," facing 306.

VI. THE CORPORATION TREASURER: What system of book-keeping is used, 302; how the church collections are counted, 302; sample page from the collection book, 303; Property Committee, when appointed, 304; duty of the, 304; form of requisition on the treasurer used by employés, 305; how the budget for the year is prepared, 304; form of budget, 306; annual statement of the treasurer prepared for the Year-Book, facing 308.

THE END

CPSIA information can be obtained
at www.ICGtesting.com
Printed in the USA
BVHW061357100419
545158BV00020B/1101/P